Sociological perspective → Occ Soc —

preparation for actual roles / occ

anti-eth. account

frequency / writing ?

means of integration ?

- Preptha
- Shelly preferred
- Self

Work —
- problem
- social dem.
- gender
- seniority ?

Characteristics

To all who faithfully combine scholarship and sacrament

Academic Vocation in the Church and Academy Today

'And With All Of Your Mind'

Edited by

SHAUN C. HENSON AND MICHAEL J. LAKEY
University of Oxford, UK

Routledge
Taylor & Francis Group

LONDON AND NEW YORK

First published 2016 by Ashgate Publishing

2 Park Square, Milton Park, Abingdon, Oxfordshire OX14 4RN
711 Third Avenue, New York, NY 10017

Routledge is an imprint of the Taylor & Francis Group, an informa business

First issued in paperback 2018

British Library Cataloguing in Publication Data
A catalogue record for this book is available from the British Library

The Library of Congress has cataloged the printed edition as follows:
Academic vocation in the church and academy today : 'and with all of your mind' / edited by Shaun C. Henson and Michael J. Lakey.
   pages cm
 Includes bibliographical references and index.
 ISBN 978-1-4724-5454-6 (hardcover : alk. paper)
1. Clergy–Office. 2. Theology–Study and teaching.
I. Henson, Shaun Christopher, editor. II. Lakey, Michael J., editor.
 BV660.3.A23 2015
 261.5–dc23

                                                              2015021924

ISBN 978-1-4724-5454-6 (hbk)
ISBN 978-1-138-59244-5 (pbk)

Contents

PART III   THE EDUCATIONAL CONTEXT

PART IV   THEOLOGY AND MINISTERIAL VOCATION

PART V   CONCLUDING REFLECTIONS

Notes on Contributors

Stephen C. Barton is Reader and Honorary Fellow in New Testament at Durham University. Alongside his articles and essays, Stephen's books include *Invitation to the Bible* (SPCK, 1997), *Life Together: Family, Sexuality and Community in the New Testament and Today* (T&T Clark, 2001), and the *Cambridge Companion to the Gospels* (Cambridge, 2006).

Mark D. Chapman is Vice-Principal of Ripon College Cuddesdon, and Reader in Modern Theology at the University of Oxford. Mark, an active educator, scholar, and priest is the author of books including *The Fantasy of Reunion* (Oxford University Press, 2014), *Anglican Theology* (T&T Clark, 2012), and *Anglicanism: A Very Short Introduction* (Oxford University Press, 2006).

Lucy Dallas is Curate at St Peter's Church, Tewin, Hertfordshire. A doctoral student in New Testament at the University of Cambridge, her academic interests include Biblical studies. Lucy is passionate about the need for theology to be done at parish level and in local churches. She has lectured on, 'Doing Theology in the Parishes' at Chelmsford Cathedral.

Peter Groves is a member of the Faculty of Theology and Religion at the University of Oxford, and is Parish Priest of St Mary Magdalen Church, Oxford. Previously Chaplain and Fellow of Brasenose College, Oxford, Peter teaches modern theology and doctrine, and advocates for the study of academic theology at parish level. His writings include the book, *Grace: The Cruciform Love of God* (Canterbury Press, 2012).

Shaun C. Henson (Editor) is a member of the Faculty of Theology and Religion at the University of Oxford, and serves as Chaplain to St Hugh's College, Oxford. He has combined his work in the academy with priesthood in the parishes near Blenheim Palace, Oxfordshire for the past decade. Shaun is the author of *God and Natural Order: Physics, Philosophy, and Theology* (Routledge, 2014) and other work.

Daniel Joslyn-Siemiatkoski is Duncalf-Villavaso Associate Professor of Church History at Seminary of the Southwest, Austin, Texas. In addition to his expertise in the history of Christianity and comparative theology, Dan's research embraces the history of Jewish-Christian relations in the early and medieval periods, Anglican theologies of religion, and comparative theology. He is the author of numerous articles and of the book, *Christian Memories of the Maccabean Martyrs* (Palgrave Macmillan, 2009).

Michael J. Lakey (Editor) is a member of the Faculty of Theology and Religion at the University of Oxford, New Testament Tutor at Ripon College Cuddesdon, and is Assistant Curate in the Dorchester Team, Oxfordshire. Michael is the author of *Image and Glory of God: 1 Corinthians 11:2–16 As a Case Study in Bible, Gender and Hermeneutics* (T&T Clark, 2010) and other work.

Christopher Landau studied Theology at Cambridge University before spending eight years as a BBC radio reporter and television news producer. He was a reporter on BBC Radio 4 before becoming the BBC's World Service Religious Affairs Correspondent. Christopher, who is currently reading for a doctorate at the University of Oxford, is Curate at St Luke's Church, West Kilburn, London. His publications include an essay in *Religion and the News* (Ashgate, 2011).

Alison Milbank is Associate Professor in the Department of Theology and Religious Studies at the University of Nottingham, specialising in religion and culture in the post-Enlightenment period. Alison is an expert on the works of J.R.R. Tolkien and G.K. Chesterton, and has authored or edited books and essays including *Chesterton and Tolkien as Theologians* (Continuum, 2009), *Dante and the Victorians* (Manchester University Press, 2009), and *For the Parish: A Critique of Fresh Expressions* (SCM Press, 2013).

Martyn Percy is Dean of Christ Church, Oxford, and a member of the Faculty of Theology and Religion at the University of Oxford. He is a Professor of Theological Education at King's College London, and Professorial Research Fellow at Heythrop College, University of London. Martyn, previously Principal of Ripon College Cuddesdon, has written among other works *Thirty-Nine New Articles: An Anglican Landscape of Faith* (Canterbury Press, 2013) and *Anglicanism: Confidence, Commitment, and Communion* (Ashgate, 2013).

Stephen Pickard is a Bishop in the Anglican Diocese of Canberra and Goulburn, Australia, and Executive Director of the Australian Centre for Christianity and Culture at Charles Sturt University. Formerly Head of Charles Sturt University's School of Theology, Stephen is the author of several books including *Theological Foundations for Collaborative Ministry: Explorations in Practical, Pastoral and Empirical Theology* (Ashgate, 2009) and *Seeking the Church: An Introduction to Ecclesiology* (SCM Press, 2012).

Joy Tetley is lately Archdeacon of Worcester in the Church of England. Her work has combined ministry and theological education, specialising in New Testament studies and ministerial theology. Joy is the author of *A Rebellious Prophet: Jonah* (Church House, 2003) and *Encounter with God in Hebrews* (Scripture Union, 1995) and essays in works such as *Apostolic Women, Apostolic Authority* (Canterbury Press, 2010).

Samuel Wells is Vicar of St Martin-in-the-Fields, London, Visiting Professor of Christian Ethics at King's College, London, and a theological canon at Chichester Cathedral. He was previously Dean of the Chapel at Duke University and Research Professor of Christian Ethics at Duke Divinity School. Sam has authored or edited 20 books including *Crafting Prayers for Public Worship* (Canterbury Press, 2013), *What Anglicans Believe* (Canterbury Press, 2011) and *Christian Ethics: an Introductory Reader* (Blackwell, 2010).

Acknowledgements

The editors and publisher gratefully acknowledge the permission granted to reproduce the copyright material in this book. Every effort has been made to trace copyright holders and to obtain their permission for the use of copyright material. The publisher apologises for any errors or omissions and would be grateful if notified of any corrections that should be incorporated in future reprints or editions of this book.

PART I
Introduction and Overview

Chapter 1

Introduction

Shaun C. Henson and Michael J. Lakey

The works of the faithful who combine academic and ministerial functions into one vocation have been vital to the Church since its first-century foundations. The Church, quite simply, would have no practically informed theology or liturgy, and arguably no New Testament, if not for those who have been as gifted at researching, writing, and teaching as at conventional ministry skills such as preaching, presiding at the Eucharist, and pastoral care. A long list of people have to date continued on this now familiar vocational track, and many millions have benefitted from their efforts both within and outside of the Church.

Yet among the varied possible roles available to those in ministry, about which numerous books have already been written, it is astonishing that no dedicated studies exist about the vocation of men and women we might today call 'academic priests' or 'academic ministers'. That this has happened is not only surprising, but is symptomatic of a serious and recently mounting problem for the Church and academy today.

The apparent abstraction of that point is easily made concrete when a multitude of intersections shared between the Church and academy are examined. These intersections can be found in local churches, Christian and secular colleges and universities, across all diverse cultures and societies where these entities exist, and in the Christian lives of everyone who has ever discerned their gifting and calling to be from God for such a lifetime of labours.

In the following collection of chapters, we and a group of carefully chosen contributors seek to address this vocational phenomenon and material dearth directly, in a way not yet attempted. We believe that this book attests in numerous ways to the need for such a clear focus, and underscores our conviction that it must be undertaken inclusive of the viewpoints of people in several locations and different venues, and at varying levels of service. The commissioned results have returned to us dynamically as wide-ranging, multi-faceted, delightfully creative, and at points deeply prophetic.

As one exemplary lens from which to view broader attendant issues, we have drawn on the experiences and expertise of voices from around the Anglican Communion, and particularly from those who are themselves good examples of an academic priestly vocation. But it is important that readers from any ecclesiastical or educational context, in any setting where religious practice and academic expertise are valued in some combination, understand that they will find here themes and challenges familiar to them. Alongside these are constructive discussion topics featuring at least embryonic notions toward solutions. We neither imagine nor offer any pretence of unambiguous answers to the challenges that we name. After all, solutions will undoubtedly differ with persons and contexts. But we believe it is unquestionable that we are identifying a vocation undertreated to the point of a dilemma, which comes with related sets of issues equally requiring study, discussion, and resolution. While one might understandably assume that the vocation and associated matters examined here must have already received proper treatment, this is simply not the case.

Within the United Kingdom context of Anglicanism, for instance, a scholar-priest vocation is ostensibly recognised. Candidates for ordination training can even be identified as 'Potential Theological Educators' (PTE). Yet added to the fact that there is no body of literature on the vocation to speak of, those so gifted are offered little advice and no obvious career path into which to fit once they have been expensively trained. Even as this book is being published the validity of a category like PTE is up for debate, and in many denominations does not exist to start with.

Further to any examples that one might name from within Anglicanism or other settings, the time is ripe for a serious discussion of academic priestly calling widely conceived. The Church is actively now considering how to fund, deliver, and maintain theological education in the wake of changes and pressures in the Higher Education sector. Parallel challenges in this regard exist in the United Kingdom, the United States, Europe, Australia, and elsewhere.

We have purposefully endeavoured upon commissioning these chapters not to take the usual approach of choosing only the most widely recognisable names possible to write each one. Some of the authors are well-known, but others are far less so. This is because part and parcel of the set of problems to be addressed exists precisely for under-represented academic priestly workers in local churches, for example, as well as in multiple other more predictable locations. For some of these people the need for a voice, and for understanding and space to function wherever chance or providence has placed them, is most acute. There exists, naturally, a converse set of equivalent problems for the best-known of well-placed priests and academics, some of whom have also contributed to this collection.

This book cannot be an exhaustive treatment of such an important and multi-faceted topic. It does include, however, offerings from a realistic array of voices and venues. To be realistic, that array necessarily takes into account people working in jobs and places not always on a mental map when considering those combining priestly and academic work, as well as those who show potential to contribute. Our hope is that the chapters so assembled will open understanding in the Church and academy to the variety of roles possible, thus stimulating creative thinking and conversation toward greater support and opportunities. The individual chapters are divided into three broad sections inclusive of scholarship and ministerial practice, educational contexts, and theological reflections on the academic aspects of specific ministerial roles.

We as the editors open the entire series of corresponding topics with an introductory section setting the stage. Chapter 2 asks rhetorically, 'Is Someone Killing the Great Academic Priests of the Western World?', while describing and explaining creatively what academic priestly vocation is, setting it in biblical, historical, and philosophical contexts. Using Austin Farrer as an exemplar, the current and growing challenges for this vital, common, yet frequently misunderstood and contested vocation are presented, introducing prospective thoughts toward constructive solutions. That chapter is followed by '"And Enjoy Him Forever": Biblical and Theological Reflections on Dual Vocation', which employs an imaginative set of theological reflections focused on recurrent aspects of all academic priestly vocations. Case studies involving St Paul (in conversation with Aristotle), John Henry Newman, Josef Pieper, and St Augustine are all presented.

Part II, 'Scholarship and Ministerial Practice', the first of three major sections, begins with 'Playing Football at Mansfield Park: Christian Doctrine and the Local Church' by Peter Groves. Groves, who is uniquely placed as a university lecturer also in charge of a prominent city congregation, shows the local church as a proper place for serious education. He asks whether the Church at large really wants to suggest that it is possible to be a priest and not also a theologian, and why only some of those training for ordination are marked as 'Potential Theological Educators'? His argument is that the work of encouraging the scholarly vocation will prove essential, but that to avoid contradicting itself, it must guard against the privileging of certain disciplines in or by certain places or people. Stephen C. Barton follows this with a multi-faceted and practically helpful piece on 'Biblical Scholarship and Preaching'. Barton, also a university lecturer and active local church priest, explores in some depth the crucial role of informed biblical scholarship in the preparation and delivery of parish preaching. Lucy Dallas, one of two Potential Theological Educators featured in the book, then explores in 'Memory and Eucharist' how the Eucharist as the focal point of Anglican worship creates and sustains 'communities of memory' in which the person of Jesus is kept central to the formation and nourishing of the identity of Christians. She highlights how the specialist skills of an academic priest can aid local worshipers in their faithful service to God. Christopher Landau, the second Potential Theological Educator, follows with a focus on a recent human guide in 'From Thought to Desire: Theology, Priesthood and the Legacy of Dan Hardy'. Landau demonstrates how in Hardy we have a worthy role model for an approach to theological education that is centred in eucharistic worship, while being at once deeply pastoral and open to God's sometimes surprising revelations through devoted theological exploration.

Part III, 'The Educational Context', turns our attentions from local churches to conventional educational institutions. The first and third chapters are to do with aspects of theological colleges and seminaries preparing people for church life, while the second gives insight into the Church functioning in secular academia. Mark Chapman writes in 'The Vocation of the Theological Educator: Listening for the Divine Voice' of the vital role of theological education in ensuring that a 'back-and-forth communication' between tradition and Scripture remains possible. His concern is that our talk of living the virtues of the Christian life and developing a Christian 'character' need not involve a corresponding downplaying of the importance of the critical faculties, which is an age-old problem when religion and academy meet. Alison Milbank follows Chapman with 'The Academic Priest as Teacher and Tutor'. She asks what the role of a priest educator might be for buffered students at a secular university. In what sense can or should one inspire in one's students an appreciation for wisdom, mystery, and transcendence, or even a desire for God, while labouring at an institution where one cannot even bear the title 'Reverend' in a faculty list? Daniel Joslyn-Siemiatkoski turns to questions of purpose crucial for every institution of Higher Education whatever its orientations in 'Pursuing a Vocation in the Midst of Crisis: Moving from Scarcity to Mission'. Joslyn-Siemiatkoski offers an insider's American Episcopal take on a growing predicament in the theological education of priests and ministers who resource the Church. Writing as a professional theological educator, he asks what ought to be the purpose of encouraging a vocation pursued in the context of theological education? Who does theological education serve and how does it advance the mission of the Church?

That all leads well into Part IV on 'Theology and Ministerial Vocation', which starts with Australian Bishop Stephen Pickard's 'The Scholar Bishop: Recovering Episcopal Vows'. Pickard contends convincingly that all who take Episcopal vows, whether or not they are personally both an academic and a priest, are called to guide and encourage those who do have this important dual vocation, in a Church that needs it in today's world. Further, he argues that combining some measure of academic and priestly ministry is not an optional extra for anyone, nor a luxury the Church can ill afford, nor the preserve of an elite – clergy, seminarians, the experts, or 'professionals'. Rather, it is a task for all the baptised enshrined in their vows and is a corollary of their diverse ministries. Martyn Percy follows this theme of getting reconnected with the roots of all Christian vocation in 'Walking with God: Vocational Vignettes from the Gospel of Mark'. Percy reflects on the Gospel to remind us that a vocation is not a career in the sense that another job might be, but is a life surrendered to God. Every Christian for this reason has a vocation. He acknowledges cultural and personal forces that have shaped ministerial vocation in the past, and will continue to do so in the present. These forces include diversities of gifts, yes, but still every vocation to ministry is an invitation to develop an academic mind. The academic vocation, like any spiritual calling, is an invitation to risk-taking, and sometimes contending for the work that God wants doing. For those who do academic priestly ministry, the start is at ordination. Hence we end with the beginning in Joy Tetley's excellent chapter on being 'Called to Account – Signposts from the Letter to the Hebrews'. She writes on the whole of life as being offered in God's service, which certainly includes the activity and exploration of our intellect. Tetley examines how this dedication makes a difference to the way academic life is approached and exercised, what God might require of the ordained academic, and she reflects on our accountability.

Samuel Wells has spent his life leading churches alongside attachments to the academy in both England and America, and writing books for these diverse audiences. He concludes in Part V by giving a comprehensive theological reflection informed by his experiences in, 'Places of Encounter: Hanging Out Where God Shows Up'. Based on first-hand encounters that occurred during his work as a priest in a major American secular academic environment, Wells demonstrates both the possibilities and the realities of meeting God in life-altering ways within academic contexts.

We all, as editors and contributors, believe that the following work raises undeniably crucial issues. It provides a distinctive and timely contribution to discussions that are not entirely unfamiliar, but which have largely been the subject of indirect discourse, sometimes borne from vocational confusion or personal difficulties in individuals seeking to respond to the vocation, and at other times by harmful dismissals from those lacking a proper understanding of people so called. A more direct approach to discourse on what is a historically common and today widespread vocation is required. Once initiated, it must continue. Our modest offering to that direct discussion in its first book form commences here.

Chapter 2

Is Someone Killing the Great Academic Priests of the Western World?

Shaun C. Henson

In the novel *Someone is Killing the Great Chefs of Europe*, Nan and Ivan Lyons serve up a madcap mystery tale of culinary mayhem and murder.[1] The main characters include an overweight gourmet magazine publisher, an American fast food magnate, and a sexy dessert chef, among a host of colourful others. The central plot has several of the greatest chefs in all of England and the Continent being killed, one by one, and deliberately in a way reminiscent of their respective gastronomic specialties. The victims had all been honoured with an invitation to prepare part of an elaborate state banquet for Her Majesty the Queen. The press had touted the feast as 'the world's most fabulous meal'. Then the systematic killings start, and food critics, with a horde of further self-proclaimed 'greatest chefs of Europe', demand that the mystery be solved and the murders stopped. The sexy dessert chef quickly realises she is the last target on the food-themed hit-list. Her survival depends on solving the mystery now threatening also her own life, while continuing to practise what she is so greatly gifted at – preparing and delivering irresistible confections to widespread delight. The entertaining book became an award-winning dark comedy film soon after its release. Lest Americans should feel put off by the title, the Ivans later also wrote *Someone is Killing the Great Chefs of America*, although to date it is not yet a film.[2]

We can all relate to the Ivans' story at some level. We all eat, and who doesn't like great food? Most of us cook, as well, and some greatly enjoy doing so, even if we are not all chefs. Chefs, one might even mistakenly think, are emphatically unimportant to eating in most cases. Does one need a chef to open a can of beans, brown toast, or pour a drink? One *might* easily have such thoughts, that

---

[1]   Nan Lyons and Ivan Lyons, *Someone is Killing the Great Chefs of Europe* (London: Jonathan Cape, 1976).
[2]   Nan Lyons and Ivan Lyons, *Someone is Killing the Great Chefs of America* (New York: Random House, 1995).

is, until realising that most of our food – including that found in a can – was designed by someone, if not a team of someones, who *can* all justifiably be called chefs. These people delight in conceiving of and fashioning into reality all that we consume, including the finest or most common of comestibles, from sophisticated hors d'oeuvres, patés, pheasant dishes, or lobster thermidors, to ordinary fare like sandwiches, sausages, or fish and chips.[3]

In the Church today, as for Christians throughout the ages, the Eucharist is incontestably 'the world's most fabulous meal'. Known variously as the Mass, Holy Communion, or The Lord's Supper, Jesus himself initiated this and other sacraments for the divine blessing and fellowship of his people, the Church Universal, who are together being called by God from the world to gather around his fellowship table. Through the practice of our feast, along with the other sacraments and all that accompanies them, we as people of faith are transformed by God's grace and the gift of the Spirit into the Son's holy bride.

We may number the sacraments differently. Anglicans officially name two, Baptism and the Eucharist, while Catholics count seven, for example. Others differ from even these counts. In addition to varying the names and numbers of the sacraments, great debates have occurred over exactly how one can believe and teach that Christ is extant in the bread and wine – whether only by faith or grace, or in memoriam – and in what way, if so, Jesus is truly a Real Presence in the elements as we consume them. We still differ over who can preside at the table, and how any priest or minister who does should. Churches, and some individual priests, will set the Lord's Table differently. Yet most would agree that the Eucharist is the greatest of all sacraments, if we had to name only one after our Baptismal birth into faith. The *Book of Common Prayer*, still the standard for Anglican liturgies several hundred years after its 1662 version,[4] depicts the Holy Communion not just as primary, but in at least one later update as the proper setting for all other sacraments and services including Baptism, Holy Matrimony, and even the Burial of the Dead.[5]

The distinctly Christian Eucharistic meal was introduced by Jesus for regular practice in holy fellowship, as a sign of our extraordinary love for God and each other. And once any master chef designs and prepares a great meal, or even we

---

[3]   With thanks for their culinary advice to Thea C. Crapper, an Academic Registrar whose father is a chef, and Nicholas French, a College Domestic Bursar who is himself a chef. Thea and Nick both work in the University of Oxford.

[4]   Church of England, *The Book of Common Prayer* (Cambridge: Cambridge University Press, 1662, 2003).

[5]   This intention is explicit in the 1979 American update of *The Book of Common Prayer* (New York: Seabury Press, 1979).

who are not chefs do so, it is never just to be carried aloft on, say, a silver platter, or in a picnic basket. One desires the meal to be blessed, served, and consumed – and always jubilantly, we hope. Naturally, the chef would like some, too.

In the good gift of the Eucharist, we honour and remember our heavenly Sovereign in what is truly 'the world's most fabulous meal'. By faith we believe that Jesus the Host is himself present with us, and within us, as we partake of it. How could anyone ever top a meal designed and instituted by a God, who then shows up to host it, participates in the fellowship with everyone lowest to highest, and *also becomes that which is being consumed*? Ours would simply *have* to be the 'world's most fabulous meal'.

Characterisations

One wonders, following Jesus' introduction of the Eucharist to his first disciples, who has since then conceived of the finer shades of meaning, and the increasingly more elaborate practices and imagery accompanying the holy meal in its various historical and present liturgical forms? Who has discussed and debated the plethora of attendant issues? Who, most importantly, has written these things down for us in a manner that we can understand and use daily, weekly, or at least occasionally in the Church? Academics, perhaps? Theologians, maybe – people who professionally think thoughts about God (the meaning of 'theology') and all things related, which pretty much is *all things* – those we find in our seminaries or universities lecturing and tutoring? But then, 'academic' seems to imply people especially concerned with the theoretical, that which is abstracted from 'real' situations, from which we get the time-worn ivory tower image. If not academic theologians, then surely priests or ministers, ordained or lay – those greatly involved in the real lives of people desiring God, who know first-hand what it means to so devote themselves, and who plan and lead others in corporate worship?

The correct answers are 'yes', 'not necessarily', and 'all of the above' to each question. Usually it is not just academic theologians who sit, discuss, think, and write about these matters in abstraction from 'real' situations. Nor is it just priests and ministers, ordained and lay, in most cases. Ordinarily, the best architects of the holy thinking and practising so central to the Church's identity and life are some combination of the two. Priests and ministers, ordained and lay, who are active in leading and participating in church practices like the Eucharist, and who also have gifts aplenty that are undeniably 'academic', all things being equal. And yes, certainly, one can find such people combining priestly and academic vocations in our seminaries, theological colleges, and universities. But we may just as well find them in our churches, in so-called secular employment, and even working from home. We may find them almost any place, and further afield. The service of each gifted individual will vary in relation to her or his larger context, personal circumstances, special abilities, and needs and choices, even if the vocational 'gift mix' and talents are essentially the same for all. We will know those with an academic vocation from God, in every case, by what they do. They are like the chefs of the Church world, and for the Church in the world, conceiving of and fashioning into reality, in written and spoken words, all that makes for our lives as Christians around God's table, and when away from it. They must ideally make pretty good waiters, too.

The Church has had these people since Saul of Tarsus' day. They are why our Eucharistic feasts and other sacraments are so beautifully designed, powerfully evoking meaning and worship, with a sense of the presence of God. They are why so much good faith material exists on illimitable subjects and branches of study. We have always needed priestly academic types whether we realise it or not, and we require them now as much as ever. Christians face increasingly complex sets of issues as aliens living out our faith, hopefully with joy and boldness, in a real, workaday, and markedly troublous world.

But who are these characters today, and what shall we call them, besides playfully calling them 'chefs' – or *sous chefs*, if Jesus is the master chef? As this book is initially for the Anglican Communion broadly, we can simply use descriptive terms like 'priest academic' 'academic priest' or 'scholar priest'. Those writing the chapters to follow may variously employ different monikers. The term I use fits well those we are primarily contemplating in this volume, and it is an agreeable enough convention. Anyone not ordained but doing similar work with the same mix of talents should consider themselves included. Our hope is that anyone with comparable concerns and vocational gifts will find equal help, advice, and encouragement throughout, whatever their ecclesiastical orientation or talents, and whether a priest or layperson. The Church is one Body, born of the same Spirit who calls and gifts us all to do God's will and work together, wherever in God's providence, by our own choices, or through life's accidents we may find ourselves labouring.

God calls and equips priest academics to a life of devoted prayer and practice, which includes thinking, writing, and teaching for the Church and its life in our world, and undertaking the same activities on behalf of the Church for the world.

Many reading this book can name some such people, even if only from common accounts. Throughout history, thinking beyond just Anglican priests for the moment, they have had names like the aforementioned Paul (Saul),

Augustine, Anselm, or Thomas – all official saints by any reckoning; Martin (Luther), Jean (Calvin), John (Wesley and Henry Newman), and Karl (Barth and Rahner). Among Anglicans they have had names like Thomas, too (Cranmer), and Richard (Hooker), Herbert (H. Henson), Austin (Farrer), Michael (Ramsey), William (Vanstone), and Henry (Chadwick). A plethora of recent names have appeared like Keith (Ward), Alister (McGrath), Tom (N.T. Wright), Sam (Wells), Sarah (Coakley) and Rowan (Williams). This list is necessarily unfair as it includes but a few well known among a greater multitude than can profitably be recounted here. Women priest academics are growing in prominence, although in the Church of England, for example, women have only been ordained priests since 1994 (which can seem a misprint to our North American cousins, as it did to me when I first read it in a pamphlet five years after the first women were priested). There have been, and are now, countless lesser-known figures, women and men, and all as vitally important in their contexts as those named. Some are reading this book.

We recognise the most famous names and may see clearly their value, especially in hindsight. But the Church has not always known what to do with such people, nor do we always now. This is especially true early in their development, or if God calls them mostly to the local church or to another context other than the university, theological college, or seminary. We have not always admirably recognised and valued the priest academic per se adequately, nor have we seen consistently how essential their work is to God's purposes, to the life of the Church, and to the mission of God's people on earth. At times, not liking what they have thought, written, or said, we have even decided it best to persecute, and in the occasional worst historical cases to kill them, especially where intense disagreements about their ideas have occurred. In the most ideal of scenarios, when recognising and valuing their contributions rightly, we are not always clear how best to employ their gifts. 'Is she/he a priest *or* an academic?', some think or say with all good intentions, however woefully misguided such a thought actually is.

That it is impossible to find a single book directly addressing the vocation of the priest academic is a sign of great lack, and of clear need. One can easily find biographies, historical accounts, and sundry resources about priest academics otherwise. Usually they are referred to as one or the other kind of person fulfilling one or the other type of function – either priestly or academic – and are addressed as 'theologians', 'priests' or 'ministers'.

There is room for improvement on all of this quite simply by taking into account the entire vocation as a unity. Not just looking at the lives, ideas, or even writings of individuals, but peering intentionally behind the scenes at their callings, gifts, and graces from a broader vocational standpoint. What do these people perceive that God is asking them to be and do? What can we learn from them, and how might we apply what we learn more widely in the Church?

In this book we seek to address directly, perhaps for the first time, the calling and work of the priest academic in these ways. That this focus is underdone and overdue is not the fault of any single person or even body – but the lack must be *un*done by someone. Even if one were to beg to disagree with the need for this volume, which is terribly hard to imagine, we hope that it will prove to be a useful tool nevertheless. Not least, we desire to help those functioning with the set of gifts explored in these pages to think creatively and positively about their God-given vocations, and to find creative direction and encouragement for their discipleship and work among us all. Our aim is to indicate the range of such people, avoiding the usual take on edited volumes in which only people who are already well-known priest academics have a voice. What of those God has called to less well-known places and roles, or to unusual ones? We have intentionally invited and attempted to feature voices from several such categories.

There are pressures within and outside of the Church that can make a priestly academic vocation difficult, if not impossible, whoever one might be. Even the gifted people themselves may find it quite a task to discern and practise their callings optimally, if at all. Our wish is not only to highlight this special vocation and function afresh, but to engender constructive thinking, reflection, and debate far beyond this book to benefit all those so called by God. We want to celebrate the existence of the priest academic, rejoicing with them in their existence and contributions. There is so much to say that we can only contribute marginally to such needful conversations. Others are invited to continue.

Charismata and Contexts

The idea of holy *charismata*, or 'gifts', has long been held to refer to special graces flowing from the love of God to humanity for its good. Broadly considered, the *charismata* include any grace fitting that description, like divine favour, or redemption itself. Ordinarily when we see *charismata*, we think of specific gifts granted to persons for building up the Church or for calling people from the world into its manifold graces. St Paul wrote to first-century Christians about these gifts. Gentle debates abounded then, as now, regarding the exact categorisation of the gifts, like how Spirit-inspired wisdom, knowledge, and teaching fit with our modern and post-modern conceptions of researching and teaching in the Church and academe. This is not to mention debates about whether certain gifts were only effective for a specific time in the Church's history, but are now not valid. All of that aside, most of us have no doubt but that God gifts and uses women and men to think, write, and teach for the Church. But we do *not* consider enough the combined gifting of the priest academic. Nor do we think broadly enough about the exercise of this particular vocation in differing locations and contexts, with the attached varied concerns, holy interests, and desires for service and employment. Just as there is much more to say than is possible here on this undertreated vocational subject itself, there are many more locations, contexts, concerns, and diverse priest academics where those known to us all came from.

St Paul made clear in his communiqués to the Corinthians and Ephesians that the Church can profitably be thought of as being quite like a human body (1 Cor 12–14, Eph 4). Jesus is the Head, and we all are parts, like organs or limbs with several functions meant to make the whole composition work together. Eyes cannot expect ears to be eyes, and tongues should not demand that hands should be feet, and on the analogies go. Rather, we recognise the gifts and vital contributions of others as well as our own. St Paul's first-century imagery is superb still today. Any group attempting to work together, whether persons of faith or not, can make constructive use of the metaphor.

There are some contexts that will foster such a mutual understanding almost automatically. One is not only nearby as I write, but exists as a helpful model literally surrounding me. St Hugh's College, in which I sit writing, is a constituent member of such a context, being the University of Oxford and its member colleges, comprising the oldest diverse centre of higher learning in the English-speaking world. St Paul's ancient body analogy is expressly apt at Oxford, as at Cambridge, which began not long after when students fled there in 1209 to escape a series of perilous conflicts with locals.[6] Oxford is worth pause not as a celebration of one university – but as an example of a place that has made this vital notion of diversity inclusive of priest academics work very well, even in its now secular setting. The Church must reproduce the same notion for the sake of the vocation of priest academics elsewhere – and even in Oxford threats to the vocation loom large and come steadily.

That Oxford was founded by Christian friars and monks who had organised regular teaching in the city as early as 1095 is part of an inherent character making this all work. Europe and England were caught up then in what one

---

6   R.W. Southern, 'From Schools to University', in *The History of the University of Oxford*, vol. 1, *The Early Oxford Schools*, ed. J.I. Catto (Oxford: Oxford University Press, 1984), 26.

historian has described as 'a spiritual whirlwind' under the Roman Church.[7] A significant aspect of this fervour was a passion for knowledge and education. Monasteries had protected diverse knowledge in their libraries, copying books and other manuscripts by hand. By so doing, these Christian communities became the greatest Western centres of learning available during the 'Dark Ages'.

New freedoms took this learning from the monasteries to developing cathedral and capital towns like Oxford, Bologna, and Paris.[8] Monastic cloisters birthed communities that were precursors to the Oxford and Cambridge college model. In these places friars and monks read, taught, and lived in societies like that named for St Frideswide, Oxford's virgin patroness.[9] Well-known teachers like Robert Grosseteste[10] gathered crowds of eager students in what would eventually develop into the famous universities named for their host principalities. Scholarly clergy, able to sing Mass and conduct church business confidently, were needed at the local parish level, in addition to any higher educational aspirations to teach others.[11] Groups including the Franciscans, Dominicans, and Benedictines among others eventually founded full colleges at Oxford.[12] Cambridge followed suit, equalling Oxford in scope by the fifteenth century. Durham, the third oldest university in England, also became a leading centre of medieval scholarship. Three of Oxford's colleges were founded from Durham – University and Balliol, and in 1286 Durham College, which was run *from* Durham to train scholars *for* Durham for 300 years, was renamed Trinity College and fully incorporated into the University of Oxford.

The main occupations among the newer Mendicant orders (religious orders dependent upon charity for their livelihood) included the usual prayer and practical living. Yet there was an increasingly greater emphasis on study, writing, and teaching, for their own education and benefit, and that of society. Educating the world became a primary aspect of the monastic mission.[13] At first the content was principally theology, philosophy, and canon law. But these subjects were rapidly matched by Greek and Hebrew, and eventually by material that would evolve to become physics and other natural sciences. Oxford produced

[7]   Keith Feiling, 'Transformation of England, 1066–1154', in *A History of England: From the Coming of the English to 1918* (London: MacMillan & Co., Ltd, 1950), 107.

[8]   Ibid.

[9]   Southern, 'Schools to University', 1–5.

[10]   Ibid., 34–6.

[11]   Ibid., 1.

[12]   M.B. Hackett, 'The University as a Corporate Body', in *The History of the University of Oxford*, vol. 1, *The Early Oxford Schools*, ed. J.I. Catto, 37–95.

[13]   Feiling, 'Transformation', 151–4.

its own influential Christian scientific ('natural philosophy') and philosophical thinkers like the Franciscans Roger Bacon (1214/1220–1292), John Duns Scotus (1265/66–1308), and William of Ockham (c. 1287–1347).[14]

The Franciscans, as that list attests, made a central contribution to Oxford and English culture generally, friars not being tied to one house and living quite actively in the world. Franciscan influence upon England as a whole was one of spreading 'holiness, public spirit, and learning'.[15] The Dominicans contributed similarly for the same reasons. An Oxford education provided students with a range of learning, from what could seem abstract, impractical,[16] and fit for the most ivory of towers, to the most useful and influential of practical arts, like preaching.[17] Not much has changed since 1095.

The University is populated by many Christians still, even if most colleges and the collective University now function as pluralist secular institutions.[18] Despite that status, Oxford retains its centuries-old Latin motto from Psalm 27, appearing on its official arms: '*Dominus Illuminatio Mea*', 'the Lord is my Light'.[19] Most colleges continue to have active chapels and resident priests, who since the English Reformation are nearly all Anglicans. Many colleges retain charitable status as church foundations because of statutory clauses ensuring that they must, in fact, have active Anglican chaplaincies. In almost every case including at St Hugh's, we who serve as chaplaincy priests are still meant to contribute to the intellectual lives of our colleges. Most of us teach and write as members of a University faculty, most often Theology and Religion.

The monastic constitution of Oxbridge colleges as communal centres of learning around diverse subjects continues. Today men and women, teachers and students, study, research, experiment and write together around their various subjects, and increasingly across disciplines. We live, eat, work, and occasionally even pray together in this resilient Christian model, despite that most people inhabiting it are unaware of the model's provenance. Dare I add that 'Common Rooms', which exist for the relaxation and banter of undergraduates, graduates, staff, and fellows, function like church venues in the sense that we gather in them

---

[14] G.O. Sayles, 'Religious and Intellectual Revival', in *The Medieval Foundations of England* (London: Methuen & Co, Ltd.), 377.

[15] Ibid., 152.

[16] Jean Dunbabin, 'Careers and Vocations', in *The History of the University of Oxford*, vol. 1, ed. J.I. Catto, 565.

[17] Ibid., 602–5.

[18] F.M. Turner, 'Religion', in *The History of the University of Oxford*, vol. 8, *The Twentieth Century*, ed. Brian Harrison (Oxford: Oxford University Press, 1994), 293.

[19] Hackett, 'The University', 94.

as varied members of the same 'body', our colleges, and share fellowship and ideas together whatever our respective academic, administrative, or practical gifts. (We never confuse the usual tea, biscuits, and sandwiches with the Mass, Holy Communion, or Eucharist, I hasten to add.) A variety of viewpoints and interests functioning productively together in one community has always been not only tolerated, but vital to the success of the model, which continues because it works so well. Reflecting changes in society at large, the healthy diversity is unsurprisingly now inclusive of enthusiastic non-believers, more who are diffidently agnostic, and many from religious viewpoints other than Christian, in addition to the continuing crop of staple Anglicans.

This context and intellectual orientation, retaining an inherited monastic model of learning and religious devotion as partnered educational concerns, has given rise over the centuries to a number of prolific and impactful priest academics. This is the crux of the Oxbridge matter for our consideration. These figures, mostly men until recently, have had a notable impact on the Church, academe, and wider society, often in equal measure. Several widely known and respected exemplars spring easily to mind.[20]

John Wesley (1703–1791) and his brother Charles (1707–1788) began their careers at Oxford as Christ Church undergraduates. John became a teaching fellow of Lincoln College in addition to his Anglican priestly ministry. In Oxford the first 'Holy Club' members met, eventually to be called 'Methodists' in mockery of their methodical religion.[21] The Wesleys sought throughout their long careers to combine erudition and religion as a unified set of activities, in an emphasis that seems to have been at least partly autobiographical in origin. Their ideal was almost certainly both an outgrowth of their natural interests, and an obvious, fruitful extension of the Oxford environment that had nurtured them. In addition to praying and preaching apace, John wrote, compiled, and edited numerous scholarly and practical works, which even during his lifetime were published and sold as a 32-volume set. Charles, also an Anglican priest, composed an astonishing estimated 9,000 poems and hymns, many of which a wide variety of churches worldwide now sing regularly. Reflecting the Wesleys' ideal of conjoined learning and devotion Charles penned, 'Unite the two so long

---

[20]   A handful of names spring to mind who would be excellent examples, now including Sarah Coakley and a few other Oxbridge postholders. I shall mention here just three widely known historical models.

[21]   Diarmaid MacCulloch, *A History of Christianity* (London: Allen Lane, 2009), 747–55.

disjoined, Knowledge and vital piety: Learning and Holiness combined, And all truth and love, let all men see', in the hymn often listed as 'Sanctified Knowledge'.[22]

John Henry Newman (1801–1890), the Anglican priest academic who famously converted to Catholicism (1845), and who was beatified in England by Pope Benedict XVI in 2010, also began at Oxford. Newman was an undergraduate and later fellow at Trinity and Oriel colleges respectively, eventually serving as Vicar of the University Church of St Mary the Virgin from 1828–1843. He produced during a very active priestly ministry as an Anglican and then Catholic, a catalogue of influential academic and devotional writings. These include 'Tracts for the Times' (1833–1841), 'The Idea of a University' (1852), 'The Dream of Gerontius' (1865), and 'Grammar of Assent' (1870),[23] along with widely-sung hymns like 'Lead, Kindly Light' and 'Praise to the Holiest in the Height'.

The Wesleys and Newman are but two examples. Many alongside them, increasingly including women, could all serve equally well as archetypal models of the priest academic. No one fits our purposes better, however, than the slightly lesser-known twentieth-century figure of Austin Farrer (1904–1968). An entire constellation of interrelated matters, like who Farrer was as a person and priest, how his environment and contacts formed and facilitated his service, and the lessons we can all learn from each issue for ourselves now, are especially relevant to priest academics today.

Austin Farrer

There is at present one main long, and several shorter, biographical accounts of Farrer's life.[24] Each says more or less the same things, albeit one or two get

---

[22] 'Sanctified Knowledge', composed for the opening of Kingswood's School by John Wesley in 1748. Charles Wesley, 'Hymn 461, For Children' in *The Works of John Wesley*, vol. 7, *A Collection of Hymns for the Use of the People Called Methodists*, eds Franz Hiderbrandt and Oliver A. Beckerlegge (New York: Oxford University Press, 1983; reprint Nashville: Abingdon Press), 7:643–44.

[23] Ian Ker, *John Henry Newman: A Biography* (Oxford: Oxford University Press, 1988, 2009).

[24] Philip Curtis, *A Hawk Among Sparrows: A Biography of Austin Farrer* (London: SPCK, 1985), and short biographical accounts in David Hein and Edward Hugh Henderson (eds), *Captured by the Crucified: The Practical Theology of Austin Farrer* (London: T&T Clark, 2004); Charles Conti, *Metaphysical Personalism: an Analysis of Austin Farrer's Metaphysics of Theism* (Oxford: Clarendon Press, 1995); Basil Mitchell, 'Austin Marsden Farrer', in Austin Farrer, *A Celebration of Faith*, ed. Leslie Houlden (London: Hodder and

some details wrong. Not one considers directly or adequately Oxford's impact in shaping Farrer's vocation, asking what about that context might have mattered for his priestly academic formation. Most importantly, no such account has yet considered what others inclined to a similar vocation might learn from Farrer, his context, and his development for themselves.

The oft-repeated facts are that following an education at St Paul's School, London, Farrer entered Balliol College, Oxford, on a scholarship. His academic gifts were indisputable by the completion of his undergraduate studies. He had earned an almost unheard of triple first in three degree examinations – Classical Honour Moderations (1925), *Literae Humaniores* (1927), and Theology (1928).[25] Following further Craven Scholarship and Lidden Studentship awards, and then training for ordination at nearby Cuddesdon theological college (where he was friends with Michael Ramsey, later the Archbishop of Canterbury), Farrer became Chaplain and Tutor at St Edmund Hall, Oxford (1931–1935). From that point onward he was daily combining priestly devotion and academic activities into one set of labours. In his next two posts, as Chaplain of Trinity, Oxford (1935–1960) and as Warden of Keble, Oxford (1960–1968), the latter job lasting until his death, the same set of priestly and scholarly activities were not only allowed, but were *required* of him. He undertook them not just by virtue of his gifts, interests, or motivations, but by the formal expectations of the posts that he occupied. Farrer had to combine priestly and academic gifts to do his jobs. What is pertinent is that this vocational mix, especially in Oxford's ethos during Farrer's lifetime, was not unusual.

Farrer seems to have been the prototypical priest academic by all accounts, embodying what one might describe as a living unity of the priestly and academic. 'More than any figure of his generation in the University', F.M. Turner has written in an official Oxford University history, 'Farrer embodied the highest ideal of the college chaplain-theologian'.[26] One would have to know something of the impact of his work, and that of other 'chaplain-theologians', to know what an understatement that is.

Those who knew Farrer well or encountered him in action often commented on his apparently seamless combination of the uppermost (and, granted,

Stoughton, 1970); Michael Ramsey, 'Foreword' and Richard Harries, 'Introduction', in *The One Genius: Readings Through the Year with Austin Farrer*, ed. Richard Harries (London: SPCK, 1987); and Turner, 'Religion', 309–10.

[25]   A 'first' in Oxford is the highest possible classification, and is by definition rarely earned. To get a triple first in Oxford's examination system is evidence of an exceptional intellect.

[26]   Turner, 'Religion', 309.

occasionally the most abstract) of thinking with the most practical of priestly applications. Farrer's academic abilities were in a sense not unlike those possessed by anyone else, having been some derivation of genetic traits, combined with the fruits of spirited study and plain hard work. Yet he was unlike the academic theologian one might otherwise meet who is not quite as good with people as paper, be that books, journals, or other media. Farrer, instead, is said to have been equally comfortable when preaching or offering personal spiritual counsel to someone in need as when thinking deeply, writing, or lecturing.[27] At once he had this excellent priestly facility along with the highest of intellects, possessing the 'qualities of originality, independence, imagination and intellectual force amounting to genius', with 'genius' having been a descriptor applied to him repeatedly.[28]

Lord Bishop Richard Harries encountered Farrer in person, and has elucidated Farrer's prodigy further by noting that it had at least three discernible facets, which together spoke of a seamless unity of gifts. These were the sheer brilliance of his intellect; his poetic imagination exemplified in the 'imaginative flair, creativity and literary sensitivity at the service of his prose'; and the depth of his spirituality and personal holiness.[29] Farrer's person and work consistently represented this 'union of academic theology and lived faith', evident even when his academic writing for specialists could be quite dense and abstract.[30]

Perhaps most unusually, it has been said that Farrer's merging of priestly and academic functions was so uninterrupted that it was not easy to tell *which* he was doing *when*, other than by noting the obvious context of church or classroom at hand. Professor Basil Mitchell knew Farrer well personally and professionally. Mitchell noted in his eulogy at Farrer's memorial, 'One had the impression that as he grew older his intellectual and devotional life and his practical activities became steadily more unified ... There was no discernible difference of tone between preaching and lecturing or between lecturing and everyday speech'.[31] This was true even of 'the sustained eloquence of his [Oxford] Bampton Lectures [which] was no more than the natural and unaffected expression of a unified intellectual and spiritual vision ... surely St Mary's [the University Church] had seen and heard nothing like it since John Henry Newman occupied that pulpit'.[32] Commentators like Mitchell indicate that Farrer never veered from this union of professional emphases as some might. As years pass, people active in priestly

27   Mitchell, 'Austin Marsden Farrer', 13–16.
28   Ibid., 13.
29   Harries, *The One Genius*, ix–x.
30   Hein and Henderson, *Captured by the Crucified*, 3.
31   Ibid., 15.
32   Harries (ed.), *The One Genius*, xi, quoting Basil Mitchell.

and academic spheres can become either more academically or devotionally inclined. But Farrer's gifts grew more conjoined over time.

Farrer's greatest accomplishments, likewise, came from a combination of what are usually disparate skills: he was a first-rate philosopher and theologian; he was also a biblical scholar, if a slightly unorthodox one; and he was a keen, even if not distinguished, poet. These predilections together made him a unique thinker and writer – but also a phenomenal preacher. His sermons especially were said to 'show the many-sidedness of his ministry and the perfect wedding in him of theologian and priest'.[33] Farrer's sermons, like his other writings, spanned his interests in theology, philosophy, and spirituality, which he commonly joined in inventive ways. *The Glass of Vision*, his 1948 Bampton Lectures, was a characteristic attempt to share his thoughts on the relations of three otherwise ordinarily disjointed things, which he described as

> the sense of metaphysical philosophy, the sense of scriptural revelation, and the sense of poetry. Scripture and metaphysics are equally my study, and poetry is my pleasure. These three things rubbing against one another in my mind, seem to kindle one another, and so I am moved to ask how this happens.[34]

The same will hold for any priest academic: in addition to activities stemming from our own combined gifts, and God-given ability to bridge gaps, our work will settle on certain areas expressive of our individual interests. These may take any number of creative amalgamations and forms.

It must be noted that not everyone will 'get' or celebrate the work of priest academics. Farrer has been judged to have produced the occasional misstep *because* of his combined gifting, even while holding together erudition and religion so well generally. Charles Conti has evaluated an apparent evolution in Farrer's academic writings from, 'the massive impressive metaphysical treatise of *Finite and Infinite*, published during the heyday of Positivism, to *Faith and Speculation*, which came out shortly before his death in 1968 ... *Finite and Infinite* was so heavy in places and so condensed throughout that it placed excessive demands on the reader'. Considering the very different *Faith and Speculation*, an American reviewer described it as 'a fireside chat with an avuncular companion of urbane wit and theological whimsy'. Yet surely, by and large, those who found *Finite and Infinite* 'heavy' were not those for whom it was intended. That work

---

[33]   Leslie Houlden, 'Editor's Preface', in Farrer, *A Celebration of Faith*, 9.

[34]   Austin Farrer, *The Glass of Vision. The Bampton Lectures for 1948* (Glasgow, the University Press, 1948), x.

was composed for an academic audience of the highest calibre, bearing particular standards for any such book, and showing specialised academic interests in a distinct area of philosophy. Farrer's sentences like, 'This demand can be met, and the facts squared, if we admit that the soul's *cogitatio* – we prefer to say its *voluntas* – can be degraded and elevated up or down a continuous scale, so that the lower is the potency of the higher', were not written with chats over tea with the vicar in mind.[35]

Likewise, those who did not like *Faith and Speculation* were again doubtless not those for whom Farrer had written that work. Farrer's thoughts in the latter self-proclaimed 'Essay in Philosophical Theology', like 'to worship means to adore, however much we may tell ourselves that *laborare est orare, das Denken ist auch* Gottesdienst ... ', where Farrer quotes Hegel's famous line that 'thinking is also worship',[36] are obviously different in character to the dense prose of *Finite and Infinite*. Critics of this latter work included academic friends like Mitchell, who upon seeing it in manuscript form was 'ashamed to say I returned it without comment'.[37] Mitchell found the work to be fideist in tone, whatever Farrer's aims. The result was that Farrer seemed to have side-stepped too sharply his usually intense appeal to reason. Still, even that book was clearly written for a thoughtful and educated audience, composed by a thinker of the same ilk.

Whatever the truth of Farrer's intentions or the judgements concerning his divergent works, one can take the point that any priest academic will at times be writing or speaking for one kind of audience and not another. This is so even when making the same points with the same sets of gifts but for different readers or hearers. Does one raise, lower, or maintain one's academic or priestly tone with respect to an audience? The answers seem obvious. As a priest who teaches in a university faculty while delivering talks and homilies in both a college chapel and in nearby parish churches, I find I certainly must modulate tone and material. And I find that doing so for the best possible effect in each case takes work, sometimes may require sacrifice of content or purpose – and sometimes may fail a bit. Yet for effectiveness, we must all bear these questions in mind, whatever our views or abilities. An aspect of Farrer's overall gifting that all priest academics must possess was precisely his ability to navigate, and bridge gulfs between, devotional and academic spheres. He was able to negotiate all sides

---

[35]   Austin Farrer, *Finite and Infinite: A Philosophical Essay* (Westminster: Dacre Press, 1943), 207. Farrer is here discussing 'The Soul and Her Faculties' in the context of a broader section on 'Examination of Finite Substance: The Self'.

[36]   Austin Farrer, *Faith and Speculation: an Essay in Philosophical Theology* (London: Adam & Charles Black, 1964), 27.

[37]   Ibid.

so effectively because he lived on all sides. Farrer's natural 'habitat' and ability will be part of the vocational package that all priest academics will have to some extent, and must exercise and develop in order to make our own offering.

Rifts between erudition and practical religion, perceived or imagined, are never far away. Such a gap emerged at Oxford during Farrer's lifetime, marked by the usual 'alienation of theology from religion', as 'academic theology became increasingly separated from personal devotional life, the priestly vocation and the corporate life of the church'.[38] F.M. Turner claims in his Oxford history that at mid-twentieth century, 'Austin Farrer to some extent overcame that alienation'.[39] If 'academic' priesthood has anything of import to offer the Church, then we must all likewise actively seek to overcome these gaps whatever their form or content, and wherever we are called, using the orientation and abilities that we have been given as best we can by God's grace.

Farrer was also an active and highly capable apologist against the best of university-level attacks from movements like positivism and scientism, both of which were enjoying a heyday during his time in Oxford. Philosopher Eleonore Stump has written that we all owe Farrer a debt for the academically credible way that he accomplished his defence of the faith, and in her view more ably than did even his friend C.S. Lewis, though Lewis was the more famous of the two.[40] And all of this Farrer accomplished while his sermons remained accessible, usually starting with 'some odd or amusing everyday incident'[41] with which most everyone would be familiar.

A key to understanding the importance of his priestly academic example is that in terms of ordering his life, he was first a disciple of Jesus Christ, and was his priest. Everything else for Farrer, including the employ of his considerable intellectual gifts, stemmed from this decisive worshipful relationship. Two have written jointly, 'think of him as one whose primary vocation was that of a priest dedicated to the care of souls, whether through the preaching of the Christian faith, the administration of the sacraments, or the writing of books for learned specialists and interested laity'.[42] A man of reputed considerable personal

---

[38]   The quote from Leslie Houldon who followed Farrer as chaplain of Trinity College, and the adjoining point, appear in Turner, 'Religion', 309.

[39]   Ibid.

[40]   Eleonore Stump, January 1992, speaking at a conference on Austin Farrer at the Center for Theology and the Natural Sciences, Berkeley, California.

[41]   Mitchell, 'Austin Marsden Farrer', 15.

[42]   Jeffrey Eaton and Ann Loades, 'Austin Marsden Farrer', in Jeffrey Eaton and Ann Loades (eds), *For God and Clarity: New Essays in Honour of Austin Farrer* (Allison Park, PA: Pickwick, 1983), xiii. Also quoted in Hein and Henderson, *Captured by the Crucified*, 3.

holiness, Farrer saw prayer as his paramount activity. He even considered thinking and the search for knowledge as types of praying. 'We know on our knees', he preached.[43]

The end result of Farrer's extraordinary life and works is that like many honourable 'saints' before him he continues to have influence now. In his case, that legacy is both priestly and academic, in accordance with the gifts and opportunities that were given to him, and by the faithful exercise of all that God granted him in his particular situations.

This can all seem so easily achievable when reading accounts of someone like Farrer who seems so easily to have achieved it. Not everyone will have his impact, of course, nor should we expect to or be disappointed if we do not. What we each must attempt is faithfulness in all that God has called us to do, with our own unique set of gifts, and in our contexts. Yet accomplishments at any level combining such diverse gifts into one 'seamless' vocation seem increasingly rare in today's real world of the Church and academe. There simply are not as many people living the life of Farrer.

Where Have All the Austin Farrers Gone?

The truth is that being an 'Austin Farrer' is not only increasingly rare, but is far more difficult than it once was. This is not mere fancy, but is a verifiable fact, and is among the motivations both positive and preventative that have generated this book. There is no single answer to the complicated question concerning why, or to what might be done to correct the trend. But there are explanations, and creative suggestions for corrections, that we can begin to explore.

Given this chapter's title, let us say for the sake of argument that all priest academics are generally in some kind of life-threatening danger – even if no one is quite 'killing' them like the gifted chefs in Nan and Ivan Lyons' story. We can instigate a thought experiment for reflection in which priest academics are at least like an endangered species. There are similarities. Endangered species are identifiable, having similar characteristics as a related group, and we have established something like that of priest academics. We could even call them something like *sacerdos academica* (priest academic) in the manner that species are routinely named. Let us say that part of the explanation for the increasing

---

[43] Houlden, *Austin Farrer, A Celebration of Faith*, 45. Also Richard Harries, 'We Know on our Knees ... ': Intellectual, imaginative and spiritual unity in the theology of Austin Farrer', in *Divine Action: Studies Inspired by the Philosophical Theology of Austin Farrer*, eds Brian Hebblethwaite and Edward Henderson (Edinburgh: T & T Clark, 1990), 21–33.

rarity of Austin Farrers is that hazards are afoot threatening the survival of this species.

There is no disputing that some species die out of existence, and that this occurs for a variety of reasons. Most species that have ever existed are now extinct, many are surprised to learn. Of greatest importance for our priest academics is to name the threats, and decide whether or not the species can and should be saved.

Extinctions usually happen for the two dynamically interrelated reasons of *habitat* and *adaptability*. Members of a species either adapt to the specifics of an environment over time, including the life-threatening aspects, or if faced with severe enough hazards within a short enough time span, they can be wiped out of existence. In the latter case, a habitat in which any species is born, eats, breathes, and survives can change naturally to their detriment. This typically happens through natural causes like droughts, diseases, fires, earthquakes, variations in temperature or precipitation, the occasional enormous asteroid striking the earth, and so on. These life-threatening natural changes to habitats are almost always beyond a species' control.

Sometimes, however, deadly changes to habitats are caused by preventable means like human activity. We can dramatically alter habitable environments, ruining the ability of a species to be born, eat, breathe, and survive. This can happen through gradual and even seemingly innocent encroachments geographically, and through avertable neglect. At times through ignorance or unthinking selfish behaviour we can damage or ruin a habitat. Pollution is among such problems. Unwittingly or not, we can effectively eliminate a species' place at the table of life. Habitats can become uninhabitable through both internal and external factors, each as deadly as the other.

Homo sapiens, human beings, are rare among earth's creatures in being able not only to so affect the habitats of other creatures, but to alter our own habitats negatively or positively, detrimentally or for maximal benefit. In the worst cases of humans versus humans, we make war or commit genocide. Yes, we do kill each other. But we can self-consciously make ingenious creative changes favourable for our lives and work, too.

Regarding habitats, increasing threats to the survival of priest academics include precisely the gradual evaporation of suitable environments, in our case being places of service. An ideal environment would make clear space for a priest academic to undertake both priestly and academic functions in a single context. Farrer was able to act as a priest and academic because he was allowed and even required to do so in each successive post. Oxford and Cambridge chaplaincies, as holdovers from a monastic history, have long been places where such conjoined activities could be undertaken, even when both were not required. Chaplaincies give priest academics 'space to think', as one of my colleagues puts it. But there are relatively few chaplaincies to begin with, and fewer remain as attractive permanent positions, especially where the parameters allow or even encourage academic work alongside priestly service.

A new trend among colleges is to limit the tenure of chaplains to just several years, a number recently reduced from five to three. This is partly to avoid the legal ramification that a post can become permanent if allowed to last long enough. At the end of their tenures most chaplains, even if exceptionally academically gifted and accomplished, are pushed back into a job market where they might have to choose parish roles likely not allowing academic work. Or they hunt for purely academic roles that are virtually impossible to land in the first place, and where they are not expected or allowed to be acting also as the priests they are ordained to be.

Pressures on universities, even like Oxford or Cambridge where so many chaplaincies exist, are making it increasingly difficult to allow any 'distractions' from focused research, writing, and teaching. The United Kingdom's government, for example, places faculties under certain expectations to produce excellent research outputs at quite a high volume. Outcomes affect the ranking and funding that even theology and religion faculties receive. The powers that be are progressively forced to choose only people who will seem entirely committed to producing the required academic work, divorcing it from any added priestly vocation. One can be told even by senior ordained faculty members who were once chaplains themselves, that one's ministry will now be seen as evidence of a discursive if not a confused career path. Priestly activity becomes an unfortunate interference. There are still Canon Professorships and similar posts historically requiring a post-holder to be ordained, but even that is now changing. For example, a major theological Chair at Oxford, held in the past by Rowan Williams and similarly celebrated priests, no longer requires an ordained person. Such scenarios and attitudes may not be inherently sinister, but they are beginning to eliminate the Austin Farrers of today. Ironically, Farrer himself would have been excluded, like so many now without the occasional exceptional set of circumstances.

What about the churches, then, local or otherwise? Parishes and churches once routinely encouraged priestly and academic activities together. Well-educated parish priests wrote books aplenty. But this time, too, has largely passed, even if there are also exceptions in this category. Upon the completion of my doctoral studies and already ordained into the Church of England, a well-known priest academic who examined my work (the physicist Sir John Polkinghorne), advised me not to take a parish role, suggesting instead a university chaplaincy, if

I could get one. That was several years before the currently increasing strictures. I also serve as a local parish priest, helping in churches near my home. We and others ministering at local levels are increasingly under pressures for numbers of different reasons, including the basic evolution of parish life, and the ways and means of life generally. Imagine the opportunities to research and write at a time in history when one had to wait to receive a visit or a letter about a Christening, Wedding, or another matter – instead of numerous instantaneous emails and voicemails per day, with most who make contact expecting an instantaneous response, please? The conveniences are great for priest and parishioner alike, and all of that work is important and most worthwhile and rewarding. But the related pace comes with a price for any kind of contemplative work, like thinking, writing, and even praying.

For now, in the United Kingdom, these encroachments and shrinking habitats notwithstanding, the scholar priest vocation is still ostensibly recognised. We do recall the well-established history that produced the Farrers, Wesleys and Newmans of the world, among so many others before and after them. Ordination candidates can be identified as 'Potential Theological Educators'. But then they must all enter the same fray of scenarios and situations just named, and are offered little or no help or advice after being expensively trained. Even the best informed bishops, because of their own pressures to fill parish churches with able staff, seem unsure of what to do with the priestly academic vocation. Alas, even if they are entirely sympathetic and understanding, as things stand they cannot just create job opportunities, or offer research funding, however worthy a project may be.

These same problems exist in other countries worldwide. An American cathedral sub-dean has recently written of talking with 'those considering calls to the priesthood who were turned away because they also happened to have a call to an academic vocation as well. They were told that they were too academic to pursue a call to priestly ministry, and that they would have to choose either a vocation to the priesthood or an academic career'. One was advised that the church required people who wanted to *do* things, not just think about them. The sub-dean remembered his own ordination process, when he had been told to 'hide any hint of an academic vocation from the committee so that they would not hold it against us'.[44] And all of this happens when much of the required reading for ordination trainees will have been written by priest academics

---

[44] The Reverend Canon Robert Hendrickson, 'The Consolation of Theology: or Why We Need Scholar Priests', 1 March 2013, http://thesubdeansstall.org/2013/03/01/the-consolation-of-theology-or-why-we-need-scholar-priests/.

and those similarly gifted across many centuries. Surely, we must not see our short-sightedness.

These are but a few examples of oft-repeated sets of circumstances, and conversations mentioned by countless people in numerous scenarios. I had coffee with a fellow priest yesterday as I write, who without knowing I was completing this chapter, raised precisely these kinds of vocational worries. She is set to face them when her chaplaincy, which comes with an academic teaching fellowship, ends soon. So much for the current state of *sacerdos academica*'s habitats. Still two hopes remain, as they do for any 'threatened' species. These are the *human factor*, and *adaptability*.

Of the *human factor*, human beings are, indeed, able self-consciously to make ingenious creative changes favourable for our lives and work. Any increasingly strained situation making the life and work of the priest academic more difficult can be changed. We are not decrying laws of nature or natural disasters, or anything else beyond our human ingenuity or powers to fix. We are talking about human choices to make space or not for a set of people clearly called by God across the centuries to do work from which the entire Church continues to reap benefits. This factor is largely *external* to the species, however. It will require those with the power to affect habitats to desist or act accordingly.

The same principles and permissions that have made priest academics like Farrer successful can work not only in environments like Oxford or Cambridge where the church and education have flourished together, but in any educational or church institution, at any level or location. The same applies in the country at a rural parish church, in the city, and whether in the poorest or richest of neighbourhoods; on the prairie or plain, and in any other location or context willing to recognise, foster, and support a similar vocation and set of priestly activities. It is the principles governing a habitat, not the location or the context, that really matter.

Adaptability is a factor largely internal to a species. Anyone truly called by God to be a priest academic must certainly try to reach for the best opportunities most helpful to the faithful performance of their vocation. But we must not forget the likes of Paul, who, having a similar set of gifts, wrote a portion of the New Testament not from a professorship but a prison cell. Those holy writings, deep, learned, and empowered by God through His Spirit, and touched by the faithful prayers and sufferings of the saint who penned them, are touching lives still. A species is as a species does, in other words. Having the right gifts does not automatically entail having the right attitudes or willingness to do whatever one can do in the circumstances one happens to be in, but that is what we must all do. Like the dessert chef in the Nan and Ivan Lyons' story, it can be tricky to fend off extinction while doing what we are made to do well. Nevertheless, as we seek to be educated and trained for our special vocations, and to teach others likewise, let us continue to do as we are called to do with all of our might. No one is trying to kill us, thankfully.

Who knows what might happen next in the long and certain history of priestly academic vocations – and in yours specifically? The possibilities seem endless. The Church may yet prove to be the best locus for academic thinking and writing – our seminaries, theological colleges, Bible colleges, monasteries, cathedrals, chapels, and local churches. The chapters to follow offer insights, clues, reality checks, and encouragements from experienced priest academics working in a great variety of such settings and at different levels. As we read, think, and continue to work, we can also pray to the Lord to send more academic priestly labourers into his fields.

Chapter 3

'And Enjoy Him Forever': Biblical and Theological Reflections on Dual Vocation

Michael J. Lakey

The Problem of Dual Vocation: Aristotle and Paul in Conversation

Aristotle

> Nature makes nothing in the mean manner that the metalworkers make the Delphic Knife. Rather, *one* tool is fashioned for *one* activity. In this way, each tool is brought to most beautiful completion, since it serves *not many activities but one*. (Aristotle, *Politics* 1252b.1–5)[1]

By strange coincidence, Aristotle, born in the northern city of Stagira, anticipated by millennia that other great northern philosopher, the unknown Yorkshireman who coined the phrase *'tis neither nowt nor summat'*. Both of these intellectual giants were profoundly troubled by things which lack a unity of identity, function and purpose. Whereas the Yorkshireman is stereotypically frank, the Stagirite expresses his discomfort by means of an illustration involving an obscure piece of cutlery: the Delphic Knife. Of course, ironmongery is an odd place to commence an exploration of academic vocation in the Church, but Aristotle deserves a hearing, especially in relation to the question of dual vocation. This is because of his argument that in an environment ordered towards certain corporate ends things and people find their fulfilment in niche activity. The question here is whether it is apt, or even possible, for one person to occupy more than one niche well, *viz.* to have a dual vocation as theologian and priest.

Beginning with Aristotle's illustration: the precise design of the blade used in the sanctuary of Apollo is something of a mystery. We know that visitors to the Pythic Oracle at Delphi routinely offered sacrifice and that the knife was cultic.

---

[1]   My translation and emphasis.

We also know that the avarice of the Delphic priests was a commonplace in Antiquity, it being possible that the knife's additional functions being somehow related to this.[2] However, Aristotle does not say. His objection seems *prima facie* to concern chiefly the design of the knife rather than its usage, since what he takes issue with is its multiplicity of function.[3] Contrast this with Nature, in which '*one* tool is fashioned for *one* activity'. That he elects to frame the contrast between singularity and multiplicity of purpose in terms of an implied though stark contrast between meanness ('the mean manner': *penichrōs*) and generosity is, for Moderns, a counterintuitive move. If competence is evidence of gratuity, why is multi-competence not a sign of even greater gratuity? That Aristotle understands this not to be the case is clear, yet why he makes *this* point in *this* way requires some explanation.

It is important to recognise that though the argument of this section of *Politics* concerns Greek social structure, it proceeds by means of a comparison with those described as Barbarians. Aristotle understands the key difference between these two modes of social organisation to be that the latter inadequately distinguish between the ranks of women and slaves. His conclusion is that barbarian culture is an undifferentiated mass of unspecialised individuals (*Pol.* 1252b.5–15). Clearly, *he* regards this arrangement as deficient. As to why he frames what is essentially a contrast between specialism and generalism in terms of liberality and illiberality, the answer lies in his discussion of various forms of *koinōnia* ('fellowship'). For the Stagirite, fellowship is a mode of social organisation involving shared interest, mutual advantage and a common life. Two aspects of this bear upon the question of niche activity and thus extend to the question of dual vocation. In the first place, niche activity is *necessary* because human beings are not omnicompetent. It is only when socially organised that humanity tends towards self-sufficiency, with differently specialised individuals providing what any given individual might otherwise lack. Secondly, niche activity is *desirable* because it is through specialisation that a member of the group fulfils his or her unique *telos*. Both aspects can be seen in Aristotle's discussion of the city (*Pol.* 1252b.30–53a.20), though the same is also true *mutatis mutandis* of smaller *koinōniai* such as villages or households. In short, specialisation is integral to Aristotle's notion of *sociopoiesis* (generation of community),[4] since a multi-competent individual needs no-one.

---

[2]   See Carol Dougherty and Leslie Kurke (eds), *The Cultures within Ancient Greek Culture* (Cambridge: Cambridge University Press, 2003), 80–81.

[3]   See Walter Burkert, *Homo Necans: The Anthropology of Ancient Greek Sacrificial Ritual and Myth* (Berkeley: University of California Press, 1983), 119.

[4]   See Stephen Pickard, *Seeking the Church* (London: SCM, 2012), 183–4.

This resonates with Aristotle's notion of 'friendship/love' (*philia*), since reciprocity in the form of giving and receiving gifts is integral to the foundation and maintenance of affective forms of social solidarity. Moreover, relationships in both domestic (*Nicomachean Ethics* 1159a.26, 62a.21), and political (1155a) associations are elsewhere described in terms of *philia*. Nevertheless, Aristotle's point here is not ultimately about reciprocity and solidarity between individuals, but rather concerns the generosity of the agency that orders the whole. It is *Nature* whose generosity he contrasts with Delphic parsimony. Apparently, his argument is that interdependent specialisation is evidence of a gratuitous, sociopoietic super-agency. This is disclosed through mutual necessity across difference.

The Apostle Paul

> There are varieties of gifts, but it is the same Spirit; and there are varieties of services, but it is the same Lord; and there are varieties of activities, but it is the same God – the one who *activates the all in all*. (1 Cor 12:4–6)[5]

The similarities between Aristotle and Paul on the topic of social formation are several. Perhaps the most striking is Paul's use of the term *koinōnia* (Gal 2:9, Phil 2:1) to describe the Church, together with the attribution of *sociopoiesis* to an activating ordering intelligence, whose agency is described in terms of gratuity, *viz.* God/the Spirit of God (1 Cor 12:4, 2 Cor 13:13). More generally, the Apostle, like the Stagirite, understands ideal social structures to involve partnership and mutual necessity, ideas which coalesce in the famous somatic metaphor of 1 Corinthians 12. This choice of metaphor is hardly inventive, since the body was a common *topos* in Antiquity (Livy, *History of Rome* 2.32.7–11).[6] In terms of direct parallels, life in the ecclesial body shares with its Aristotelian counterparts the traits of diversity, directedness and cooperation. A 'diversity of ministries' (*diareseis diakoniōn* 1 Cor 12:5) is directed towards the one Lord; individual gifts towards common 'advantage' (*sympheron* v.7); and the body metaphor itself towards a practice of mutual care and honour (v.25).[7]

The structural similarity between these two models is apparent in Paul's discussion of the interrelationship between gifting (1 Cor 12:7–11) and

---

[5]   My translation and emphasis.

[6]   See Michael J. Lakey, 'Body', in *Dictionary of the Bible and Western Culture*, eds Mary Ann Beavis and Michael J. Gilmour (Sheffield: Sheffield Phoenix Press, 2012), 64–5.

[7]   Margaret Mitchell, *Paul and the Rhetoric of Reconciliation* (Louisville: Westminster John Knox Press, 1991).

function (vv.28–9). The specific examples he chooses ('foot', 'hand', 'ear', 'eye' vv.15–17) all suggest a one-to-one correlation between a particular member's capacity and that person's role in the body (esp. vv.16–17). In short, Paul, like Aristotle, understands the common life of a community in terms of niche activity and divine gratuity (v.24). Nevertheless, unlike Aristotle, the correlation between individual identity and purpose is not always one-to-one. Apostle and tongue-speaker both appear on Paul's list of ecclesial activities in 1 Cor 12:28, and yet Paul claims to exercise both (1 Cor 14:18). Likewise, 'not all are prophets' (1 Cor 12:29), but the gift of prophecy is universally commended (1 Cor 14:1). It is telling that when Paul employs the body metaphor *elsewhere* (Rom 12:3–8), there is a direct correspondence between a 'grace entrusted' (*hē charis hē dotheisa* Rom 12:3, 6), *viz.* a ministry, and the possession of 'gifts commensurate with' (*charismata kata* v.6) the exercise of that grace. It may be that Paul's preferred position resembled Aristotle's, which begs the question of whether he too had a preference for singularity of purpose.

At this point, a key difference between the Stagirite and the Apostle should be noted: specifically the latter's narrative soteriology. Despite their models of social formation resembling one another, Paul differs fundamentally from Aristotle regarding the nature of things. Whereas Aristotle is concerned with things and persons fulfilling their inherent potential appropriately, Paul understands the world and its teleology to be shaped by a theology of Creation and Redemption. Though these two moments correspond to one another, they are not identical, as the Adam-Christ comparison indicates (Rom 5:12–21, 1 Cor 15:42–9). Also, both moments are instances of radical Divine gratuity: things and persons do not inhere of themselves, but because God speaks new being and new potential into existence where and when he wills (Gen 1, 2 Cor 4:6, 5:17). As a consequence, the relationship between the world and a Pauline Christian is doubly – perhaps even triply – ambiguous (1 Cor 7:29–31). It is as if Creation requires re-framing *from within*, returning to its deepest primal structures at the very moment at which it is drawn forward in Christ towards an imperfectly known future (2 Cor 3:18, 4:6).[8] This may be why Pauline communitarian discourse is so very conventional in its logic, yet so left of field ideologically that it can describe the 'natural' Aristotelian categories of humanity (men, women, slaves, ethnicity) as irrelevant to the baptismal identity (Gal 3:26–8). Paul's basic intuition seems to suggest that vocation involves the revivification of what is already there, but also its transformation through the

---

[8]   See further Michael J. Lakey, *Image and Glory of God*, Library of New Testament studies (London: T & T Clark, 2010), 92–5.

addition of something novel. The questions remain as to how this impacts Paul's broadly Aristotelian approach to community and the question of dual vocation.

Aristotle, Paul and Dual Vocation

None of the preceding material ought to be taken to imply that Paul was either knowingly or straightforwardly Aristotelian. That he knew Aristotle's *Politics* cannot be excluded; Aristotelian ideas were certainly current during this period. However, since the Stagirite is hardly the only Ancient to have reflected on the nature of community in terms recognisable here, how would we know what Paul knew? Besides, it would not be wise to assume too much about the scope of his education.[9] Though he has considerable rhetorical ability, and does not appear ignorant of Graeco-Roman ideas, slogans and literary forms, he rarely cites Graeco-Roman literature as such.[10] In any case, the genealogy of Paul's model of community is irrelevant to the present discussion, it being sufficient only to note the strong structural similarity with Aristotle.

By way of drawing together the discussion: both Aristotle and Paul have a strong preference for niche specialisation as a driver of concord and cooperation within their respective communities (*homonoia*). Both make connections between specialised activity, the necessity of cooperation and affective social solidarity (*philia/agapē*). Both treat this as foundational to *sociopoiesis*. Both treat *sociopoiesis* as the work of a gratuitous ordering agency. Where they differ is in their underlying view of the world, Paul's thought being filtered through a matrix of biblical Creation ideas and a narrative cosmological soteriology. This informs his ecclesial social radicalism, which contrasts Aristotle's rather conservative defence of the aristocratic ideology of his own context. In short, the difference between the Stagirite and the Apostle seems to turn not on the shared logic of *sociopoiesis*, but on the latter's distinction between life *kata sarka* ('according to flesh') and a hitherto unprecedented form of life *kata pneuma* ('according to Spirit', see Rom 8:5–9, 2 Cor 5:16–17). For Paul, ritual transitional moments such as baptism appear to coincide with the reception of a pneumatically mediated *charism*, which is directed towards the gift of a definite function within the eschatological community, *viz.* a *new creational*

---

[9]   See E.P. Sanders, 'Paul Between Judaism and Hellenism', in *St. Paul Among the Philosophers*, eds John D. Caputo and Linda Alcoff (Bloomington, Ind.: Indiana University Press, 2009).

[10]   See Lakey, *Image and Glory*, 79–92; also Abraham J. Malherbe, *Paul and the Popular Philosophers* (Minneapolis: Fortress Press, 1989).

teleology. The similarity with Aristotle at the level of logic would suggest that Paul tended to regard this as singular in form.

The consequences of this for ordained academics are substantial. If the nature of vocation is such that the Divine call is to perform one particular function in particular, then the challenge to those called to two distinct types of Christian service will always be that of integrating these tasks, or at least of ordering them appropriately. More is at stake than the logistics of integration; this discussion suggests that singularity of purpose demonstrates, indeed enacts, the *sociopoietic* generosity of a God who is not so under-resourced that He asks individuals to double-up (Matt 3:9). According to this, the question facing priest-academics is not simply how to make ministry work; it is how to achieve narrative unity[11] in a *single-yet-apparently-dual* pattern of life and in so doing honour the sheer abundance of God. This process of narrative integration is summed up by Rowan Williams, who likens the discernment of vocation to hearing one's true name.[12]

Naming is a helpful metaphor for the discernment of vocation, since it assists in organising the various options faced by scholar-priests. One approach might be to insist that the ordained-theologian's true name is *either* scholar *or* priest! Another might be to suggest that one vocation or name is proper to the Academy whilst the other is proper to the Church. These seem to me to be extremely difficult positions to defend. The one inadequately attends to the historical phenomenon of scholar-priests in the Church and the experiences of those who continue to find themselves called to this pattern of ministry, whereas the other relegates scholarship to the Academy, thereby neglecting that theology is the proper language of Christian faith. Of course, the dynamic aspects of Paul's anthropology might be cited to support the idea that, despite there being stable locations within the ecclesial body, an individual is not required to occupy only one such location in perpetuity. This is correct; ministerial duality might be experienced simultaneously *or* in temporal succession. Common to both cases is the challenge of integration: to discover how the graces, practices, virtues and proximate ends peculiar to the one ministry might inform, modify, expand and be recapitulated in the other. *Inter alia*, this involves asking not only how activities intrinsic to scholarly life might contribute to prayer, pastoral formation, mission

---

[11]   See Alasdair MacIntyre, *After Virtue*, 2nd edition (London: Gerald Duckworth & Co., 1985), 219.

[12]   Rowan Williams, *A Ray of Darkness* (Cambridge, Mass.: Cowley Publications, 1995), 152.

and preaching but also how worship, especially the celebration of the Liturgy, might contribute to research and teaching.[13] It is to this task that we now turn.

The Vocation to Theology: Newman, Pieper and Augustine

John Henry Newman

> If ... Theology, instead of being *cultivated as a contemplation*, be limited to the purposes of the pulpit or be represented by the catechism ... [it] is not simple knowledge, but rather is an *art or a business making use of* Theology.[14]

One of the more interesting discussions of the place of theology in the scholarly life of a university is found in John Henry Newman's seminal work *The Idea of a University* (1854). Aimed at providing a rationale for a distinctively Catholic higher education, the argument of this piece draws heavily upon the *artes liberales* (liberal arts) tradition of Antiquity.[15] As such, like Aristotle (*Politics* 1337b.1–20) and Seneca (*Epistles* 88.1–5) before him, Newman carefully differentiates between two types of intellectual activity, the former (liberal) pursuing knowledge for its own sake and the latter (useful/servile) for its utility in regard to some commercial, professional or ministerial end. That Newman chose theology and ministry to illustrate this distinction is particularly apt for present purposes, since he offers a starting point for thinking about the role of the discipline in the academy, the Church and the seminary. Of course, the excerpt above begs certain questions, such as whether he offers us a realistic view of the academy and whether he is correct in talking of theology for ministry in utilitarian terms. We touch on some of these issues in the remaining discussion.

Nevertheless, Newman's appropriation of the antique tradition is not uncritical. Ancient models of *paideia* understood the attainment of knowledge, broadly construed, to be the proper end or goal of human intellectual activity (Cicero, *On Duties* 1.6.18). The same is true of Newman's work. He treats each of the liberal arts as having its own proper place in any coherent, intellectually rich account of the world: knowledge, including theological knowledge, is simply

---

[13]   See further Daniel W. Hardy and David Ford, *Jubilate: Theology in Praise* (London: Darton, Longman and Todd, 1984).

[14]   John Henry Newman, *The Idea of a University* (London: Longmans, Green & Co., 1907), 108–9. Emphasis added.

[15]   See further Werner Jaeger, *Paideia: The Ideals of Greek Culture* (Oxford: Blackwell, 1939).

worth having. Despite this, ancient writers tended, with occasional exception (Seneca, *Epistles* 88.2), to associate intellectual formation with formation in moral virtue (as in Aristotle, Cicero and Quintilian), whereas Newman strictly maintains that these processes are unconnected. He writes: 'philosophy ... gives *no command over the passions*', suggesting that 'Liberal Education makes not the Christian, not the Catholic, but the gentleman'.[16] Whilst this approach is common to much of the Christian tradition, Newman's specific stance is shaped in particular by his confessional position regarding the relationship between nature and grace. Take, for example, his careful teasing apart of the real but temporal good of education and humanity's eternal end in God: 'we perfect our nature, not by undoing it, but by adding to it what is more than nature'.[17]

Despite his overarching aim of a formational environment in which Nature and Grace might be integrated – the confessional liberal arts university – it is doubtful that the normative secular expectations of the present-day university environment encourage this sort of integration. Not least, there is the problem of the present-day academy's liability to profound utilitarian pressure.[18] At most, Newman's aims are practically attainable only intermittently. The intellectual formation of university students is increasingly directed towards occupational ends, even in notionally liberal subject areas. Outside of the lecture hall, students are rarely unaffected by the need for paid work or untouched by the ubiquity of consumerist models of recreation. The result is a deficit of time and space for the acquisition of the habits necessary to cultivate knowledge as the 'good' Newman understood it to be. More ominously, this state of affairs is hardly restricted to students; academic staff, ordained or otherwise, subject to the demands of institutional exercises such as the UK's Research Excellence Framework (REF) are in the same boat.

Beyond the academy, Newman's observation that the ministries of teaching, preaching and pastoral care in churches and seminaries utilise theology has qualified merit. Whether this is a complete account of its role is another matter. It is worth noting the unusual occupational location in which ordained ministers find themselves. Priestly activity differs from other occupations traditionally designated as servile by being directed *in scope* towards human life in its entirety and *in orientation* towards humanity's final rather than its proximate end. As such, a priest is not straightforwardly a professional, since ministry is more expansive than the exercise of expert knowledge over a limited area of occupational practice.

---

16   Newman, *Idea*, 120. Emphasis added.

17   Ibid., 123.

18   See Mike Molesworth, Elizabeth Nixon, and Richard Scullion (eds), *The Marketisation of Higher Education and the Student as Consumer* (London: Routledge, 2011).

Neither is he or she a third sector activist, an ecclesiastical version of the 'organic intellectual' whose job it is to help a community to articulate its own practical wisdom. Rather, a priest is someone *called*: called to participate in a divine life which is pure excess; called to witness to this life through proclamation and service; and called to enact this life through sacramental action. These activities require virtue, insight and imaginative depth as much as they do skill, expertise and acumen. Such a person must know God and be shaped by this knowledge. This signals the importance of theological vision as a fundamental vocational category (Prov 29:18, Isa 6:1), one that is intensified when the life and character of priesthood coincides with scholarly calling.

Josef Pieper

In regard to theological vision, vocation and scholarly activity, the work of Josef Pieper on leisure is highly illuminating. Like Newman, Pieper draws upon the liberal arts tradition, though by contrast with Newman he is less concerned with the question of education *per se* than he is with the preconditions for cultural activity. He makes two principal claims. First, he argues that the connection between knowledge and leisure in Antiquity is far from incidental; it is common, though in different ways, to both the liberal arts tradition and the Jewish practice of Sabbath. Second, he proposes that leisure time free from resource pressure is epistemologically crucial. It cultivates the dispositions and habits by which one is enabled to see, to receive and to understand the world aright. Pieper's notion of leisure is highly specific; it is not merely time spent away from work, for the sake of work; it is time devoted to doing no-thing.[19] Thus spent, leisure time involves intentional inactivity and festivity. It is gratuity at work. Unsurprisingly, Pieper finds these qualities to be present *par excellence* in practices such as worship.[20]

Pieper's analysis turns upon an epistemological taxonomy that differentiates between reason in its active-investigative (*ratio*) and in its receptive-contemplative (*intellectus*) moments. Making space for leisure disciplines one to encounter one's object of knowledge as a gift to be received (*intellectus*) rather than to be made subject to an instrumental, reductive and ultimately domineering form of scrutiny.[21] This is to posit a close relationship between rest and receptivity to phenomena such as intuition, faith and epiphany – in short, between the cultivation of non-utilitarian space and time and openness

---

[19]   Josef Pieper, *Leisure, the basis of culture*, trans. Alexander Dru (New York: Pantheon Books, 1952), 31ff.

[20]   Ibid., 65ff.

[21]   Ibid., 25–43.

to genuine theological vision. In terms of its implications, Pieper's work could indicate that the situation in some ministerial settings constitutes a potential, though profound, theological challenge to the vocational integrity of those environments. When time poverty, resource pressure and, dare it be added, an ethos underpinned ideologically by the rhetoric of sacrifice combine to militate against the cultivation of habits of receptivity, then there is a risk that vision might be bounded by utility and thus be cut off from its own source.

In terms of the significance of Pieper's work for the present discussion, note the participatory nature of his epistemology. Pre-Modern epistemologies tended to assume that only like could know like (Aristotle, *On the Soul* 1.404b–05b), that apprehension occurs by means of some form of substantial participatory correspondence knower and known (1 Jn 3:2). Though Pieper's work does not entail precisely this position, his stance is redolent of it nonetheless. His point about leisure is not chiefly concerned with our use of time, as if evacuating time of activity would solve our problems; it concerns re-*creation* or restoration, with leisure as the apt orientation of oneself as a creature in a world of fellow creatures. As such, there is a connection, albeit tacit, between participation in the world and the capacity to see it whole (*intellectus*). In terms redolent of the Apostle Paul (1 Cor 2:10–11), Pieper makes a similar point in regard to receiving the Spirit and the knowledge of God.[22] In both cases, grace is epistemologically central. It is not merely that through leisure knowledge is received as a gift; rather, through re-*creation* one receives *back* one's knowing self. Of course, this begs the question of whether the liberal/useful dichotomy is sufficient to account for the practices and dispositions that sustain theological activity. If Pieper is correct, leisure is ultimately an ontological move oriented towards participation in God's own rest, towards entry into the overflow of the Divine life and towards the giving and receiving of love (Matt 11:28, Heb 4). This indicates that there is a third theological moment alongside the contemplative and the active, one that is erotic, unitive, ecstatic *and basic*. The correspondence is inexact, but these categories are redolent of the tripartite taxonomy in Catholic thought of dogmatic, moral and mystical theology.

By way of further comment, this helps to give some leverage over the question with which the first half of this chapter concluded: how might worship, especially the celebration of the Liturgy, contribute to research and teaching? If the preceding observations hold then it follows that participation in the festal and the sacramental has the capacity to function as a wellspring of the sort of theological vision that ought to sustain and enliven scholarship.

---

[22]   See ibid., 20; also Lakey, *Image and Glory*, 56–65.

This is because activities such as prayer, praise, proclamation and presidency are not, in Pieper's terms, work; they are gratuity. They generate and sustain the erotic, unitive and ecstatic orientation of both individual Christians and the Church towards God. As an entry into God's rest worship hones the spiritual senses, educates the desires, decentres and reorients the self.[23] Consequently, though liturgical involvement is no guarantee of theological insight, one might nevertheless expect to find scholarship that has been divorced from worship to be impoverished in one way or another. Of course, in the case of scholar-priests a combination of roles is not only an opportunity for scholarship to be illuminated and energised by intimate involvement in the cultic; there is also the risk of combined ministry multiplying pressures, especially as both academic and parochial settings are occupationally intense. However, the foregoing argument would suggest that attending to the centrality of leisure puts work, including theological and pastoral work, in its proper place.

Augustine

> Suppose, then, we were wanderers in a strange country, and could not live happily away from our fatherland, and that we ... determined to return home ... But the beauty of the country through which we pass, and the very pleasure of the motion, charm our hearts, and *turning these things which we ought to use into objects of enjoyment*, we become unwilling to hasten the end of our journey. (Augustine, *On Christian Teaching* 1.4.4)[24]

By way of moving the present discussion in the direction of a conclusion, we leave modern debates regarding education and culture and instead turn back to the world of Late Antiquity in the form of this brief allegory from Augustine's *On Christian Teaching*. The passage is situated towards the beginning of a discussion of things and signs, itself the opening move in an argument devoted to constructing a distinctively Christian reception of Graeco-Roman *paideia*. It alludes to, or at least evokes, the biblical narratives of the Exodus and the Parable of the Prodigal Son (Lk 15:11–32), thereby giving concrete, scripturally evocative form to a positive account of the Christian life as a narrative quest for God. Particular attention should be given to Augustine's mention of utility and enjoyment in this passage. Note his description of enjoyment as 'rest[ing] with

---

[23]   See Samuel Wells, 'How Common Worship Forms Local Character', *Studies in Christian Ethics* 15 (2002): 166–74.

[24]   Translation J.F. Shaw; emphasis added. In Vol. 2 of *Nicene and Post-Nicene Fathers, First Series*, eds P. Schaff and H. Wace (Edinburgh: T & T Clark, 1887).

satisfaction [in something] *for its own sake*' (*Christian Teaching* 1.4.4), with the implication being that utility involves treating it as a means to some other end (1.4.4). Later in the work (1.22.20), he expands upon this by insisting that only *God* is sufficient in which to rest, indeed that God is *only* to be rested in and never utilised. The corresponding position, that the world is insufficient for true enjoyment but apt for utility, is found here.

Since Augustine was a significant figure in the Christian appropriation of the liberal arts tradition, it is unsurprising that his terms overlap those of Newman and Pieper. Indeed, Augustine's reception of the ideas of use and enjoyment is significant for what follows, from Thomas on human teleology (*Summa Theologica* I–II qq.11, 16) to Reformed confessional materials (*Shorter Westminster Catechism* A.1). The motif of the journey through temporal things in search of the eternal is also significant, having echoes in the Collect for Trinity IV (*BCP*) and even in John Bunyan's *Pilgrim's Progress*. Unlike Newman and Pieper, Augustine is not chiefly concerned with either the distinction between free and useful occupations or with the epistemological effects of leisure. His principal concern is for the apt use of creation; indeed, he employs the terms *uti* ('use') and *frui* ('enjoy') in a manner reminiscent of Graeco-Roman moral reasoning about this topic.[25] Significantly, aesthetic experience is central to his argument, since it is uneducated desire for beauty and pleasure that threatens to misdirect the pilgrim from his or her destination. Again, the relationship between untutored desire and the misdirection of the self is a common *topos* in Antiquity, not least in Stoicism and in Pauline Christianity (see 1 Cor 6:12, Epictetus, *Discourses* 3.12.4–6, Seneca, *Epistles* 116.5).

If Augustine is correct and God alone is to be enjoyed, then it logically follows that human beings, including ourselves, are objects of utility. The difficulty arising from this, as Augustine himself notes (*Christian Teaching* 1.22.20), is the problem of utility and love. Understanding there to be an unconditional obligation to both the first and second Great Commandments, he poses the question: ought one's human loves to be characterised by enjoyment or use? Though this question does not have the same force here that it came to have in the work of subsequent thinkers, it is nevertheless important for Augustine to address. His particular proposal is that, whilst God is to be loved for Godself, all other things 'are to be loved in reference to (*propter*) God' (1.27.28). Of course, this suggests that one's loves require intentional ordering if they are to

---

[25]   See Carol Harrison, *Augustine: Christian truth and fractured humanity* (Oxford: Oxford University Press, 2000), 98 nn.40–41; also Allan Fitzgerald and John C. Cavadini, *Augustine through the Ages: An Encyclopedia* (Grand Rapids: Eerdmans, 1999), 859–61.

be proportionate to their various objects. For Augustine, the order of love (*ordo amoris*) requires one to love God first (Deut 6:5), then one's own soul, then one's neighbour (Lev 19:18) and after that one's body.[26]

This point regarding the intentional ordering of affections bears upon the theology and practice of ministry. To assert that God is *summum bonum* (final good) is to imply more than that we ought to order our loves. It is to make a bold claim about God's absolute primacy as the organising principle of an authentically Christian approach to the world (1 Cor 8:6). It is also to necessitate a consequent intentional ordering of activities (1 Jn 3:18), such that the glory of God, the good of one's soul and the good of one's neighbour receive due attention practically as well as affectively (*Christian Teaching* 1.28.29). In short, *if* one's chief end is 'to glorify God and to enjoy Him forever' (*Shorter Westminster Catechism* A.1), *then* it follows that all other ends are subordinate to this, contributory to it or in competition with it. To minister ordinately (as a priest, a scholar or both) in the light of this is to accept that ministry is not the sole or even the most important ministerial imperative. Augustine hints at this in his discussion of the balance to be struck between the active and contemplative lives. Though he describes ministry as the 'necessity of love', it never entirely obscures the need for 'holy leisure' (Augustine, *City of God* 19.19).

In terms of the pursuit of *theology*, it is worth offering a final reflection upon the significance of the first Great Commandment for Augustine. As the following epexegetical comment indicates, he clearly understands the implications of the instruction to love God in cognitive and not merely affective or volitional terms: 'concentrate all [one's] thoughts, [one's] whole life and [one's] whole intelligence upon Him' (*Christian Teaching* 1.22.21). Moreover, the noetic terminology Augustine employs here, 'thoughts' (*cogitationes*) and intelligence (*intellectum*), would indicate that he has in view the life of the mind broadly construed. This is an insightful reading, since the reference to 'mind' in the Gospel accounts of this logion (Mk 12:30, Matt 22:37, Lk 10:25–28) is itself a gloss on the expansive anthropological terms used in the Deuteronomic version, which denote the interior person in his or her entirety.[27]

The implications of this reading for the relationship between theology and vocation are significant. It suggests a deep integration between the three theological moments mentioned above in the discussion of Pieper (contemplative, active and unitive). Any or all of these can be movements of love.

---

[26]   See Harrison, *Augustine*, 97–100, esp. 99; Oliver O'Donovan, *The Problem of Self-Love in St. Augustine* (New Haven: Yale University Press, 1980).

[27]   See Johannes Behm, '*dianoia*', in *The Theological Dictionary of the New Testament*, 10 vols, ed. Gerhard Kittel (Grand Rapids: Eerdmans, 1964), vol. 2, 963–7. See esp. 965–6.

Indeed, as accounts of the totality of the erotic dimension of theology, they are incomplete without one another. To borrow from the world of human relationships: it would be an odd form of marital love in which partners had no interest in either mutual knowledge or mutual service; indeed, such circumstances would probably indicate some underlying problem at the level of unitive desire. In concrete terms, this is to signal the importance of theological activity as an aspect of a rightly oriented interior life, without which ministry cannot be done aright. It is to treat it as a spiritual discipline as basic as prayer, as integral to the pursuit of holiness. This is also to go some way towards answering the question posed in the first part of this chapter, namely how to unify the *single-yet-apparently-dual* pattern of life of the scholar-priest in a theologically apt manner. Theology, liturgy and pastoral ministry are all bound up with the soul's *eros* for God; it would be surprising if they could not be pursued in combination!

Summary and Conclusion

The present chapter has set out to contribute to the discussion of academic vocation by considering some of the issues attached to the call to the study of theology, what this call might mean for the life of the Church and, in particular, the implications of this for those called to both priestly and scholarly ministries. It is apt, though coincidental, that a chapter devoted to addressing the question of dual vocation should come in two parts. The first part explored some of the issues attached to the idea of vocation, and some of the ways in which these issues and concerns become more pressing in the specific case of a dual vocation. This was done by means of a comparison of Aristotle and Paul on the question of the relationship between individual purpose and social formation. For Aristotle and Paul there is a relationship between vocation and grace. This is principally concerned with signification, with the way in which specialised individual activity discloses the generosity of the agency that organises and animates the group. Both authors see the disclosure of gratuity in the call to be one thing in particular, since this fosters interdependence, solidarity and reciprocity with differently specialised individuals. The question of identifying and ordering the calls to both scholarship and to priesthood is closely related to the question of whether an ordained academic is one thing or two, and also to the further question of how his or her vocation can be understood ecclesially as a gift.

The second part of this chapter sought to examine various aspects of the nature and purpose of theology so as to illuminate its role alongside priestly ministry. This took the form of an exploration of the ideas of utility and enjoyment in the work of Newman, Pieper and Augustine. Newman proved to be a helpful entry point, partly for the way in which he employs the classic liberal arts tradition, but also for the way in which his application of this tradition to mid-Victorian notions of the Academy casts into relief some of the present-day occupational pressures experienced by theological scholars in universities, seminaries and churches. Pieper's work was particularly significant. His emphasis on the epistemological centrality of leisure addresses some of the issues arising from the discussion of Newman. What is more, though he does not tackle theological study directly, his work is directly relevant to the vocational question of the integration of scholarship and priesthood; leisure, festival *and worship* educate participants in the art of attending receptively to the graced elements of human existence. To bring scholarly and particularly liturgical activity together, is thus to put theology into close relationship with its animating principle. Augustine's discussion of use and enjoyment and of the order of love entails the converse position, namely that human existence in its entirety is properly theological and that, regarded thus, scholarship can itself be an act of service, of liturgy (*leitourgia*), an outworking of love. This is to draw attention once more to the way in which, in Augustine, all of human life can be drawn together in God in a profound unity and a deep integrity. In short, it is to observe the way in which the call to holiness underpins all vocation, including that of the scholar-priest.

PART II
Scholarship and Ministerial Practice

Chapter 4

Playing Football at Mansfield Park: Christian Doctrine and the Local Church

Peter Groves

It would be wrong to call Jane Austen an Augustinian, not least because recourse to long words and labels would be likely to invite her pointed disapproval. However, the similarity between the Georgian novelist and the late antique theologian runs further than her name being an abbreviation of his, at least in this respect: the dangers of misplaced desire concerned them both. Danger is perhaps too gentle a word to describe the disastrous consequences of the Fall which so alarmed Augustine, consequences which, for human beings, meant that disordered reason and will were bound inevitably to reproduce themselves in other human beings, since it was impossible for children to be conceived without lust, and both sin and guilt were physically transmitted from one generation to another. Sadly, the author of *Mansfield Park* has left us no critique of *The City of God*,[1] and no explicit account of human sin. However, she was far from theologically unaware. Danger is perhaps more of an Austen word than an Augustinian one, but control of style and lightness of comic touch should not lead us to doubt the enormity of turmoil and suffering which might be the lot of the young man or woman whose misplaced desire is allowed to triumph over their reason.

In *Mansfield Park*, the kind, pious and slightly dull Edmund Bertram is the Christian facing danger, and the danger is presented to him in the attractive form of Miss Mary Crawford. Her arrival, and that of her brother Henry, is a consequence of the close relationship between social and financial power, and the parochial system of the early nineteenth century. In *Mansfield Park* it is the elder brother who is the prodigal. Edmund's brother Tom has accrued a level of

---

[1]   *The City of God Against the Pagans (De Civitate Dei Contra Paganos)*, completed around 426CE, is a theological treatise by Augustine of Hippo in 22 books. A milestone of Christian thought, it covers a vast range of theological issues, including creation, humanity, sin and salvation. Augustine, *The City of God against the Pagans*, ed. R.W. Dyson (New York: Cambridge University Press, 1998).

debt through gambling that prevents his father bestowing the Mansfield living upon his younger son.[2] Instead, he takes advantage of the then common practice of selling the right of presentation to someone else. This practice was lucrative: in *Sense and Sensibility* John Dashwood values presentation to a living worth £200 a year at £1400.[3] Sir Thomas Bertram makes his arrangement with a Dr Grant, whose wife, younger than he by 15 years, is sister to Henry and Mary Crawford. It is not long before these 'young people of fortune' are added to the society of the village, and to the dramatis personae of the novel in which they both take central parts. Henry's interest in the heroine, Fanny Price, is motivated chiefly by the piquancy of the new: this is the first time he has encountered a young woman inured to his charms. Mary's interest in Edmund takes her by surprise, as she has previously had eyes only for eldest sons. Having been determined to dissuade Edmund from ordination, she finds her interest revived on learning of the dangerous illness of his brother Tom, a crisis which presents the very real prospect of Edmund succeeding not to the family's other living, but to the title and estate.

Mary Crawford, as well as being 'remarkably pretty', is intelligent, witty and vivacious, easing herself naturally into contrast with the shallow Bertram daughters so indulged by their aunt, the monstrous Mrs Norris. Edmund is, unsurprisingly, much taken by one so attractive, but their morals and priorities are very different. Mary is startled when she first discovers that Edmund is to be ordained.

'But why are you to be a clergyman? I thought that was always the lot of the youngest, where there were many to choose before him'.

'Do you think the church itself never chosen, then?'

'Never is a black word. But yes, in the never of conversation, which means not very often, I do think it. For what is to be done in the church? Men love to distinguish themselves, and in either of the other lines, distinction may be gained, but not in the church. A clergyman is nothing ... .

One does not see much of [his] influence and importance in society, and how can it be acquired where they are so seldom seen themselves? How can two sermons a week, even supposing them worth hearing, supposing the preacher to have the

---

[2]   Jane Austen, *Mansfield Park*, ed. Tony Tanner (London: Penguin, 1966), 58.
[3]   Jane Austen, *Sense and Sensibility*, ed. Tony Tanner (London: Penguin, 1969).

sense to prefer Blair's to his own, do all that you speak of? govern the conduct and fashion the manners of a large congregation for the rest of the week? One scarcely sees a clergyman out of his pulpit. ... '[4]

Edmund replies with all the romantic piety of the ordinand fresh from Oxford:

'A fine preacher is followed and admired; but it is not in fine preaching only that a good clergyman will be useful in his parish and his neighbourhood, where the parish and neighbourhood are of a size capable of knowing his private character, and observing his general conduct, which in London can rarely be the case. The clergy are lost there in the crowds of their parishioners. They are known to the largest part only as preachers. And with regard to their influencing public manners, Miss Crawford must not misunderstand me, or suppose I mean to call them the arbiters of good breeding, the regulators of refinement and courtesy, the masters of the ceremonies of life. The manners I speak of, might rather be called conduct, perhaps, the result of good principles; the effect, in short, of those doctrines which it is their duty to teach and recommend; and it will, I believe, be every where found, that as the clergy are, or are not what they ought to be, so are the rest of the nation.'[5]

There is much to contest in Edmund's analysis, not least the anti-metropolitan tone and the idealisation of the small rural parish. But the basic point is clear. The teaching of 'doctrines' is not something limited to the pulpit. Mary's assumption is that an incumbent is likely to be absent except on Sundays, and even then might well be expected to rely on the sermons of the popular Edinburgh preacher Dr Hugh Blair. Edmund insists that the basis of good teaching is the presence of the parson among his parishioners, and not simply his residence, but his living of the Christian life through the practice of his ministry, in such a way as to teach by influence the living of that life to those for whom he is pastorally responsible.

It is a view echoed strongly later in the novel by his father, who is adamant that his son, once presented to his living, must reside in the parsonage house.

'He knows that human nature needs more lessons than a weekly sermon can convey, and that if he does not live among his parishioners and prove himself by

4   Austen, *Mansfield Park*, 120.
5   Ibid., 121.

constant attention their well-wisher and friend, he does very little either for their good or his own'.[6]

The author has laced this reminder of what constitutes good ministerial practice with heavy irony. Sir Thomas, a character so compromised by the fortune he makes from his slave plantations, is himself an absentee, choosing disastrously to entrust his children's education to their Aunt Norris. The consequences of his neglect are, finally, the elopement, adultery and divorce of his elder daughter, Maria, who receives perhaps the harshest reward of any Austen character: she is sent to live with Mrs Norris, 'where, shut up together with little society, on one side no affection, on the other no judgment, it may be reasonably supposed that their tempers became their mutual punishment'.[7]

Edmund's idealism and his father's hypocrisy are two among many instructions for pastors which can be found in the writings of the Rector of Steventon's daughter. Some of her better known clergy are so amusingly presented as to distract the reader from the substantive theological point being made. In *Pride and Prejudice*, the ludicrous Mr Collins – 'Mr Bennet's expectations were fully answered. His cousin was as absurd as he had hoped'[8] – is introduced by way of a letter. It is a missive justly famous for its unctuous pomposity, which so amuses the reader as almost to obscure the telling reaction of Elizabeth, no stranger to delusion herself but still the novel's sharpest observer and principal truth-teller. We are told that 'Elizabeth was chiefly struck with his extraordinary deference for Lady Catherine, and his kind intention of christening, marrying and burying his parishioners whenever it were required'.[9] How good of a parish priest to do the bare minimum, that and only that which will be publicly and legally noticed.

Even more damning is the characterisation of the incumbent of Highbury, Mr Elton, in *Emma*. Although the patrician society of Jane Austen's novels is a barrier for some readers, others are encouraged by the importance, throughout her work, of Christian charity and generosity towards those less fortunate. Such charity is one of Emma Woodhouse's more attractive features, despite her edgy emotional naivety. The early part of the novel is dominated by Emma's ridiculous plan to bring together in marriage her orphaned friend Harriet Smith, and the remarkably venal Mr Elton, who seeks a marriage of considerable financial advantage. Emma and Harriet make a visit to a needy family struck by sickness, and as they return they bump into the vicar, who is, it seems, concerned for

---

6   Ibid., 255.
7   Ibid., 450.
8   Jane Austen, *Pride and Prejudice*, ed. Vivien Jones (London: Penguin, 1996), 59.
9   Ibid., 56.

the same unfortunate people. He intimates that he had been going to call on the family, but would defer his visit for a while now that others had attended them. However, in half a sentence two pages later, Austen offers a detail which condemns Mr Elton as starkly as any of her erring clergy. Emma deliberately breaks her lace, which excuse necessitates a stop for them all at the vicarage, with Elton and Harriet left alone. When their brief conversation is reported back we learn that 'he had told Harriet that he had seen them go by, and had purposely followed them'.[10] He had, in other words, no intention of visiting the family which needed his pastoral care, he had simply wanted an excuse to talk with Emma (who is, of course, the object of his grasping affection). So we see depicted a parish priest who not only neglects the visiting of the sick which is his duty, he lies about that neglect to two of his parishioners in order to ingratiate himself with the rich young woman on whom he has his eye. When measuring just how unpleasant a man Austen is portraying, we should set his reprehensible actions not simply against the genteel social world of the novel's setting, but also and more importantly against the scriptural injunctions to generosity and truth which were the basis of the author's moral world. Mr Elton is a hypocrite, a sham of a parish clergyman, and he does not go unjudged by the events of the narrative. Rejected by Emma, he quickly runs off into the arms of one of English literature's most ghastly characters, who will soon be heard complaining loudly about her husband's parishioners, people who have the gall to want their vicar to be a vicar and not a society fop.[11]

Of course Jane Austen is not the timeless schoolmistress of the Church, and the world of her characters is, on the whole, even more privileged than her own. But through her condemnation of absenteeism, and her disdain for poor pastoral practice, we can see something of the importance of context for Christian teaching. However, it would be easy, and misleading, to make that simple point alone, to remark unremarkably that theological teaching is not something to be separated from the context of the parish, that the local church is the framework into which we must fit the work of Christian doctrine. But such an account is not nearly adequate to Austen's examples. Edmund Bertram's defence of the parson's doctrinal practice suggests something much more than the necessity of residence in the local parish. Rather, he is maintaining that all the pastoral activity of the local priest in his local setting constitutes the teaching ministry to which he is called. Sermons are one thing, but there are other things, and it is all the things together which are the effect of the 'doctrines' which the parish priest

---

[10]   Jane Austen, *Emma*, ed. Ronald Blythe (London: Penguin, 1966), 114.
[11]   Ibid., 439.

is called to teach and recommend. The ministry of teaching is not the repetition of particular 'doctrines', it is the practice of them. Doctrine – teaching – is much more than 'doctrines'.

'A New Teaching'

This double contention – that Christian teaching is much more than verbal communication or the making of statements, and that there is an organic relationship between the activity of doctrine and its particular setting – is basic to the theology of the gospels. The narrative of the Gospel of Mark makes those points explicitly. Mark throws us into the adult ministry of Jesus with very little preparation, presenting Jesus' proclamation of the kingdom and call to repentance immediately before their practical parallel in the call of the fishermen. Another 'immediately' places us on the Sabbath and enacts for us the first of many dramatic conflicts between Jesus and the powers which enslave, in this case the unclean spirit which possesses the man in the Capernaum synagogue. Having heard Jesus' rebuke and witnessed the man's deliverance, the onlookers respond in telling fashion. 'What is this? A new teaching ... ' (Mk 1:27) Jesus has not, in any ordinary sense of the word, offered any 'teaching'. He has demonstrated authority, power and control, and he has liberated a person from suffering. But he has said very little. Seeing his action described as 'teaching' would puzzle us if we read this text in isolation or if we were to forget that those whom Jesus has called are those who are called 'disciples', that is, those who learn.

Mark's is a narrative of the truth of Christ in action: calling, teaching, healing, travelling, calming, saving, assuring, challenging, comforting, questioning, giving, submitting, dying and rising. These actions take place not at a distance from their intended objects and audiences, but within the world which both inhabit. Nowhere is the importance of presence made clearer than in the crafted double story of the healing of Jairus' daughter and the woman with the flow of blood. The latter account is deliberately sandwiched within the longer story of the little girl's healing, presenting a mimetic textual reference to the events of being enclosed and pressed upon, of the intimacy of close proximity on which both these healings depend.

The story is familiar (Mk 5:21–43). Jesus responds to Jairus' call for help by setting off for his house, but during the journey he encounters another who seeks wholeness, the woman whose years of suffering have only been exacerbated by those to whom she had previously turned for help. The merest touch of the hem of Jesus' garment is enough for her, but anonymity is impossible. Jesus is shown in control by his knowledge that power has gone out of him, but this is a compromised control. It was the woman who touched him. Her action was made possible by his being embedded in the crowd. She can touch him because he is as close to those around him as he can possibly be, being pressed and put upon as he struggles through the crowd. The power has gone out from him, as the text puts it, precisely because he was in the midst of the crowd and could be touched. Had he been at a distance, the woman – afraid to speak – would have had no hope. The physical intimacy, the connection which she is able to make with the one who is in the midst, is the key to her salvation, and that intimacy will be replayed as the tale is completed, when Jesus dismisses all but a few and then takes the daughter of Jairus by the hand. These are simple and obvious examples of a simple gospel truth – that the teaching of Jesus himself is the life he incarnates by coming among us as human.

Doctrine as Practice

The practical nature of teaching suggested by both the gospel and the novelist chimes loudly with some important debates in modern and postmodern theology. The American theologian George Lindbeck[12] is just one of many writers who insist that to understand the content of Christian faith and life as reducible to a series of propositions – whether verifiable or not – is to reduce Christianity to something infinitely less than itself. Interpreters of Augustine and Aquinas have reminded us that their use of the Latin term 'doctrina', though different in those two different authors, nevertheless assumes something quite essential: that 'doctrina' is not an act of intellectual reflection or ratiocination, but rather an action, and in particular an action of the Church. Whilst critics of a propositional model of theological language vary in their proposals, the need to understand doctrine as practice, as something done, and to recognise that truth claims and forms of life are inseparable, is one which many affirm.

The work of the Austrian philosopher Ludwig Wittgenstein lurks near the surface of these discussions. That the term 'language game' is now so familiar to many is testimony to the influence of Wittgenstein's later writing. By that image, he expresses the diversity and rule-governed nature of language, and the impossibility of identifying any single essence or rule of meaning which will explain how human beings understand everything. He notes that there is no

---

[12] In his much discussed essay *The Nature of Doctrine: Religion and Theology in a Postliberal Age* (Philadelphia: Westminster Press, 1984).

single thing common to all games, hence the appropriateness of the coinage. (Whilst, in the context of a discussion of doctrine, it might be tempting to see theological discourse itself as a language game, Wittgenstein himself lists much smaller and more specific linguistic events as 'language-games' – examples include giving orders and obeying them, reporting an event, forming and testing a hypothesis, making a joke.[13]) Along with Wittgenstein's use of game imagery goes his contention that 'the speaking of language is part of an activity, or of a form of life',[14] that is a pattern of human activity which need not and cannot be justified, but provides the basis for the network of shared meanings which enable human linguistic communication to take place.

The influence of Wittgenstein upon theological conversation has been various – enormous in some quarters, and minimal in others. But those who have offered accounts of doctrinal practice and meaning which build upon that influence include Lindbeck (though his non-realist approach to theological truth claims is not one which Wittgenstein would have shared), and also some of his critics, in particular Rowan Williams,[15] whose reflections on the history of doctrinal language, and especially on the work of John Henry Newman, offer a distinctive approach to the definition of doctrine which will help us reflect on the parish as a theological setting.

Commenting on Newman's study of the controversies surrounding the Council of Nicaea in AD 325, the book he called *The Arians of the Fourth Century*, Williams observes a distinct lack of propositional rigidity in Newman's interpretation of early Christian thinkers. This nascent theology 'maintains orthodoxy by a constant process of self-correction, the endlessly mobile, circling reference of metaphor to metaphor'.[16] What comes to be called orthodoxy is not 'a matter of just getting one set of formulae right'.[17] (Newman's insistence on the need to understand patristic theology in its widest possible linguistic context is explicitly noted by Williams as an anticipation of Wittgenstein: 'to find meaning, look for use'.[18]) The use of definitions, the emergence of dogmatic statements

---

[13]   Ludwig Wittgenstein, *Philosophical Investigations*, trans. Elizabeth Anscombe, Peter Hacker and Joachim Schulte, 4th edition (Oxford: Wiley-Blackwell, 2009), §23.

[14]   Ibid., §23.

[15]   Rowan Williams, 'The Judgement of the World', in *On Christian Theology* (Oxford: Blackwell, 2000), 29–43.

[16]   John Henry Newman, *The Arians of the Fourth Century* with an introduction and notes by Rowan Williams, (Gracewing, 2001), Introduction p. xlii. See also Rowan Williams, 'Newman's *Arians* and the Question of Method in Doctrinal History' in *Newman after a Hundred Years*, eds Ian Ker and Alan G. Hill (Oxford: Clarendon Press 1990), 263–86.

[17]   Williams (2001), xliii.

[18]   Ibid., xliii.

such as those which emerged from Nicaea itself, is something almost to be regretted. It represents, perhaps, a failure of theological engagement whereby the early flowering of Christian truth is necessarily narrowed and codified.

The distinction between doctrine and dogma which is at work here (similar but not restricted to a traditional Roman Catholic account) is one which depends on the vitality of doctrine as something which is done, and something which is ongoing. (There are connections, of course, with Newman's later *Essay on the Development of Christian Doctrine*.) The pre-Nicene theology which Newman seems to idealise undoubtedly qualifies as doctrine – as the practice of Christian teaching. But it is the reaction to conflict and disagreement which gives us dogma. The arguments which we now call the 'Arian controversy' called for response, and so what had earlier been a mobile set of overlapping metaphors had to give place to something which could be more clearly 'either / or', a statement or series of statements by which the positions of others could be measured. The reticence of earlier theologians in the face of mystery is necessarily overcome in response to what Newman sees as the distortion of doctrinal truth. In this case, the arguments concerning the divinity of the Son made inevitable the refinement of terms and adherence to particular forms, which we now associate with the language of creed, definition and dogma. The expression of theological claims in a set of statements called a 'creed' and promulgated by a 'council' is what qualifies as dogma – as that which is defined and fixed at a point in history – and constitutes a channelling and a particularisation of the activity of doctrine, which is the ongoing transmission of Christian truth in the life of the Church.

Drawing this contrast allows us to understand doctrine both as something fluid and something practical. The connection with Edmund Bertram's idealism, and the motive urgency of Markan teaching, is not hard to make. The practice of doctrine is just that, a practice. The transmission of Christian truth is far broader an activity than the accumulation of propositional truth claims. This practice – doctrine – is not something preconceived which is then dropped into an existing context. Rather the life of the Church is both context and practice where Christian theology is concerned. The neat delineation of general and particular, or essential and contextual, will not do justice to doctrine as something which is done, and continues to be done.

Playing the Game

A metaphor along the lines of Wittgenstein's imagery may help. Football, or soccer, is the world's most popular participation sport. Part of its universality is the ease with which it can be played – one needs only a ball and some players. The players must, however, share certain common assumptions about what constitutes the game. They must, broadly speaking, know the rules of football. Those rules are well known to many who have never read the official 'laws of the game', but those official laws, agreed by the international governing body of the sport, provide ultimate arbitration when football is being played to a high standard (and often when it is not: the present writer holds a season ticket at Queens Park Rangers). Now it would be highly unreasonable to suggest that, because a professional match in the UEFA Champions League involves all sorts of things absent from a playground kick about, the latter should not be called a game of football. And in both cases, most of what was needed to make the game work would be understood by all. The playground player might, if he or she wishes, pick up the ball in the centre of the pitch, and run with it. But to do so and claim that this still constituted a game of football, would be daft. Likewise, the playground fixture may be an extremely serious one, so serious that any disagreement caused one set of players to leave the pitch and start a parallel game on the other side of the playground. Were they to do so, they would still clearly be playing football, but they would certainly not be playing this particular game of football.

Doctrine, in my forced metaphorical account, is the game of football. It has lots of different aspects. Tactics, shirt colours, physical fitness, psychology, skill are a few. We might propose liturgy, preaching, prayer, fellowship, pastoral case and evangelism as a few ecclesial parallels. Dogma constitutes those definitions which the game requires in order to make it work. At a serious level, the pitch on which the game is being played will be delineated by white paint. In a social game, the pitch may be agreed. Either way, the existence of a pitch is a common assumption, as is the position of the goals, whether marked by jumpers or goalposts. Likewise, the rules – however sophisticated – are agreed among the players so that the game may take place. Of course there are complexities and arguments over definition, such as we may find in newspaper columns calling themselves 'You are the ref', which invite the knowledgeable reader to suggest a course of action in a strange footballing circumstance. But the very fact that such minor boundary disputes take place is testimony to the existence and function of the rules. The game is there to be played.

Doctrine – teaching – is an activity analogous to the playing of a game. Christian doctrine is a particular activity, playing this game and not another one. If I suggest that a sensible ecclesial course of action is the abandonment of the doctrine of the Trinity, then I am no longer playing this game, no longer practising Christian doctrine. To borrow again from Rowan Williams, in forcing my own practices upon the game to which they are alien, I am guilty of assessing the language of doctrine as if it were primarily illustrative, that is, it tells us something about what is already the case. So if, for example, the human Jesus of Nazareth manifests a truth about the love of God, in order for me to be aware of this, I must have a notion of the love of God with which this Jesus of Nazareth somehow fits. Williams's contention is that the narrative of Jesus is not illustrative but constitutive: there is no truth about God which is independent of the particular historical individual who is Jesus of Nazareth.[19] Likewise, the particular historical circumstances of Christian language – the history of doctrine, in other words – is not a neutral, untheological area of study, but part of the Church's reflection on its own identity which makes up so important a part of the game. That reflection, being part of this game, is not in a vacuum, but here and now in this particular context, in the life of the Christian Church.

Theology and the Parochial Church of England

No doubt a great deal could be said about these metaphorical stretches, but in concluding this chapter I shall dwell on some questions for theologians and for the Church of England in particular. The claim being made is that doctrine is nothing more nor less than the ongoing witness to and delivery of Christian truth in the life of the Church. The relationship between the parish as setting and doctrine as activity need hardly be stated. There is no need whatsoever to provide any apology for the parochial setting as a properly doctrinal context, one whose ongoing life testifies to the interdependence of place, word and action in the doctrinal narrative. Rather, we may suggest, it is any other setting, in particular any non-ecclesial setting, which needs to justify itself as a possible context for 'doctrine'. The assumption made by many that the phrase 'professional theologian' means 'university academic' is, or ought to be, open to significant question.

---

[19] Rowan Williams, 'Maurice Wiles and Doctrinal Criticism' in *Wrestling with Angels*, ed. Mike Higton (London: SCM Press 2007), 275–99.

Of course doctrine is far more than the Christian life of any individual minister (which the fictional Edmund Bertram would be quick to affirm). It is the worshipping life of the Church, the calendrical observance of properly Christian time, the enactment in mission and action of the call to preach the good news, proclaim liberty to captives, to tend the sick, bind up the broken hearted, comfort the dying and pray for the dead. It is the study and the centralising of scripture, the celebration of the life of grace in the Christian sacraments, the building up of the community – Christian and beyond – in fellowship and generosity. All these are the life of the Church, and hence all of these are 'doctrine', they are the teaching that the Church does. Discussing and reflecting upon them, particularly but not only through intellectual study, is what we call Christian theology. Undoubtedly one can reflect from a distance, and we can study theology in all sorts of different situations, but we are mistaken if we think we can practise doctrine anywhere other than in the Church and, in the Church of England, that will almost always mean a parish church.

What must be challenged, therefore, is the assumption that different Christian theological practices are restricted to certain spheres only, that academic theology is merely a preparatory discipline for the practice of 'pastoral' or 'contextual theology'. Our universities and our training institutions are adept at providing instruction in the traditional areas of study which we associate with 'academic theology', and we are all too familiar with the sense that this study is to be left behind once the practicalities of Christian ministry have begun, replaced by the 'real' theology of parochial or sector ministry. However, much of what calls itself 'academic theology' would not qualify as doctrine in our sense, but rather as something which supports or contributes to doctrine when undertaken as an ecclesial task. Its value is not to be doubted, but if it is the task of the Church it is not something which can be separated from Christian practice, certainly not something which belongs to some people rather than others, ordained or otherwise. A simple example concerns the study of scripture. The uncomfortable sense that 'Bible teaching' and 'biblical studies' are very different things is deeply problematic for the Church. Centralising the text of scripture is essential to doctrine, and is something the Church does in many ways – liturgical as well as rhetorical or traditionally didactic. The Church must own 'biblical studies' whilst not being enslaved to it, but it must also promote and practise 'biblical studies' as part of its doing of doctrine.

The same is true of the study of the Christian past, which forms a necessary part of theological reflection on Christian identity. Christian history is also an aspect of 'doctrine', it is something theological because it is practised as part of the life of the Church. Doctrine is always a present activity, an activity which is not dropped into an ecclesial context, but which shapes and provides that context even as it is practised. It is the activity of Christian teaching, the doing of doctrine, which makes these intellectual tasks theological. So 'contextual theology' or 'pastoral theology' or 'academic theology' are not neatly distinct, just different members of the same family, different playing positions on the same football team.

The laudable practice of nurturing young clerical scholars has recently been given expression in the Church of England's 'Young Priest Theologians Network'. Important work is being done. Parallel to this development is the classification made of some candidates for ordination, who are marked out at an early stage as 'potential theological educators'. But if our suggestions about doctrine are worthwhile, some serious questions arise: they are linguistic, but it has been insisted throughout this chapter that meaning is not a matter of language alone. Have we really thought our terminology through? Does the Church of England really want to suggest that it is possible to be a priest and not be a theologian? What could that mean? And why are only some who are training for ordination 'potential theological educators'? Language and nomenclature are important parts of formation in particular. The work of encouraging the scholarly vocation will prove essential, but if it is to avoid contradicting itself, it must guard against the privileging of certain disciplines in or by certain places or people.

The danger which Mary Crawford presents to Edmund Bertram is only finally overcome when he is stunned by the cool shrug of her shoulders in response to the scandalous elopement of her brother and his sister. It is this final conversation which brings him to the recognition that he had been in love with 'the creature of [his] own imagination'. The conclusion of the novel is, in part, Edmund's recognition of the love which has been present to him throughout in the person of the heroine. The ongoing task of Christian doctrine is not something which the Church will find anywhere other than within its own life. Or, to put it another way: the Church should know what it is that it is doing.

Chapter 5

Biblical Scholarship and Preaching

Stephen C. Barton

'Scribes Trained for the Kingdom of Heaven'[1]

Given that it is customary in some quarters for the preacher to begin with a text, my text for the reflection that follows is Matthew 13:51–52. Strategically placed at the conclusion of Jesus' teaching in parables about the kingdom of heaven, Matthew has Jesus challenge his disciples as follows:

> 'Have you understood all this?' They answered, 'Yes'. And he said to them, 'Therefore every scribe who has been trained for the kingdom of heaven is like the master of a household who brings out of his treasure what is new and what is old'.[2]

The metaphor of the disciple as a 'scribe trained for the kingdom of heaven' offers a suggestive scriptural warrant for exploration of the role of biblical scholarship in preaching. The image of the 'scribe' (*grammateus*) is of a person so schooled in the sacred traditions, so immersed in the disciplines of reading and interpretation, that true discernment and communication of God's (new and old) ways with the world becomes possible.

Of course, we live in a world markedly different from the world of the scribe in the time of Jesus. One of the differences is the marked *plurality* which characterises the social and institutional contexts in which texts are studied and knowledge is pursued. Even sacred texts like the Bible are the subject of intense scholarly engagement, not only in ecclesial contexts such as churches, seminaries and denominational universities, but also in secular state-funded institutions of higher education. There is no doubt that this plurality generates tensions of all kinds. Is the Bible to be studied as Scripture to inspire faith or as ancient source

---

[1]   I dedicate this chapter to Michael Lakey on the occasion of his ordination as a Deacon in the Church of England, Christ Church Cathedral, Oxford, 5 July 2014. My thanks to Michael and to Keith Beech-Gruneberg for their helpful comments on this chapter.

[2]   Biblical quotations are from the NRSV unless otherwise indicated.

to inform historical reconstruction? Is the Bible to be read as a canonical witness to divine revelation and the coming of God or as a religious classic within a wider literary canon? Should the Bible be interpreted according to the traditions and practices of the Church or like any other book? Should the Bible be celebrated as a summons to life or held in suspicion as a weapon of oppression? Does the Bible belong to world-wide communities of faith or to the world of reason as institutionalised in university departments of biblical studies?[3] So there *are* tensions. In my opinion, however, such tensions, although serious, can be over-dramatised. They can also be enormously creative, not least in relation to the ecclesial practice of preaching.

'And How are They to Hear Without Someone to Proclaim Him?'

Before proceeding further, however, a word is needed on the nature of preaching itself. What are we talking about?[4] Suggestive are the words of Paul in Romans 10:14–15:

> But how are they to call on one in whom they have not believed? And how are they to believe in one of whom they have never heard? And how are they to hear without someone to proclaim him [*kērussontos*]? And how are they to proclaim [*kēruksōsin*] him unless they are sent? As it is written, 'How beautiful are the feet of those who bring good news [*tōn euangellidzomenōn ta agatha*]!'

From Paul's impassioned cry in its context in Romans we may infer at least the following. First, in Stephen Wright's pithy formulation, preaching is 'the oral proclamation of God's good news'.[5] Second, the 'good news' concerns the disruptive eschatological reality of Jesus Christ risen from the dead and exalted as Lord of all. Third, the proclamation is a practice whose goal is transformation:

---

[3]   For representatives of opposing views, see Angus Paddison, *Scripture: A Very Theological Proposal* (London: T&T Clark International, 2009), and Philip Davies, *Whose Bible is it Anyway?*, 2nd edition (London: T&T Clark, 2004).

[4]   For present purposes, I am ignoring the common distinction between evangelistic preaching and preaching for the edification of the faithful. As Rowan Williams puts it in 'The Sermon' in *Living the Eucharist*, ed. Stephen Conway (London: Darton, Longman and Todd, 2001), 47: 'The more deeply I am converted, the more hungry I become, the more deeply I realise my unconversion. I preach into and out of that situation'.

[5]   Stephen I. Wright, 'Preaching, Use of the Bible in' in *Dictionary for Theological Interpretation of the Bible*, eds Kevin J. Vanhoozer et al. (Grand Rapids: Baker Academic, 2005), 617–21, at 617.

the salvation and conversion of life of humankind. Fourth, for the proclamation to be heard, a proclaimer is required. Fifth, the practice has scriptural warrant and draws upon scriptural resources. Sixth, the practice is apostolic and therefore ecclesial: it is an outworking of the mission of God to the Church and to the world.

Theologically speaking, therefore, whatever we say about the relation between biblical scholarship and preaching has to take with full seriousness the nature of preaching as a spiritual (but also embodied) practice within the life and witness in Christ of the Church. Indeed, in at least one of its modes, the practice of preaching is an integral part of the liturgy. Taking its rise from the readings of Scripture which precede, and finding formal articulation in the words of the Creed which follow, preaching has its place as a central element of the Ministry of the Word which reaches its fulfilment in the Ministry of the Sacrament. God's grace mediated orally (and aurally) through sacramental word, reaches its climax in God's grace mediated materially through sacramental meal.[6]

'By the Renewing of Your Minds'

Against the backdrop of preaching so understood, biblical scholarship is necessarily a subordinate partner. This is so on theological grounds, since proclamation of God's good news is a spiritual charism given, irrespective of intellectual capacity and scholarly training, to whom the Spirit wills, as evidenced in Acts 4:13, where Peter and John, although powerful preachers, are identified pejoratively by the Jerusalem authorities as 'uneducated and ordinary [*agrammatoi kai idiōtai*]'.

It is also evident on historical grounds. Historically speaking, biblical scholarship was never intended to be an end in itself. Rather, the very *raison d'être* of biblical and theological learning in the life of the Church was for the edification of the faithful and the evangelisation of unbelievers – not least, through the preaching of sermons. Speaking of the importance of preaching in the period of the Church Fathers, for example, Carol Harrison[7] says this:

> The sermon is indeed the most common genre among the fathers' writings, and for most of them, it represents at least two-thirds or more of their literary output.

6   On the significance of the interrelation of 'Word and Table', see Gordon W. Lathrop, *Holy Things. A Liturgical Theology* (Minneapolis: Augsburg Fortress, 1993), 43–53.
7   Carol Harrison, *The Art of Listening in the Early Church* (Oxford: Oxford University Press, 2013), 147.

This is, first and foremost, because they thought of themselves as pastors rather than academic theologians; that any theology was generally done through exegesis of Scripture with a sermon, rather than apart from it ... ; that biblical commentary often took the form of a series of sermons rather than an independent work; and that other concerns (such as the suppression of heresy) was met most effectively through the sermon.

But to acknowledge that biblical scholarship plays a subordinate role in the ecclesial practice of preaching is by no means to diminish its importance. That Paul could exhort the Roman Christians to 'be transformed by the renewing of your minds [*tēi anakainōsei tou noos*]' (Rom 12:2, also Eph 4:23) is more than adequate testimony to the high value placed on the role of sanctified reason in the life of the Church. And, as Ellen Charry has demonstrated, disciplined, scholarly, scriptural inquiry into the truth about God, humanity and living well was a dominant feature of Christian thinkers for the first sixteen centuries of the Church's life, from Paul to Calvin.[8]

Having touched on these important introductory matters, in what follows, I want to do two things. First, I will offer several constructive ways of thinking about the business of biblical scholarship in its relation to Christian practices like preaching. Second, and following good precedent,[9] I will offer a 'sermonic exhibit' of my own, in order to show what I believe to be a constructive homiletic outworking of biblical scholarship in practice, as it touches on a subject of considerable doctrinal, liturgical, and emotional sensitivity.

Performing the Text

One does not have to have seen the 1997 film *The Apostle*, starring Robert Duvall as a charismatic Pentecostalist preacher, to acknowledge that preaching is a dramatic act. It is a way of 'performing' the biblical text. The preacher's communication through words, gestures, postures, inflections, tone of voice, facial expressions, mood, and interaction with the congregation are all acts of interpretative engagement and appropriation which, when done well, allow the biblical text to 'speak' and the congregation to 'hear'.

---

[8]   Ellen T. Charry, *By the Renewing of Your Minds. The Pastoral Function of Christian Doctrine* (New York: Oxford University Press, 1997).

[9]   See Stanley Hauerwas, *Unleashing Scripture. Freeing the Bible from Captivity to America* (Nashville: Abingdon, 1993), Part Two.

But a skilled performance of any kind has to do justice to *the kind of text* being performed and to the context in which the performance is taking place. For example, take a musical score. A skilled performance of a Beethoven symphony presupposes an ability to interpret the score; and that in turn involves, not just a knowledge of the symphonic form, but also an understanding of the composer and his times, the circumstances in and for which the music was composed, and the history of its interpretation in previous performances. It also involves well-rehearsed collaboration between conductor and orchestra, as well as sympathetic engagement with the audience in such a way that the audience itself is enabled to enter into the overall performance-event.

By analogy, one way of appreciating the role of biblical scholarship in preaching is to think of the biblical scholar as a member of a large and ongoing interpretative community helping to sustain skilled performance of the text of Scripture. By 'skilled performance' I mean practices (including preaching) that allow the text to come alive for its hearers (and readers) in ways that enable both conversion of heart and transformation of life through participation in the transcendent life of the God to whom Scripture bears witness.[10]

Just as a performance of a Beethoven score is predicated upon the practice of the various musical disciplines, or (as a comparable analogy) the performance of a Shakespeare play is predicated upon the practice of the disciplines of the stage, so also the performance of Scripture demands the practice of the various disciplines of reading and interpretation – disciplines at which the biblical scholar is especially adept by virtue of his or her intellectual formation and academic vocation. There is a technical aspect to apt performance of the Scriptures, and this is where the biblical scholar has a role to play. The role is important, in so far as expertise may be required in, say, offering historical background, or addressing semantic problems, or deciding on a translation, or describing how texts have been taken (or *mis*taken) in the past. But the role is subsidiary. It is subsidiary to the main drama: and the main drama is the Spirit-inspired life of the Church in its praise, prayer and preaching, and in its sacrificial witness to God in the world. As Nicholas Lash[11] puts it:

> [T]he poles of Christian interpretation are not, in the last analysis, written texts (the text of the New Testament on the one hand and, on the other, whatever appears today in manuals of theology and catechetics, papal encyclicals, pastoral

---

[10] Seminal is Nicholas Lash, 'Performing the Scriptures', in *Theology on the Way to Emmaus* (SCM: London, 1986), 37–46. See also, Stephen C. Barton, 'New Testament Interpretation as Performance', *Scottish Journal of Theology*, 52/2 (1999), 179–208.

[11] Lash, 'Performing the Scriptures', 42 (author's emphasis).

letters, etc.) but patterns of human action: what was said and done and suffered, then, by Jesus and his disciples, and what is said and done and suffered, now, by those who seek to share his obedience and his hope. We talk of 'holy' scripture, and for good reason. And yet it is not, in fact, the *script* that is 'holy', but the people: the company who perform the script.

This, it seems to me, is a useful (implied) corrective to temptations to any kind of biblicism, including a kind that biblical scholarship itself may encourage. It also puts the emphasis in the right place: on the people and the ways of faithful living and dying in times past to which Scripture bears witness, and on the response which Scripture invites of its readers and hearers in times present and future.

Deepening Practices

Another way to situate biblical scholarship constructively within a larger framework, is to draw on metaphors of 'deepening' and to think of biblical scholarship as a *deepening practice*. Such a practice – and in this it is like prayer, is even *a form of prayer* – has as its goal the gaining of insight into what really matters: and in relation to Scripture, what really matters is Scripture's witness to God, Christ, the Spirit, and the way to life. In so far as it draws upon such deepening practices, preaching (and other forms of communication) is more able to go to the heart of things, opening up ways of living which are more fully attuned to reality in all its complexity, human and divine.

But that goal is hard-won. Like any worthwhile achievement it takes time, effort and skill. A deepening practice, therefore, is an *ascetic* practice. It is a *discipline*. Indeed, it is a discipline of *love*: the love of wisdom and truth, both for the sake of good community and for growing up into God who *is* Wisdom and Truth.[12]

Biblical scholarship, I suggest, is one such deepening practice, with good reading and wise interpretation of Scripture among its particular concerns. Such good reading and wise interpretation require disciplined ways by means of which the meaning(s) of the text may be opened up and appropriated. The testimony of Bishop John V. Taylor[13] to his own engagement with scholarship (both biblical and in the Humanities more generally) makes the point well:

---

[12]   See David F. Ford, *Christian Wisdom. Desiring God and Learning in Love* (Cambridge: Cambridge University Press, 2007), esp. 225–72.

[13]   John V. Taylor, 'Divine Revelation through Human Experience', in *Bishops on the Bible*, eds John V. Taylor et al. (London: Triangle/SPCK, 1993), 2–3.

It was [while] reading English and history at Cambridge that ... I began to appreciate the relation between the meaning of any piece of literature and the historical situation within which it was written. I learned to guess at the period, and even the author of an unidentified passage of prose or poetry from its style. I could tell myth from epic, romance from scholarly chronicle, a spontaneous report from a well-worn anecdote, and both from a literary narrative. Instinctively I could recognize all these, and many other kinds of writing, in the Old and New Testaments; and I wanted to read them as such, as myth or epic or song or history or sermon, if that was their nature. For I felt that was how God had intended them to be the vehicle of his voice.

As I went to take a degree in theology I discovered the prophets of Israel. Up till then they had merely contributed some purple passages to my anthology of personal comfort, reproof and doctrine. Now I was exhilarated by the distinct individualities that emerged from their recorded outbursts, their heroic outbursts against social wrongs, political follies, religious apostasy, their daring vision of a suffering, passionate God. I felt like someone well stocked with Shakespearean tags, who had just emerged, for the first time in his life, from a performance of one of Shakespeare's plays.

Acquiring the kinds of literary and historical skills to which Taylor refers, along with the understanding, appreciation, inspiration and correctives they generate, is the goal of biblical scholarship. Broadly speaking, it is possible to characterise the practice in terms of three overlapping kinds of inquiry.[14]

Author-Centred Approaches

First, there are approaches which attend to the world 'behind' the text. Here, using the methods of historical criticism, the focus is on reconstructing the intention of the original author(s) or editor(s), along with the originating context from which a particular text comes and for which it was written. Such an approach reflects the conviction that what the original author(s)/editor(s) meant *matters*.[15] It also offers doorways into the worlds long past of ancient

---

[14] See W. Randolph Tate, *Biblical Interpretation. An Integrated Approach* (Peabody: Hendrickson, 1991).

[15] It matters in terms of the conviction of Christian faith that Scripture is Spirit-inspired (2 Tim 3.16–17); and it matters because, however much the text is justifiably open to multiple interpretations, it cannot be the case that there are no limits to legitimate interpretation.

Israel, Jesus, and early Christianity, and therefore into the vital originating – indeed, revelatory – moments which were decisive for grounding and shaping Christian faith.[16]

At the same time, questions of a self-involving kind naturally arise, out of a recognition that, while the past (including the past of the Bible) is indeed a foreign country, nevertheless *their* world – the world inscribed in the text – is *ours* also. This is so, not least because we belong to communities (such as the Church) shaped by *traditions of reception and interpretation* that mediate the past to the present. Hence, reflecting analogically, and with a sense of the pressure exerted by tradition, we cannot help but ask: 'If that was the shape of holy living in God's presence *then and since*, what does it mean to be God's holy people *now?*'; 'If that was how Jesus' followers responded to him *then and since*, what does it mean to be a follower of Jesus *now?*'

Indeed, some traditions of reception and interpretation are so strong that the so-called 'gap' between scriptural past and existential present is transcended and a powerful kind of inspired identification takes place. A wonderful example comes from Thomas Merton's reading of the psalms in the context of monastic prayer:[17]

> The kings of strange desert tribes have survived in the psalms; they were the enemies of Israel. Their mysterious names do not mean anything definite to us. These kings emerged from the verses of psalms like the weird symbolic enemies that menace us in dreams and fade away. They are the powers of evil that are still around us today. We know that Sisera is dead with a tent peg in his temple, and Jabin's bones long ago whitened in the ravine of Cisson. Yet Jabin and Sisera still rise up to plague us though they cannot prevail. But we know, on the nights when their names pass before us, in the small hours, at the chanting of Mattins, that the old battles we are celebrating are more than ever actual. Actual too are the same miracles by which Israel overcame her enemies and entered glorious through divided Jordan to occupy the Promised Land. These battles and these victories go on without ceasing, generation after generation and century by century, because the whole church is still passing out of Egypt, company by company. The shining tribes of Israel are still crossing the desert in the slow interminable march that

---

[16]   Good on this is J.D.G. Dunn, 'Criteria for a Wise Reading of a Biblical Text', in *Reading Texts, Seeking Wisdom*, eds David F. Ford and Graham N. Stanton (London: SCM, 2003), 38–52.

[17]   Thomas Merton, *Bread in the Wilderness* (London: Burns & Oates, 1976), 80. The passage is quoted by David Hope in his essay, 'Prayer and the Scriptures', in *Bishops on the Bible*, eds John V. Taylor et al., 75–6.

Balaam saw from his mountain when his curse against them choked in his gullet
and turned into a song of praise.

Noteworthy here is how the 'I' of the psalmist speaks to the perennial situation of
the believer such that the 'I' and the believer become one. By a kind of tradition-
shaped imaginative fidelity, Merton *finds himself* – indeed, finds the story of the
Church – in the strange world evoked by the psalms.[18]

Text-Centred Approaches

Second, there are approaches which attend to the world 'within' the text
understood as a product of the literary artistry and rhetorical power which the
text displays. Here, as well as focusing on what the text 'says', the focus is on
how the text 'speaks', including the use made of rhetorical devices such as plot,
setting, characterisation, point of view, irony, ambiguity, metaphor, allusion,
and so on. Put another way, by deploying the resources of literary criticism in
its various modes, the text-centred approach deepens our grasp of the text by
bringing to the surface the literary and rhetorical techniques by means of which
the text grasps us.

Not only does this help us read the text in ways stimulated by aesthetic
appreciation and emotional engagement, it also helps us to avoid egregious
misreadings. One way it does this is by the appreciation it makes possible of the
genre and poetics of the text. Thus, biblical myth can be appreciated as depth
symbolism of the human condition expressed in narrative form, rather than
literal reportage of historical events; apocalyptic can be taken as the Scripture-
inflected visions of eschatological reality granted to prophets and seers to inspire
hope among the persecuted faithful, rather than *Da Vinci Code*-style cryptic
riddle; an epistle can be taken as one side of a lively correspondence in contested
historical circumstances, rather than universal moral rule-book; and so on.

What text-centred approaches offer overall is a recognition of the wide variety
of ways Scripture 'speaks' to the human person at every level. To put it in a way
that inevitably oversimplifies: narrative engages us at the level of imagination,
law at the level of the will, the psalms and the Song of Songs at the level of the
emotions, the wisdom and epistolary literature at the level of the heart and
mind, and apocalyptic at the level of our intuitions and dreams. There is, in

---

[18]　For another witness to the immediacy of the psalms to the interpreter, see Ellen
F. Davis, *Wondrous Depths. Preaching the Old Testament* (Westminster: John Knox Press,
2005), 17–32.

other words, a *spaciousness* to Scripture that text-centred approaches open up; and this gives the reader, hearer and preacher plenty of room for (serious!) play.[19]

Reader-Centred Approaches

Third, there are approaches that attend to the ways in which the meaning of the text is actualised in often quite different ways by different readers according to the experience, presuppositions, and commitments which they bring to the text. The focus here is on the world 'in front of' the text and how meaning is generated in the interaction between text and reader, or between text and reading community. Reader-centred approaches, with their focus on how meaning arises on *this side* of the text, help us to recognise that our performance of the text – including our preaching from the text – is *not value neutral*. It always comes from somewhere, and is shaped by traditions of one kind or another.

This is where ideological criticisms, often finding articulation in theologies of liberation – themselves indebted variously to the intellectual tradition of the 'hermeneutics of suspicion' – make a significant contribution.[20] They help the preacher to recognise how easy it is for Scripture to be used (consciously or unconsciously) for pernicious ends, usually to do with the maintenance of oppressive power relations and the silencing of people who are 'other' in one way or another – for example, on account of their ethnicity or gender or sexual orientation or social class or age or (dis-)ability. There is a nice irony here. Against the backdrop of ideological criticism, biblical scholarship is itself implicated.[21]

As such, what is required of the preacher, as of every interpreter of Scripture, is the exercise of moral-theological discernment – in other words, *wisdom* – itself shaped by prayer, learning and holy living in the context of the transformative practices of Christian community. Implicated in the practice of wise interpretation, therefore, is the issue of the Spirit-formed *character* of the interpreter and the interpretative community.[22] Not coincidental, in the quotation I gave at the outset from the Gospel of Matthew, is the representation

---

[19] See Daniel Migliore, *Faith Seeking Understanding* (Grand Rapids: Eerdmans, 1991), 47: 'The witness of Scripture accomplishes its purpose in a polyphonic rather than homophonic manner. Its faith discourse is extraordinarily rich. ... [T]he literary genres of the scriptural witness are fittingly diverse ways of bringing us into relationship with God'.

[20] For one account see Anthony C. Thiselton, *New Horizons in Hermeneutics* (London: HarperCollins, 1992), 411–71.

[21] See Zoë Bennett and Christopher Rowland, 'Contextual and Advocacy Readings of the Bible', in *The Bible in Pastoral Practice*, eds Paul Ballard and Stephen R. Holmes (Grand Rapids: Eerdmans, 2005), 174–90.

[22] See Stephen E. Fowl, *Engaging Scripture* (Oxford: Blackwell, 1998).

of the discerning scribe-disciple as one 'trained for the kingdom of heaven' – that is, one shaped by following Jesus and living according to the precepts of the Sermon on the Mount.

A Sermonic Exhibit

I conclude with a 'sermonic exhibit'. I hope that, in some small way, it displays the constructive potential of the relation between biblical scholarship in its literary-historical modes and preaching. I hope too that it demonstrates how biblical scholarship has the potential to move the reader or hearer to what Paul Ricoeur called a 'second naïveté', where the meaning and significance of the text can be appreciated at a more profound level, not in spite of critical reflection, but because of it.[23]

The sermon, which focuses on Matthew's story of the events surrounding the birth of Jesus, was prepared for Advent 4, and preached at my two local parish churches, Holy Trinity Widdrington, and Saint John the Baptist Ulgham, in the Diocese of Newcastle of the Church of England, on 22 December 2013. The Old Testament and Gospel lections for the day were, respectively, Isaiah 7: 10–16 and Matthew 1:18–25.

The Vulnerability of God: A Sermon on Matthew 1:18–25 [24]

"The other day, my wife Helen and I went to see a wonderful film called *Philomena*. It's based on the true-life story of an Irish Catholic girl, ignorant of

---

[23]   Representative of Ricoeur's approach is the following quotation from his essay, 'The Language of Faith', in Charles E. Reagan and David Stewart, eds, *The Philosophy of Paul Ricoeur* (Boston: Beacon Press, 1978), 234–5: 'I think that any modern hermeneutics is a hermeneutics with a double edge and a double function. It is an effort to struggle against idols, and, consequently, it is destructive. … But we understand better that this task of destruction pertains also to the act of listening, which is finally the positive aspect of hermeneutics. What we wish is to hear through this destruction a more original and primal word, that is, to let speak a language which though addressed to us we no longer hear, which though spoken to us we can no longer speak. It is this access to interpretation which is the driving force of hermeneutics'.

[24]   The sermon, naturally, has no annotation. It is indebted, nevertheless, to the following works of New Testament scholarship: Raymond E. Brown S.S., *The Birth of the Messiah* (London: Geoffrey Chapman, 1977); David Catchpole, *Resurrection People* (London: Darton, Longman and Todd, 2000); and Andrew T. Lincoln, *Born of a Virgin?* (London: SPCK, 2013).

how babies are made, who gets pregnant out of wedlock. When she gives birth, she and the baby are committed to an institution run by an order of Catholic nuns called the Magdalen Sisters. Here, as a kind of penance, Philomena is made to work long hours in the laundry. She's allowed to be with her little boy each day for only brief intervals between shifts. One day, something heart-rending happens. A car arrives and her beloved son is taken away for adoption without her permission, by people she does not know, and to a destination she can only imagine. The story tells of Philomena's quest, in later life, to find her son. Philomena, played by Judi Dench, is aided in her quest by the journalist Martin Sixsmith, played by Steve Coogan.

The story, and the film of the story, is very moving. A box of tissues is a recommended accompaniment! If I ask myself why it's so moving, I think it's something to do with the sense of *the preciousness of human bonds* evident in the love of Philomena for her son, someone whom she's never forgotten. But the story also speaks of *love's vulnerability* – vulnerability to ignorance, tragedy and wickedness. Life and love *stand on the brink*: they are precarious in the face of disaster and death. So I think the story of Philomena is so touching because – in one way or another – it is *our story* too.

But if you haven't seen *Philomena*, think of a BBC TV series like *Call the Midwife* starring Miranda Hart. Why is it so popular? There's even a Christmas special promised! Apart from the nostalgia it evokes, the appeal must be something to do with the tension between the wonder of birth-giving and the courage of mothers and midwives ... and the accompanying circumstances of pain, poverty, ignorance, and human folly. There's always that tension between life and death, good and evil; and always that sense that life is as precious as it is precarious.

That brings us to the story of *another* birth, as told in the first chapter of the Gospel of Matthew. And what I want to offer this morning is a kind of 'minority report'. What I mean is: there is a way of reading Matthew's account of the conception and birth of Jesus that offers an alternative account of what really happened. In this alternative account, it's the vulnerability of the babe and his mother – indeed, the vulnerability *of God* – that comes to the fore.

The *majority report* takes Matthew's account at face value. While Joseph and Mary were still only at the betrothal stage, and before they had had sexual intercourse, Mary is found to be pregnant. How has the pregnancy come about? The Holy Spirit has taken the initiative and, as the ultimate, divine source of life, has brought about a miracle: a virgin has conceived! When Joseph learns of the pregnancy, he does what is required by Torah: he plans to divorce her – but quietly, so as to minimise her shame. But there's another divine intervention, this time in the form of an angelic messenger who appears to Joseph in a dream. The angel reveals to Joseph that the one conceived by Mary is 'from the Holy Spirit'. What is more, it's a boy, and the boy, Mary's son, is to be named 'Jesus'. And, as if that's not remarkable enough, the whole episode has been known of in advance. It had been revealed to Isaiah: 'Look, the virgin shall conceive and bear a son, and they shall call his name Emmanuel' (Isaiah 7:14). Joseph wakes from sleep, and, in obedience to the angel's command, marries Mary, but – again in accordance with Torah piety – refrains from sexual intercourse with her while she is pregnant. And when Mary gives birth, Joseph gives the babe full legal status as his son by naming him; and he names him Jesus.

That's the 'majority report'. It's summed up in the words of the Nicene Creed where, in speaking of Jesus, we confess that, 'for us men and for our salvation [he] came down from heaven, and was incarnate by the Holy Ghost of the Virgin Mary, and was made man'.

The *minority report* offers a somewhat different reading. It suggests a reading that takes into consideration a number of critical observations. First, Matthew's way of telling the story of Jesus' birth is *conventional*. That's to say, it follows a well-known Old Testament pattern – namely, that for a leader or saviour-figure to be born, an obstacle has to be overcome, often of a gynaecological kind, such as the barrenness of the mother-to-be. Think of Sarah, the mother of Isaac; think of the mother of the strongman Samson; think of Elizabeth, the mother of John the Baptist. The sign that the one born is special is that God gets involved by giving life to the woman's dead womb. But the fact that God gets involved does not preclude normal marital relations. A man still plays his part: but it is God or God's Spirit who makes their intercourse fruitful. So it could be that when the angel in Matthew tells Joseph that 'the child conceived in her is *from the Holy Spirit*' (1:20), the participation of a man in the act of procreation is not precluded. It's just that, on this occasion, God's Spirit is specially involved, since the one to be born is special.

But doesn't Matthew say that Mary conceived *before* she and Joseph had come together in marriage, and quote Isaiah to the effect that 'a *virgin* shall conceive'? Doesn't that make the case of Mary's pregnancy a case of conceiving miraculously, *without* a man? However, at this point, the minority report will draw attention to the fact that the word for 'virgin' in the quotation from Isaiah 7:14 (Hebrew *almah*; Greek *parthenos*) usually has a more general meaning of 'young woman', that is, a young woman who is not necessarily a virgin in the strict sense of the word. In other words, in our Old Testament reading from Isaiah 7, the sign of God's faithfulness given to King Ahaz of Judah is not that a 'virgin' shall conceive, but that a son will be born! It's the birth of the son that signifies God's providence and ongoing commitment. Similarly with Matthew's story, including his quotation from Isaiah 7. What is important as a sign of God's renewed commitment to his people is not a miraculous, virginal conception, but *the birth of the Messiah*. And the main reason why Matthew quotes from Isaiah 7 is that it identifies the one to be born as no less a figure than 'Emmanuel', which means 'God with us'.

One more thing. The story Matthew tells focuses, not so much on Mary, but on *Joseph*: his plan to divorce Mary when he learns of her pregnancy, the message he receives from the angel in a dream, his taking Mary as his wife, and – the climax of the whole episode – his naming of the baby. Now: why the focus on Joseph and his naming of the baby? The clue comes in the genealogy which Matthew puts right at the beginning of his Gospel. What is important for Jesus to be acknowledged as the Messiah is the claim that Jesus is of the royal lineage of King David: and the only way that can happen is for Joseph, himself descended from David, to own the baby as his son. So, in Matthew's story of the conception and birth of Jesus, what seems to be most important is, not virginal conception, but the birth of one who, by virtue of his adoption by Joseph as his son, can be claimed as of King David's lineage, and therefore the Messiah of Israel.

In the light of considerations such as these, the minority report offers the following kind of reconstruction. First, Mary's pregnancy came about through the normal process of sexual intercourse. The man involved was someone other than Joseph. Indeed, in Jewish circles from the second century on, a common view was that the birth of Jesus was the result of a relationship between Mary and a Roman soldier by the name of Panthera. A much later Jewish tradition even claimed that the conception was a result of rape. Second, in consequence of his conception out of wedlock, Jesus' status at birth was that he was illegitimate, with all the associated social and religious stigma. Third, against this background, Joseph had good reason in terms of Torah to divorce Mary, but for reasons not made explicit refrained from doing so. Instead, he married Mary and regularised the status of the baby by acknowledging him and giving him a name.

Now, I wonder what we are to make of this minority report? My guess is that for some, it will sound shocking, while for others it may be the kind of thing they had thought all along. For some, the wonder will be in the miraculous account of virginal conception, angelic intervention, and scriptural fulfilment; for others, the wonder will be in the miracle that, out of precarious beginnings, a human being was born through whom great blessing would come on the whole world.

It seems to me that, whichever view we hold, *both* attest to what is fundamental to Christian faith. Both attest to the conviction that this man Jesus is the revelation of God in human flesh. The 'minority report' provides no less a warrant for Christian belief in the Incarnation than the traditional view. Indeed, it is worth pondering whether the doctrine of the Incarnation is given new depths of meaning if God entered the world as an illegitimate baby, born to a vulnerable young woman – born to someone like Philomena. If the Messiah's life could *end* in the vulnerability and shame of the cross, it could surely also *begin* in the shame and vulnerability of illegitimacy.

It's important that we don't *sanitise* the story of the Incarnation. I think that's what tends to happen at Christmas, with the idyllic crib scenes, and the innocence of the school nativity plays, and the purity of the carol-singing from King's College, and the general fog of nostalgia round the nut roast and mulled wine. The thing is: when we sanitise the story of the Incarnation, we also sanitise the world.

But the world *cannot* be sanitised! Human history *cannot* be sanitised! There is too much suffering, too much injustice, too much pride, too much folly. It's into *this* world, *this* history that God came, as an ordinary – yet also extraordinary – human being. It's into the world of Philomena that God came, as a baby, conceived out of wedlock, and born (if the minority report is right) with the stigma of illegitimacy. And by coming into this world, by becoming one with us, God in Jesus *redeemed* the world.

That's the good news we celebrate, as Advent gives way to Christmas: God, in the humble circumstances of Jesus' birth, brings to birth a new world. So, in the words of the carol, by God's grace, may Jesus Christ 'be born in us today'.

And to Jesus Christ our Saviour and Lord be all glory and honour, now and forever. Amen."

Conclusion

In a recent reflection on the contribution of biblical scholarship to Christian life and practice, John Rogerson says this:

> [T]he main purpose of biblical scholarship is to enable the Bible to be better understood. Much of its work is highly technical and of little direct relevance to the average person. While its results may appear to be negative, calling into question traditional theories of the authorship and inspiration of the Bible, arguing that not all the words of prophets or of Jesus are authentic, or questioning the historical accuracy of the Bible, the religious significance of the Bible has been enhanced rather than diminished by biblical scholarship. ... Biblical scholarship can liberate modern people from the guilt of not being able to believe literally

in everything that the Bible contains. It can enthuse them with the message of the Bible, and transform their conception and practice of Christian discipleship.[25]

Rogerson's comment is particularly pertinent in a context of *polarisation* between people who take the Bible literally and 'modern people' in quest of liberation from 'traditional theories'. Of course, his formulation begs a number of questions including, not least, what it means to take the Bible literally, and what assumptions underlie the characterisation of 'modern people' as guilt-ridden freedom-seekers! Now, heard (or read) in a certain way, the 'sermonic exhibit' I have offered – with its account of the traditional interpretation of the conception and birth of Jesus and the 'minority report' offered by (some) contemporary scholarship – speaks into and from this kind of polarisation.

Nevertheless, drawing on biblical scholarship, what I have tried to offer are readings which show that Matthew's is an *open* text which invites (or at least, allows) hearings and readings *in different ways*, ways that may speak to people marked by experiences like that of Philomena or like those portrayed in *Call the Midwife*. For in so far as we live in a world marked by love, loss, vulnerability and tyranny, Matthew's narrative speaks with saving power of a God who, quite remarkably, is 'with us' in the birth to an unwed young woman of a baby.

---

[25]   John Rogerson, 'The Gift and Challenges of Historical and Literary Criticism', in *The Bible in Pastoral Practice*, eds Paul Ballard and Stephen R. Holmes, 121–34, at 133.

Chapter 6

Memory and Eucharist

Lucy Dallas

Memory in the Church

In the church of which I am curate there stands a memorial book, kept under glass and open to the current month of the year. It names local people who worshipped and served God in that church, and it reminds the community of all who have gone before them in that place. The church building is, in effect, a monument to memory; plaques and masonry on the walls recall prominent local families, and stained glass windows, saints. Outside, the churchyard is nothing if not a place of memory, a place in which to remember among the graves and flowers. At particular times, these memories are heightened; November is a month of memory, the month in which people are, increasingly, more likely to attend church than at any other time except for Christmas, to remember those killed in conflict on Remembrance Sunday, and their own loved ones on All Souls' Day. The focal point of the church, like most Anglican churches, is the altar, and the focal point of the church's activities is the celebration of the Eucharist; 'doing this in remembrance' of Jesus. This is all exactly as it should be; churches have been described as 'communities of memory'[1] and must necessarily be so, as the truths borne by the Church's tradition are rooted in historical, particular times and places, just as the truths we learn as individuals are rooted in particular experiences and places.[2] In this chapter I explore how the focal point of much Anglican worship, the Eucharist, creates and sustains 'communities of memory' in which the person of Jesus is kept central to the formation and sustaining of the identity of Christians.

Eucharistic theology, of course, spans a spectrum of belief, and has done at least since the Reformation; eucharistic definitions and controversies most often centre on the presence of Christ in bread and wine, with accusations of idolatry on the one hand, and reductionism on the other. As Herbert McCabe

---

[1]   Stanley Hauerwas, 'Remembering as a Moral Task', in *The Hauerwas Reader* (Duke University Press, 2003), 327.

[2]   Ibid., 327.

put it, the Catholic view of the Protestant view of the Eucharist has often been portrayed as 'merely symbolic ... [and] Catholics ... leaned over backwards to say the opposite', in doing so, paying insufficient attention to the profoundly rich symbolism of the Eucharist.[3] Resistance to 'bare resemblances or memorials of things absent'[4] can often mean a failure to reflect on what we mean when we say that the Eucharist is the 'memorial of our redemption', whose words of institution are recalled at every celebration; 'Do this in remembrance of me'. Indeed, early Christianity is clearly concerned with remembering the person of Jesus; Paul's narrative of the institution of the Eucharist in 1 Corinthians 11:24 and Luke's later portrayal of the same event in Luke 22:19 validate the Christian sacred meal 'in remembrance of me'.

So rather than arguing against the real presence of Christ in the Eucharist, I suggest that deepening our understanding of memory and memorialism cannot but deepen our understanding of the Eucharist, and is, ultimately, the best antidote to 'bare resemblances or memorials'; as I argue here, there is nothing 'bare' about memory at all. Rather, the way in which memories are created and sustained is a profound insight into the identity of any given community. The vocabulary of memory is telling, and in English, a distinction can be justifiably made between 'reminding' and 'remembering'; whereas 'reminding' indicates the bringing back to the mind of that which once was there, 'remembering' in its etymology suggests that in the process of memory, something is 're-membered', brought back together where it had become dissociated. In 'reminding', the locus of memory is the mind; in 'remembering', the locus of memory is the body to which the individual members are re-connected. One suspects that Hooker's repudiation of the Eucharist as 'bare resemblances or memorials of things absent' is a reaction against the implication that 'doing this in remembrance of me' is a cognitive exercise. This reaction has arguably become more pronounced in the twentieth century, in response to the impact of Freudian psychology on western European understanding of memory, as I shall discuss below. Therefore, it is an important task for the Church to explore what kind of memory-event the Eucharist is, and, as I argue here, some pertinent insights are offered by sociological theorists of memory, notably Maurice Halbwachs and scholars influenced by him. Although theologies of the Eucharist and memory have been written,[5] the impact of cultural memory studies on eucharistic theology has

---

[3]   Herbert McCabe, *The New Creation* (London: Contiuum, 2010), 14.

[4]   Richard Hooker, *The Works of Richard Hooker*, vol. 2 (Oxford: OUP, 1841), 3–4.

[5]   See J. Gittoes, *Anamnesis and the Eucharist* (Aldershot: Ashgate, 2008), B. Morrill, *Anamnesis as Dangerous Memory: Political and Liturgical Theology in Dialogue* (Congeville: Liturgical Press, 2000).

yet to be fully explored,[6] and this short chapter offers, hopefully, stimulus for theological discussion of what we mean when we say we 'do this in remembrance' of Jesus.

At the outset, it is worth saying that the Eucharist is a 'remembering event' in the sense that it re-members its people by drawing them once again to that which makes them a body in the first place, the identity of the people of God through the faith of Jesus Christ, and connects them in this body to all who have participated in that faith. In this way, in celebrating the Eucharist 'in remembrance of me' we do not simply remind ourselves of the long-ago event of Jesus' death, but rather, we re-member ourselves as a part of the whole Christian community of faith as members of one body of which the gathered congregation is a representation. Thus, 'doing this in remembrance of me' forms the basis for Christian identity. To understand the implications of this link between group identity and memory, it is helpful to consider some theoretical approaches to memory.

Memory in Freud

One person who understood the centrality of memory to human identity and experience, and whose theorising about memory has been pervasively felt in western psychology is, of course, Sigmund Freud. For Freud, memory is self-evidently personal and individual, so that the task of the psychoanalyst is akin to that of a midwife,[7] or, to use another metaphor, specialist librarian who can access the cognitive equivalent of the bookstacks, the 'unconscious ... memory's fundamental repository'.[8] Freud recognised the power of memory, repressed and consciously explicit, over the lives and experiences of his patients. However, it is important to bear in mind that this individualistic approach to memory derives directly from an individualistic theory of human identity; being an integrated, healthy person means the overcoming of the id, those impulses, governed by

---

[6]   However, studies of anamnesis in early Christianity, based on Halbwachs's theorising, include L. Stuckenbruck, S. Barton and B. Wold (eds), *Memory in the Bible and Antiquity* (Tübingen: Mohr Siebeck, 2007); A. Kirk and T. Thatcher (eds), *Memory, Tradition and Text: Uses of the Past in Early Christianity* (Leiden: Brill, 2005); R. Rodriguez, *Structuring Early Christian Memory: Jesus in Tradition, Performance and Text* (London: T & T Clark, 2010); D. Joslyn-Siemiatkoski, *Christian Memories of the Maccabean Martyrs* (New York: Palgrave Macmillan, 2009).

[7]   Richard Terdiman, 'Memory in Freud' in *Memory: Histories, Theories, Debates*, eds Susannah Radstone and Bill Schwarz, (New York: Fordham University Press, 2010), 94–5.

[8]   Ibid., 100.

suppressed memories of which we are not consciously aware and therefore powerless over, by the ego, that is the capable, conscious self, and the super-ego, the self as assimilated from other people such as teachers, family members and therapists. In this way, the individual is the focus of Freud's theory of memory, and the integration of the individual is the ultimate aim of Freudian therapy. Memory is regarded as that which is contained within the individual's psyche, and therefore concerns events which have taken place within the individual's lifetime. Ultimately, the Freudian approach is predicated on an individualistic anthropology; people are regarded as primarily self-referential beings.

Memory in the Hebrew Scriptures

Within this paradigm, Jesus' commandment to 'do this in remembrance of me' makes perfect sense to his first disciples, but much less so to future generations of Christians. Indeed, it seems that this approach to memory has been that which twentieth-century Protestant Christianity has taken for granted; as Alan Kirk and Tom Thatcher suggest, 'Biblical scholarship has invested deeply in the traditional understanding of 'memory' as an individual faculty of recollection, and, moreover, has tended to discount the possibility of vital connections between 'memory' and 'tradition'.[9] This observation makes perfect sense within a Freudian paradigm of memory; Biblical scholarship has tended to discount the link between memory and tradition because it has inherited a frame of reference for understanding memory in which tradition has no obvious place. However, whereas Freudian anthropology and theory of memory are individualistic, the Biblical tradition seems to understand memory as essentially relational or covenantal; the refrain 'God remembered his covenant' echoes through the Hebrew Scriptures[10] and one verse suggests that the opposite of remembering the covenant is the breaking of it,[11] so that remembering the covenant is synonymous with keeping faith. Through the Hebrew Scriptures, 'remembering' is used far more often of people than of facts,[12] and where 'remembering' relates

---

[9]   Alan Kirk and Tom Thatcher, 'Jesus Tradition as Social Memory' in *Memory, Text and Tradition: Uses of the Past in Early Christianity* (Leiden: Brill, 2005), 25.

[10]   See Genesis 9:15, 9:16, Exodus 2:24, 6:5, Leviticus 26:42, 1 Chronicles 16:15, Psalm 106:45,

[11]   Jeremiah 14:21; 'remember and do not break your covenant with us'.

[12]   The many examples of this remembering of people include Genesis 8:1, 'God remembered Noah' and the prayer of Deuteronomy, 'Remember your servants, Abraham, Isaac and Jacob' (9:27).

to facts, the facts are related so as to recall their hearers to their identity as the people of God. Arguably, the whole Deuteronomic tradition is a call to this type of remembering.[13]

Memory in Halbwachs

This Hebrew relational or covenantal understanding of memory resonates with the theorising offered by Maurice Halbwachs, whose approach to collective memory has had a profound impact on the way in which memory is regarded sociologically, and whose influence is felt in humanities disciplines, although somewhat ironically, whose influence is felt least in the discipline with which it has an obvious affinity, theology. Halbwachs, a student of Durkheim and influenced by Durkheim's insistence on the importance of shared memory in traditional societies, widened this insight to all communities and all types of community.[14] '*La topographie légendaire des* évangiles *en terre sainte: Etude de mémoire collective*' and '*Les cadres sociaux de la mémoire*', both published in 1941, became programmatic for the articulation of 'collective memory', which Halbwachs had already formulated in his 1926 study 'On Collective Memory'. For Halbwachs, all memory is mediated socially or culturally, even the most intensely personal or solitary memories; as Kirk and Thatcher summarise Halbwachs's argument, 'social frameworks of memory are indispensable for the very possibility of remembering, for they give coherence and legibility to memories, arranging them within dominant cultural systems of meaning'.[15] The use of 'legibility' suggests the inherent illegibility of individual memories in isolation; it is only within a community of others that we may 'read' our past. This is not to say that an amorphous 'collective' is the locus of remembering; as Halbwachs suggests, 'while the collective memory endures and draws strength from its base in a coherent body of people, it is individuals as group members who remember'.[16] Indeed, individuals cannot be thought of as separate

---

[13] See Deuteronomy 5:15, 7:18, 8:18, 9:7, 11:2, 15:15, 16:12, 24:9, 25:17, 32:7, and in the Deuteronomistic History, 1 Samuel 1:11, 2 Kings 20:3. Also G. McConville and J.G. Millar, *Time and Place in Deuteronomy* (Sheffield: Sheffield Academic Press, 1994) and W. Brueggemann, *Theology of the Old Testament: Testimony, Dispute, Advocacy* (Minneapolis; Augsburg Fortress, 1997).

[14] See Barbara Misztal, *Theories of Social Remembering* (Maidenhead: Open University Press, 2003), 51.

[15] Kirk and Thatcher, 'Jesus Tradition', 2.

[16] Maurice Halbwachs, *On Collective Memory* (Chicago: University of Chicago press, 1992 edition), 25.

from 'coherent bodies of people'; even in our most solitary moments, 'we are never alone'.[17]

In other words, for Halbwachs, the repository of memory is not the unconscious individual psyche, but the shared, articulated memories of the community in which the individual participates. Therefore, for Halbwachs, the community is somewhat akin to Freudian therapist, making the illegible legible for the individuals within the community. In this framework, remembering Jesus in the Eucharist is both possible and meaningful; in the Eucharist, the individual participant draws on the 'collective memory' of generations of Christians and finds his own experience of faith articulated and deepened within the context of this collective memory. As the prayer used in the Church of England baptismal service suggests, 'our' faith is only articulable within the 'faith of the church'.

Memory in Assmann

However, communities are anything but static entities, churches maybe especially so, hence an account of collective memory needs to consider how successive generations relate to the 'cultural memories' of the community. Jan Assmann, a German Egyptologist, inspired by Halbwachs and formed by an academic discipline with a keen awareness of cultural specificity, nuances Halbwachs's concept of collective memory by distinguishing between the relatively short-term 'communicative memory' of oral societies and the longer, 'objectivised' 'cultural memory' arising out of 'communicative memory', notably in *Kultur und Gedächtnis*,[18] published in 1988. For Assmann, the most important characteristic of 'communicative memory' is its 'limited temporal horizon' which 'does not extend more than eighty to (at the very most) one hundred years into the past'.[19] Anecdotes and sayings passed down in an oral society are obvious examples of such 'communicative memory'. Therefore, the category 'communicative memory' invites the question of what happens once the generations who sustained such communicative memories pass away. One obvious example of this juncture between communicative memory and cultural memory in the United Kingdom is that of Remembrance Sunday, which remains vitally meaningful and, in many places, gives rise to the largest congregations of the year. However, the generation of those who lived through the two world

---

[17]   Ibid., 23.

[18]   J. Assmann, *Kultur und Gedächtnis* (Frankfurt / Main: Suhrkamp, 1988).

[19]   J. Assmann, 'Collective Memory and Cultural Identity' in *New German Critique*, No. 65 (Spring-Summer 1995): 127.

wars will shrink in coming decades, and the cohort of those who fought will shrink even more quickly, and it is at this point that Remembrance Sunday may take on a different form, probably widening its scope of collective memory to include a wider range of conflicts and wars.

This critical juncture at which the remembering generation passes away, Assmann argues, is not addressed by Halbwachs in his formulation of 'collective memory'; 'he probably thought that once living communication crystallised in the form of objectivised culture – whether in texts, images, rites, buildings, monuments, cities, or even landscapes – the group relationship and the contemporary reference are lost and therefore the character of this knowledge as mémoire collective disappears ... "mémoire" is transformed into "histoire"'.[20] In contrast, Assmann argues that rather than denying, or indeed being anything other than collective memory, 'objectivised' culture represents a 'concretion of identity' in which 'a group bases its consciousness of unity and specificity upon this knowledge and derives formative and normative impulses from it, which allows the group to reproduce its identity'.[21] Thus, it is not that successive generations are less able to enter into the cultural memory of the group than the cohort who lived through the events; in a sense, it can be inferred from Assmann's analysis that successive generations are equipped to enter into these cultural memories more fully, as the 'objectivising' process is, essentially, the process of sifting aspects of the communicative memory which are most pertinent to the identity of the community.

Thus, published texts and public buildings, to name a few examples of 'objectivised culture' do not contradict the notion of 'communicative memory' but rather intensify it by distilling its most pertinent features so as to sustain it beyond its otherwise 'limited temporal horizon'. In the case of Remembrance Sunday, the poppy is likely to remain a potent symbol of conflict whose meaningfulness in relation to the First World War will not be undermined but which may take on new meanings and resonances as Remembrance Sunday itself takes on new meanings. To suggest a very different cultural context which may be illuminated by this theorising, Assmann's emphasis on the critical juncture between the remembering generation and the successive generations may provide an insight into the timing of the writing of the Gospel narratives from as early as the late 60s onwards; as the first generation of Christians passed away, the need to 'objectivise' the Jesus tradition so as to preserve it for future generations is a historically feasible motivation for the Evangelists. Although

---

[20] Ibid., 128.
[21] Ibid., 128.

Birger Gerhardsson, in his thorough 1961 study of remembering in the Hebrew Bible and in early Christianity, *Memory and Manuscript*, does not define or analyse the category 'memory', his account of the development of the Gospel tradition seems to follow the trajectory of Assmann's posited junction between communicative and cultural memory; as he feasibly suggests, 'in the course of [pondering the Hebrew Scriptures and the Jesus-traditions], sayings of Jesus were "remembered", repeated, expounded and applied'.[22] This account posits the conscious recollection of Jesus' spoken words in an inherited Hebrew scribal cultural context, and a re-evaluation of that Hebrew scribal tradition in the light of Jesus' authoritative spoken words which attests to the identity-formational need to create a new scribal culture which articulates the identity of the nascent Christian community. Similarly, the liturgical handbooks of the post-apostolic era such as *The Didache* and *On the Apostolic Tradition* bear witness to his distillation and sustaining of communicative memories by objectivising them as written texts.

Therefore, by its nature, 'cultural memory', the distillation of communicative memory, is characterised by its temporal distance from the present moment and is made up of 'figures of memory', or 'islands of time, islands of a completely different temporality suspended from time'.[23] As well as Remembrance Sunday, Christmas Day and the day of a funeral[24] may be seen as examples of such 'islands of time', and the distinction between the Greek *kairos* and *chronos*[25] may suggest a similar distinction between 'islands of time' and simply 'time'. These 'islands of time' are intensifications of the more diffuse shared memories of a community because they are meaningful insights into the community's identity; arguably, one reason why Remembrance Sunday does remain such a powerful act of cultural memory is because the Second World War in particular is so emblematic in constructing a British identity, embodying virtues which are claimed as 'British' and forming a narrative of Britishness which may compensate for a lack of these virtues in contemporary life.

So for Assmann, cultural identity is constituted of cultural memory, comprised of 'that body of reusable texts, images, and rituals specific to each society in each epoch, whose "cultivation" serves to stabilise and convey that

---

22 Birger Gerhardsson, *Memory and Manuscript* (Lund: C.W.K. Gleerup, 1961), 332.

23 J. Assmann, 'Collective Memory', 129.

24 It is interesting that W.H. Auden's famous poem 'Funeral Blues' begins 'Stop all the clocks ... '

25 See F.W. Danker, *A Greek-English Lexicon of the New Testament and other Early Christian Literature* (Chicago: Chicago University Press, 2000), 498 and 1092.

society's self-image'.[26] This cultural memory is made up of 'islands of time' which are 'objectivised' in texts, performances or physical constructions such as buildings and monuments. In this way, cultural memory is a distillation of communicative memory. What drives such cultural memory formation, Assmann argues, quoting Hans Mol, is not 'theoretical curiosity', but rather 'the need for identity',[27] resonating with Marc Bloch's distinction between 'knowing' and 'understanding' history.[28] This need for identity generates the capacity of cultural memory to 'reconstruct', or to relate to contemporary situations. Such relationships are not necessarily unproblematic; Assmann suggests that the relationship of cultural memory to contemporary cultures may be characterised by 'appropriation ... criticism ... preservation ... [and] transformation'.[29] Moreover, Assmann argues that the relationship between cultural memory and contemporary culture is not a one-way street; rather, cultural memory exists 'in the mode of potentiality of the archive of accumulated texts, images and rules of conduct' which 'act as a total horizon',[30] and also in the 'mode of actuality, whereby each contemporary context puts the objectivised meaning into its own perspective'.[31] In other words, identity is constantly negotiated between the 'cultural memory' of the inherited past, and the contemporary experience of those who inherit such memory.

Memory in the Eucharist

The dynamics theorised by Assmann are observable in church worship, and in particular, in the celebration of the Eucharist. Sunday morning is for many Christians an 'island of time' in which to visit an 'objectivised memory' in the form of a local church building, so as to re-connect with their Christian identity, drawing from the 'total horizon' of the variegated traditions and experiences of two millennia of Christian faith, and, by participating in this tradition, bringing to it contemporary contexts which contribute to its development by putting it into contemporary, particularised and localised perspective. Thus, it is not

---

[26] J. Assmann, 'Collective Memory', 132.

[27] Ibid., 130.

[28] M. Bloch, *The Historian's Craft* (Manchester: Manchester University Press, 1992), 8: 'the nature of our intelligence is such that it is stimulated far less by the will to know than the will to understand'.

[29] J. Assmann, 'Collective Memory', 130.

[30] Ibid., 130.

[31] Ibid., 130.

that the worshipper passively receives the tradition but rather, that every act of worship and every celebration of the Eucharist is a kind of negotiation between the tradition to which the worshipper comes, and that which the worshipper brings to it.

What emerges from these negotiations is the transmitted 'culturally institutionalised heritage of a society',[32] as ideas and memories crystallise into a particular shape. Assmann suggests a distinction between the 'formation' of ideas which are to be transmitted through writing or other forms of 'linguistic, pictorial or ritual formation', and the act of writing itself,[33] pointing out that the 'formation' of ideas necessarily precedes writing. Transmitted, or 'formed' cultural memories, Assmann argues, are 'organised' or 'cultivated' in a way that 'communicative memory' never is; the 'institutional buttressing' by 'specialised practice' carried out by particular 'bearers of cultural memory'[34] indicates the importance of particular 'figures of memory' in group identity. The reading of a Gospel narrative in a church by an ordained deacon is an obvious example of this kind of 'organising' of cultural memories; the ritual by which the reading of the Gospel is accompanied indicates the text's importance within the formation of the group's identity. As Assmann points out, 'in special cases of written cultures with canonised texts, such cultivation can expand enormously and become extremely differentiated'.[35]

Such organisation or cultivation suggests the various obligations which cultural memory imposes on a cultural group, which may be greater or lesser pending on the respective importance or unimportance attached to it.[36] The various ways in which Scripture may be read, or evoked, within a single act of worship suggests something of the relative importance of the Biblical texts to the identity of the worshipping community. Assmann argues, then, that the obligation imposed by cultural memory is twofold, both 'formative ... in its educative, civilising, and humanising functions and ... normative ... in its function of providing rules of conduct'.[37] Finally, Assmann suggests that cultural memory is 'reflexive', in that it theorises common practices by interpreting them through, for example, sayings,[38] and it relates to itself 'hypolectically', or within its own systems of logic, and finally that it 'reflects the self-image of the

---

[32]   Ibid., 130.
[33]   Ibid., 131.
[34]   Ibid., 131.
[35]   Ibid., 131.
[36]   Ibid., 131.
[37]   Ibid., 132.
[38]   Gender identity is frequently theorised in this 'reflexive' manner.

group through a preoccupation with its own social system'.[39] Thus, through this process, Assmann argues that 'through its cultural heritage a society becomes visible to itself and to others. Which past becomes evident in that heritage and which values emerge in its identificatory appropriation tell us much about the constitution and tendencies of a society'.[40] The Barthian account of Christian faith is, perhaps, the most extreme hypoletic system, with its assertion that it is only through the revelation of God in Jesus that people may understand anything of the Christian gospel.

Commemoration and Memory in the Eucharist

As inheritors of a community of the followers of Jesus, it is important to recognise that at the heart of all Christian remembering stands not a system of doctrine or a text but a person. In this way, Christian remembering is as relational and covenantal as that of the Deuteronomists; Christians are commanded to 'do this in remembrance of me', not in remembrance of information about Jesus. Theorists of memory have recognised the potency of remembering people as 'figures of history', rather than facts; in his work on Abraham Lincoln as the archetypal American 'figure of history', Barry Schwartz emphasises the stabilising influence which collective memory has on societies, and the negotiations between continuity and change which occur within the process of cultural memory.[41] Schwartz argues that acts of commemoration of significant individuals are an important medium for such negotiations; echoing Assmann's concept of 'islands of time', Schwartz notes that 'commemoration lifts from an ordinary historical sequence those extraordinary events which embody our deepest and most fundamental values'.[42] Thus, 'in commemoration a community states symbolically what it believes and wants itself to be'.[43] In this way, commemoration is the most highly distilled form of cultural memory. Furthermore, the political implications of commemoration as an expression of idealised identity are not lost on Schwartz; 'interpretations of the past ... are, in important respects, political acts'.[44] The summary at the end of the

[39]   J. Assmann, 'Collective Memory', 132.

[40]   Ibid., 133.

[41]   B. Schwartz, *Abraham Lincoln and the Forge of National Memory* (Chicago: University of Chicago Press, 2000), 302.

[42]   Schwartz, quoted in Kirk and Thatcher, 'Jesus Tradition', 7.

[43]   Quoted in Ibid., 8.

[44]   Quoted in Ibid., 12.

account of Polycarp's martyrdom encapsulates the power of commemoration as a political act; '[Polycarp] was arrested under Herod, during the time when Philip of Tralles was high priest and Statius Quadratus was governor – while Jesus Christ was reigning eternally'.[45] The martyrdom is commemorated in the assertion of the reign of Jesus, suggesting a narrative of power and authority to rival that of the Roman Empire by which Polycarp's death was brought about. Therefore, to 'do this in remembrance of me', to commemorate Jesus, is to assert that, against whatever contemporary heroes or villains may loom large in our society's cultural imaginations, Jesus stands as the one to whom to aspire, the one who embodies all that Christians believe and want to become through participation in the commemorative act of worship in the Eucharist. This in itself is a deeply political act; the post-communion prayers hint at the political nature of the Eucharist: 'send us out by the power of your Spirit to live and work to your praise and glory'.

So 'doing this in remembrance of me', commemorating Jesus in the Eucharist, is anything but a 'bare memorial'; rather, the act of commemoration is an act of aspiration and articulation of all that it means to call oneself a Christian. Helpfully, Schwartz offers the metaphors of history as both a 'lamp' to shed light on the present, and a 'mirror' reflecting the concerns and values of the present; in a very insightful description which is worth quoting in full, he suggests that this is an:

> Analytic, not empirical distinction; both aspects of it are realised in every act of remembrance. Memories must express current problems before they can program ways to deal with them. We cannot be oriented by a past in which we fail to see ourselves. On the other hand, it is memory's programmatic relevance that makes its expressive function significant: we have no reason to look for ourselves in a past that does not already orient our lives … .in its reflective (model of) aspect, memory is an expressive symbol – a language, as it were, for articulating present predicaments; in its second (model for) aspect, memory is an orienting symbol – a map that gets us through these predicaments by relating where we are to where we have been.[46]

For Christians, the Eucharist is all of these: lamp, mirror, language and map. In other words, it gives us the means to both perceive the Christian life, and to follow it.

---

[45] 'Of Polycarp' in *Acts of the Christian Martyrs*, vol. 2, ed. H. Musurillo (Oxford: Clarendon Press, 1972), 19.

[46] Quoted in Kirk and Thatcher, 'Jesus Tradition', 22.

As Christians perceive and follow the life of Jesus by commemorating Him in the Eucharist, they are drawn back to the formational narratives of Jesus' life, the life from which their own lives take their meaning. Again, memory theory can help in articulating this process, particularly the work of Eviatar Zerubavel. Whereas Assmann's formulation of 'commemorative' and 'cultural memory' are unashamedly rooted in his work as an Egyptologist and contain a strong sense of awareness of the cultural specificity of memory,[47] Eviatar Zerubavel seeks to articulate a 'transcultural as well as a transhistorical perspective on social memory as a generic phenomenon'.[48] Zerubavel is particularly interested in collective memory as aetiology, seeking out as the most enduring and significant memory 'the event that marks the group's emergence as an independent social entity'.[49] From there, Zerubavel seeks to understand collective memory as 'evolutionary narratives'[50] of social identity, using the language of a 'sociomental topography of the past'[51] to elucidate the present. It is important to note the forward-facing thrust of Zerubavel's analysis; in contrast to Schwartz's categories, for Zerubavel, the past is not so much a map, or a language, but rather a 'copiously branching bush'[52] which spreads out from a single point, in many different directions. This account of cultural memory is one which embraces diversity very easily; after all, it is obvious that the 'copiously branching bush' will branch out in many directions and that, therefore, eucharistic practices, whilst drawing on the formative narratives of the New Testament, can be simultaneously and validly divergent and faithful.

Therefore, commemorating the person of Jesus in the Eucharist is a far cry from Hooker's feared 'bare resemblances or memorials of things absent'; rather, making the 'memorial of our redemption' is such stuff as Christian identities are made on. Moreover, as Zerubavel's metaphor of the copiously branching bush with its verdant growth implies, memorialising Jesus in the Eucharist not only unites us to the past event of Jesus' death but also unites us in the coming kingdom, in the forward-straining proleptic foretaste of the fulfilment of all memory. To return to the church of which I am curate, it is a true 'community of memory', yet it is also a community of growth and life. Maybe such growth and life can only be energised by a deep re-membering, and being re-membered as a Christian community by the presence of Jesus in the Eucharist.

---

47 See, for example, his work on 'Moses the Egyptian'.
48 E. Zerubavel, *Time Maps: Collective Memory and the Social Shape of the Past* (Chicago: University of Chicago Press, 2003), 9.
49 Zerubavel, 1995. Quoted in Kirk and Thatcher, 'Jesus Tradition', 5.
50 Zerubavel, *Time Maps*, 23.
51 Ibid., 2.
52 Ibid., 22.

Chapter 7

From Thought to Desire: Theology, Priesthood and the Legacy of Dan Hardy

Christopher Landau

It may be that archaeologists are on the brink of discovering an early gospel fragment where Jesus is found to gather his disciples around him, encouraging them in their status as Potential Theological Educators. Perhaps James and John would vie to sit as vice-principal and senior tutor in the Great Commission Training Partnership. There might even be a role for the Pharisees in quality assurance.

But in the absence of such new discoveries, it may be that our discussions of vocation and theological education need a gentle reminder: that we should try to ensure that any consideration of the challenges facing theological education in the contemporary Church doesn't lose all sense of connection with our community's decidedly un-scholarly origins.

Whatever challenges we may perceive facing those with a particular vocation to academic priestly ministry, they are simply one facet of the challenges faced by the whole people of God, each with their own responsibility as theological educators. Disciples should tell and re-tell the Christian story afresh in each generation. Those called to specialist theological study face what one might call peculiar challenges in perhaps increasingly peculiar contexts. But the simple task of making sense of the Gospel is shared both by the volunteer in Sunday School and the university lecturer; we should not lose sight of the common nature of this endeavour within the Church as a whole.

That said, there are clearly specific challenges that face those with an academic priestly vocation. They might include bewilderment at the latest set of Ministry Division criteria; disillusionment at government policy towards universities; dismay at the state of some theology departments within those universities.

And so writing as one just setting out on this journey, and conscious of its complex and not entirely encouraging context, this chapter seeks to find inspiration for theological educators, in the form of food that might sustain, and even delight us, and which might encourage us to discern what sort of steps are faithful to the particular calling we have received.

Dan Hardy and the Inseparability of Priesthood and Scholarship

Our key guide will be Dan Hardy, speaking through the words of his posthumously published book, *Wording a Radiance – Parting Conversations on God and the Church*.[1] Hardy died in 2007, just six months after the diagnosis of an aggressive brain tumour. The book records conversations he held with three of the people closest to him as death approached – so we encounter reflections with his daughter, the Anglican priest Deborah Hardy Ford, her husband, Cambridge theology professor David Ford, and the Jewish philosopher Peter Ochs. The conversations are described by David Ford in these terms:

> I think the best way to begin to say what was distinctive ... is that while he [Dan Hardy] was having them he was simultaneously living out their content, and that content was the culmination of a lifetime combining Christian living and theological thinking.[2]

It is this 'intense integration of theology and life', as David Ford puts it, that I suggest should be our focus as we consider what inspiration Dan Hardy, at the end of his theological career, might offer to those of us continuing to journey as theological educators.

So firstly: a stark reminder.

> Dedicated attention to the intensity of God; that's the source of theology; it's not about academic contrivances.[3]

Hardy reminds us that at the heart of theological study is something distinctive and divine which means that true theology is a different sort of discipline from other academic pursuits. His words raise, from the outset, unavoidable questions about how the contexts in which theology is studied thus enable or suppress such an approach. But Hardy is unapologetic about this searching after the mystery of God as being the undeniable heart of theological

---

[1]   Daniel W. Hardy et al., *Wording a Radiance: Parting Conversations on God and the Church* (London: SCM Press, 2010).

[2]   Ibid., 112.

[3]   Ibid., 2.

endeavour. The practice of theology is inseparable from the Christian spiritual quest. Theology:

> has a doubling role: to explain but also to invite deeper into the mystery. It's a form of prayer done deeply within the Spirit and it requires sustained inquiry in many directions, by testing the major theologies, philosophies and sciences of modernity.[4]

This is, of course, not an argument against sustained intellectual examination of Christian claims – but it is a caution against an approach to theology as an academic discipline that simply acts like any other humanities subject. Hardy insists that our context is the 'dedicated attention to the intensity of God', and that has implications – particularly concerning how we relate to the institutions within which we work.

We might ask ourselves, for example, how content we are – or would be – to work within departments that appear to have to try and justify their continued existence within their university in terms that would make absolutely equal sense if the subject under consideration were history or geography. Is there an often unspoken nervousness about theology's relationship to faith and spirituality? Is it conceivable that the practice of theology might be described in an official university document, even in part, as 'a form of prayer done deeply within the Spirit'?

I may not be alone in responding to some of Hardy's claims with something of a sense of 'it's easy for *him* to say' – in the sense that they are the sort of sentiments that can be articulated confidently by a celebrated theologian at the *end* of their career, but may not be the most judicious utterances by a novice theologian yet to complete his doctorate and seeking to work in a mainstream university. But we should also note that Hardy's convictions grew out of the difficulties he encountered in his early career. Of his years as a postgraduate student in Oxford, where his DPhil thesis was rejected, he writes:

> At the time, Oxford philosophy – and such was its influence, much else besides – was largely in the grip of logical positivism, a movement that reduced Christian belief either to nonsense or simple moral guidance ... the options open to theologians like me were very limited, and it was a deeply frustrating time.[5]

---

4 Ibid., 2.
5 Ibid., 16.

Such frustrations were, however, always placed in the broader context of the worshipping life of the Church: tellingly, that was always an essential component to Hardy's life, and not one that could be conveniently demarcated from academic work. In her introductory pen portrait of her father, Deborah Hardy Ford follows a discussion of testing times in Oxford, and later in Princeton, with an underlining of the importance of the worshipping context within which her father approached his scholarly work. It was during a pilgrimage to the Holy Land, just weeks before his diagnosis with a brain tumour, that Dan Hardy experienced a seemingly unprecedented moment of spiritual transformation, with substantial implications for his understanding of theology: as he puts it, 'my thought about God was transformed into desire for God'.[6]

One might note that this is not the sort of quotation that one might anticipate being highlighted on a departmental website. I am yet to find a banner headline inviting students to study at a particular mainstream university so that their 'thought about God' can be transformed into 'desire for God' – and yet, this becomes Hardy's definition of what it is to engage in truly theological study and reflection. The vocational and the spiritual become inseparable. So when he reflects on the process of supervising graduate students, he describes it as 'gently edging forward the things that are being prompted in them'.[7] His task is to nurture and make known the work that the Spirit is already undertaking. And that observation is made in the context of his disclosure of the way in which he had

> for years experienced light suffused around other people, especially in a pastoral
> context ... now I also experience the light separated from others, in itself and then
> suffusing and illuminating virtually everything. I believe this frees my pastoral
> activity ... this includes graduate students, with whom I find that our pastoral
> discussions move further away from academic topics and allow students to make
> vocational discoveries of their own.[8]

These visions of light intensified on his pilgrimage to Jerusalem, with a particularly significant moment at the front of St George's Cathedral shortly after the consecration of a new Anglican bishop of Jerusalem:

---

6   Ibid., 45.
7   Ibid., 36.
8   Ibid., 101.

> I have been deeply interested in the question of the infinitely intense identity of
> the Lord. I have tended to articulate my findings through words and ideas, but, in
> Jerusalem, the reality of this intense identity was embedded in a visual experience
> of a pillar of light, making graphic what was otherwise only conceptual. The light
> magnified the meaning of God's infinite identity for me hugely.[9]

The light that Dan Hardy saw – as a pillar in St George's Cathedral, or emanating
from a graduate student making vocational discoveries – was the light of God.
A light that prompts and energises what he later refers to as 'an ongoing process
of envisioning and re-envisioning'; a glimpse of God, and a fleeting moment of
comprehension of the energy of the Spirit.

That theme of the intensity of God's light is developed alongside a theme
concerning the importance of movement. For Hardy, the Church must resist
a damaging turn inward; instead, our response to God's attraction must be to
go into the world, maintaining our unity with God as we do so. This is why,
for Hardy, the Eucharist must be at the heart of the Church's life and at the
heart of the life of the theologian: it is 'a means of educating the pilgrim's desires
in service to the Church. Enacting this education is to walk a path of church
formation and scriptural enactment'.[10]

This sense of movement is perhaps best expressed in his statement that
'ecclesiology is embodied: in Jesus' walking'.[11] For the Church to really *be* the
Body of Christ, each individual Christian faces the task of walking as Jesus
walked, and engaging with those along the journey as Jesus did, if the Body of
Christ is to fulfil its calling in a world where Jesus himself no longer walks. And
there is a freedom to be found on this walk – in the sense that 'engaging with
Jesus, we are rationally puzzled and frustrated as well as healed'.[12] It is not that
by walking with Jesus we solve all of our own problems or those of the people
around us, but it is in this journey of discipleship that we fulfil our own vocation
and that of the Church, referred to by Hardy as 'a mobile order ... measured and
guided by Scripture, by the Eucharist and by Jesus' steps'.[13]

This walking with Jesus may also offer ways forward for inter-faith engagement
in a pluralist society. Hardy writes of a 'triple hermeneutic' as Christians walk
with Jesus along a road where they also meet Muslims and Jews:

---

[9]   Ibid., 74.
[10] Ibid., 71.
[11] Ibid., 83.
[12] Ibid., 84.
[13] Ibid., 85.

> Walking with Jesus allows you to walk with other traditions. It provides a
> wonderful opening because you can imagine Jesus walking with others too ... Just
> imagine the Emmaus Road story as a story of Jesus coming and walking among his
> disciples: Christian, Jew and Muslim.[14]

This image of walking together finds concrete expression in Dan Hardy's
enthusiasm for Scriptural Reasoning – the practice where Christians, Jews and
Muslims meet together to discuss their respective scriptures, deepening their
engagement with their own faith as they also learn about other traditions. His
reflections on friendship and interaction with those of other faiths, not least seen
in the context of his giving voice to these visions of light that marked encounters
with other people, suggest that Dan Hardy was just beginning to consider an
emerging theology for inter-faith engagement, rooted in a conviction that the
mystery of God's Spirit was working in the world in ways so extraordinary as to
be generally beyond articulation.

David Ford reflects on this aspect of Hardy's work by asking:

> If the discernment of 'Church' is closely tied to discernment of God's fullness and
> abundance, and that fullness is found in some inter-faith engagement, what are
> the boundaries of the Church? It is not that there are no boundaries, no limits
> to what God is understood to fill; but we have no overview of them, and may be
> frequently surprised by the movement of the Spirit 'welling up in the group'. To
> change the metaphor from water to air: who can identify the edge of the wind?[15]

It is an attractive question, not least to those who may feel challenged to ask
what sort of context best suits a vocation to theological education. Should those
with a calling to teach simply serve those who have already made Christian –
even ministerial – commitments, or is 'the edge of the wind' a more appropriate
place, bringing with it greater religious diversity? Such reflections by Hardy
and Ford might well affirm the vocation of those theologians who feel called
to sometimes costly work in contexts where their own particular convictions
may be regarded with some bemusement or embarrassment by colleagues or
secular university authorities. The sense in which the Spirit is large enough to
guide and inspire the Christian on a journey of multi-faith encounter is crucial
here: such dialogue and journeying is built, for Dan Hardy, upon a foundation

---

[14] Ibid., 36.
[15] Ibid., 127.

of faith that is always open to the surprise of God's light being made manifest in unexpected ways.

Fundamentally, the calling is to the pursuit of a wisdom which speaks of the truth that lies at the heart of creation; it was this ongoing seeking after theological truth which animated Dan Hardy even as he approached his own death. In the closing stages of her father's illness, Deborah Hardy Ford accepted an honorary Doctorate of Divinity from General Theological Seminary on his behalf. Reading her father's words, she voiced his reflection on his own vocation, paying tribute to Coleridge, his constant influence:

> It has been about the seeking of God's wisdom. It has been prophetic insofar as it has attempted to engage more deeply with life in all its particularity. It has been priestly in tracing that prophetic wisdom to its source in the divine intensity of love, and in seeking to mediate that love through the Church for the whole world, concentratedly in the Eucharist: light and love together.[16]

In the life and work of Dan Hardy, we meet a determined commitment to hold together a pastoral and sacramental ministry with a vocation to theological learning and exploration. Each constantly resources and interprets the other, but – crucially – the task of theology cannot be separated from pastoral engagement and human interaction. For Hardy, the true theologian cannot simply resemble an excellent historian or textual critic with a specifically Christian focus. The theologian's relationship with God, and desire to seek God, places their work in a very different sort of context – with accountability not merely to earthly authorities.

Contexts for Theological Education

We cannot avoid the question of what represents the best sort of context in which to pursue the sort of theological work championed by Dan Hardy. David Ford's recent Blackwell Manifesto, *The Future of Christian Theology*,[17] offers a hopeful and optimistic account of the way in which mainstream universities can cherish and grow the study of theology alongside a broader commitment to the study of religion, by developing departments that deliberately focus both on theology *and* religious studies. Ford sets this move in a historical context

---

[16] Ibid., 12.

[17] David F. Ford, *The Future of Christian Theology* (Oxford: Wiley-Blackwell, 2011).

where religious studies once failed to flourish because of church domination of theology departments, and in the more recent context of 'traditional' theology feeling squeezed by religious studies in secularised institutions. He now advocates the potential for fruitful cross-pollination, by affirming the presence of both disciplines within single university departments.

As I have already suggested, it may well be that younger 'theological educators' begin their professional journeys at a time when the purpose of theological study is all too frequently uncertain, and when the faith that acts as its engine for advocates like Dan Hardy is all too frequently denied, or at least downplayed, for reasons of academic political expediency. We may well be worrying about shrinking staff numbers in theology and/or religious studies departments, or concerned by the paucity of funding opportunities; but David Ford's manifesto for the future of the discipline within mainstream university contexts, and not least in pluralist societies, provides some hope that there are ways of enabling the discipline to flourish without entirely removing the possibility that university lecturers in theology will undertake their work from a clearly articulated position of Christian faith.

But the ordained theologian who chooses to work in a university department, however labelled, is – with the exception of the small number of senior posts still tied to clerical positions in a handful of British universities – unlikely to find much time for sacramental ministry in the job specification of what is a full-time position purely on academic grounds. We may once again salute Dan Hardy while also recognising the very specific ministerial and theological niches he occupied.

In an English context, however, the potential of university chaplaincy remains considerable for ordained ministers with academic theological interests who might wish to pursue ministry that combines theological learning with pastoral engagement. But just as academic theologians need David Ford's model, or one like it, to justify the place of Christian theological work within pluralist university settings, I suggest that chaplaincy – not least in the universities of Oxford and Cambridge, with their disproportionately high numbers of chaplains per student compared with any other institution – may also need to engage in a process of creative self-examination, if it is to survive and flourish in a secularising university sector.

Chaplaincy and an Exercise of Imagination

One might imagine a government consultation issued by the department for Business, Innovation and Skills (which is, *obviously*, the natural home for university policy in a society where value seems increasingly to be defined in purely monetary terms). With the ineptitude of the government's 2012 consultation on the future of marriage borne in mind, we may not be surprised to be confronted by a glossy front cover with an abstract montage of spires, minarets and other religious architecture, intersected by a vibrant rainbow on a glossy cover.

The government-speak title, 'Accessing higher education faith provision: removing barriers to equality', may give a clue to what lies ahead; inside, a photograph of a beaming junior minister – with a background of that same rainbow – graces an introduction that promises 'the opening of a new dialogue about access to faith provision in today's universities'.

It continues, 'This government's commitment to equality of opportunity is well known. As legislation for equal civil marriage is drafted, we are now proposing to consult on removing barriers to equality as they present themselves in the context of faith provision in the higher education arena'. So far, so abstruse.

But it is in a dense sub-paragraph of an Appendix, 'Options for equality implementation', that a specific proposal emerges: 'In light of the government's desire to ensure equality of access to faith provision, in accordance with The Equality Act (Sexual Orientation) Regulations 2007, and to ensure a level playing field for access to pastoral and spiritual care for those of all faiths and none, one option to consider would be the ending of disproportionate provision of Anglican faith input in multi-(and non-)faith student populations'.

Or, to put it more bluntly, in the words of a prominent equality blogger who quickly picked up the story: 'Government backs sacking of anti-gay establishment religionists – Oxbridge chaplains fight for survival!'.

This is, of course, a fantasy. Isn't it? Perhaps not.

The presence of Anglican clergy in British universities, and, in particular, the large number serving at Oxbridge, is indefensible using the sort of criteria that might be found in a current government consultation. We have the 1871 Universities Tests Act to thank for some aspects of this curious anomaly; for the Act made explicit provision for the continuation of Anglican morning and evening prayer in college chapels, even while at the same time repealing restrictions on the religious affiliation of those admitted to university. And so, in the years since, while the proportion of practising Anglicans attending Oxbridge has declined, not least as the number of foreign students has ballooned, the number of chaplains has remained largely unchanged.

While other chaplaincy provision paid for by what are generally deemed secular institutions – in particular, the military and the NHS – has faced recent public criticism (and, in the case of the health service, some significant funding reductions), Oxbridge chaplaincy has continued to exist largely unchallenged. They may come from a variety of church traditions, and minister with varying degrees of eccentricity, empathy and missionary zeal – but they remain. 'Gloriously unpredictable' might be one way of putting it; 'a mixed economy of chaplaincy', Rowan Williams might have said.

What we can be clear about is that Oxbridge's Anglican chaplains represent a specific example of a complex religious presence in the modern university that makes very little sense to the contemporary secular mindset, and is – potentially at least – difficult to justify in today's prevailing political climate. So, I suggest, such chaplains need to begin thinking very carefully about how they justify their existence – if they are to present credible arguments in response to likely future challenges.

One such speck on the horizon involves as-yet-unforeseen consequences of the 2013 Marriage (Same Sex Couples) Act.[18] Given the precedent concerning Catholic adoption agencies, forced to close when deemed to be discriminatory in their service provision, one could certainly envisage a legal challenge to the privileged presence within Oxbridge colleges of Anglican chaplains who represent their church's seemingly discriminatory approach to marriage – whatever those chaplains' personal convictions. It is in such contexts that chaplains need to be prepared to justify their establishment credentials and privileges.

So how could they respond in language that a government consultation might comprehend? They might argue that they act as a credible bridge between university scholarship in theology and the life of faith on the ground; they could point to moments of tragedy when they are uniquely well-placed to gather and serve their college community, or to occasions when they create spaces for moral, ethical and spiritual reflection; they might even note the number of times they are called on to teach when esteemed faculty colleagues are on sabbatical leave.

The point is that they exercise a ministry for which it is very difficult to draft an adequate job description. It would certainly be challenging to arrive at an agreed or shared understanding among chaplains of what qualifies as time well spent; each individual will, inevitably, arrive at a different sense of ministerial

---

[18] See http://services.parliament.uk/bills/2012-13/marriagesamesexcouplesbill.html (accessed 16 January, 2015).

priorities. I suspect there may well be a shared sense of never quite managing to have enough time for either their pastoral engagements or their academic work or other priorities – though such a sense of inadequacy may simply point to the practical difficulties of sustaining the varied aspects of the calling envisaged by Dan Hardy for those who truly seek to be priestly theologians (or scholar-priests). That sense of being pulled in different directions perhaps needs to be overcome by the appropriation of new metaphors that celebrate the kaleidoscope of contexts and roles within which a university chaplain might carry out their role.

Equipping the Church

As one who began writing this while still at theological college, I can hardly ignore the contribution of those priests who choose to forgo much of the potential to give sustained attention to their own research, in order to teach ordinands in the context of a college or course. In 2003, the Church of England's Hind report into ordination training noted that for those teaching in such settings:

> the pressure of day-to-day work and the small size of institutions means that study and research can often get squeezed out ... if staff are expected to contribute to the wider life of the Church through their broader teaching and publications, then the place of research needs a much firmer footing in our establishments.[19]

Currently, an ordained theological educator is unlikely to find much time in which to pursue their own research if they have a full-time position at a theological college or course – the teaching, administrative and pastoral demands on them will be too great. But in their ability to combine teaching with eucharistic presidency, to blend pastoral care with theological conversation, they may yet afford themselves the opportunity to exercise the sort of ministry that Dan Hardy commends. Crucially, they will be able to teach theology that is open to challenge and critique, but still taught in a context where Christian faith is not tentatively assumed, but celebrated.

Compare this with the situation facing an ordained theologian in a mainstream university. Professor Nigel Biggar, beginning a series of lectures in Christian Moral Reasoning to Oxford undergraduates in October 2010,

---

[19] Archbishops' Council Working Party, *The Hind Report* (London: Church House Publishing, 2003), 21.

encouraged students to 'suspend their disbelief' as necessary, in order to engage fruitfully with subject matter that pre-supposed a Christian narrative framework. Such a moment of negotiation of Christian space is, in fact, an example of exactly the sort of move made necessary for the study of theology to thrive if departments follow David Ford's 'theology and religious studies' model. Indeed, Oxford's own faculty has recently been re-branded as a department of 'Theology and Religion' – and Professor Biggar's invitation to students provides evidence that such a shift need not mean an inevitable move towards secularised religious studies. But it also reveals the sort of moments of imaginative negotiation that will be required from ordained theologians seeking to teach Christian theology in modern university contexts.

On Realising Potential

At the 2008 Lambeth Conference, questions of theological education were, often implicitly, a constant element in the discussions among bishops. Indaba groups, formed to enable honest and fruitful discussion between participants based on an African model for dialogue, became places where the astonishingly different levels of biblical literacy became apparent. One bishop's normative hermeneutic is another's heresy, but this did not prevent a measure of agreement in the conference's concluding 'Indaba Reflections' document, which noted that the Bible studies had been a shared highlight for participants.

I attended Lambeth as the newly appointed religious affairs correspondent for the BBC World Service, so heard the variety of reflections on the Indaba process from both trusted contacts and those bishops who were prepared to defy official encouragements never to speak to journalists. But I mention this experience now as it seems clear to me that much of what I was doing then, as a Christian journalist attempting to make sense of Anglican affairs to a global audience, was theological education. Admittedly, it is difficult to get much detail into a despatch lasting less than a minute – but if an international audience is going to learn anything about the Anglican Communion, the BBC World Service may well be one of the places it starts to do so.

It is, then, with some sense of irony that I write this as a newly termed *'potential* theological educator'. Indeed, a fellow ordinand with a doctorate in theology suffers the same fate, as have a number of former school teachers during my time at Ripon College Cuddesdon.[20] There is a danger that the Church, in its institutional desire to affirm the educative potential of certain ordinands, implies that not only is their role as a theological educator something that cannot yet begin, but that it certainly didn't happen in their life prior to training. Sometimes, this simply feels like the sort of irritation to be shrugged off – the comprehension of irritating official acronyms is surely part of ministerial formation? – but on occasion the terminology of 'PTE' risks saying rather too much about how the Church values the prior experience of those seeking ordination.

Questions of terminology sit alongside unpredictable and inconsistent support offered to those designated as PTEs at their Bishops' Advisory Panel (or BAP – another delightful acronym that all too quickly trips off the tongue without a second thought). While I am in the very fortunate position of being given dedicated doctoral study time within a curacy, such an arrangement is by no means guaranteed even for PTEs with firm backing for the pursuit of a teaching role as part of their future ministry. One might consider a comparison with Pioneer Ministers, whose curacies look very different from those of most other ordinands; from this trainee minister's perspective, there could be a greater sense of clarity about what exactly is meant by the PTE designation, and how the Church supports the flourishing in ministry of those who sense an academic theological dimension to their priestly calling.

I am not aware, for example, of any formal gatherings for those who have been designated as theological educators as they develop in their ministry. While colleagues with shared theological interests may well expect to meet informally on the academic conference circuit, it seems to me that there could be real value in some form of association for the Church's theological educators (and think of the potential acronyms!). Such gatherings could offer mutual support in the negotiation of this very particular vocation, but could also act as a way of reminding the Church of the theological resources it has previously invested in. Theological consultation within the Church can often seem to be undertaken in a way that overlooks the potential input of the Church's own theologians – the group that recently advised the House of Bishops on sexuality, chaired by Sir Joseph Pilling, did not in its original composition contain any academic theologians, for example – so there are legitimate questions about whether the Church as a whole does as much as it might to harness the potential contribution of those with particular theological skills.

---

[20]   One of the Church of England's largest seminaries, linked with the University of Oxford.

Conclusion

There is something reassuringly Anglican about the sort of dilemmas faced by those who aspire to combine a vocation to priesthood with some element of academic theology. Like so many other Anglicans in varied settings around the world, we face the tension of neither wanting to exclude ourselves from mainstream (often secular) culture, nor simply wishing to assimilate and lose our distinctiveness; we are likely to be deliciously varied in our priorities, and indeed our clerical dress, but we will unite – at least some of the time – in affirming the place of the Eucharist, whatever other dimensions there are to our calling; we rather take for granted the freedom to minister in a variety of contexts in a way that would be less straightforwardly open to some of our ecumenical colleagues; and we almost certainly take for granted the lack of a curia to regulate our output.

We are free to work in a university or in a seminary; to choose our balance between academic and pastoral work; to move from parish work into theological education and back again, or combine the two; to write without fear of censure. So notwithstanding the bleak financial climate, or those ongoing questions about whether the Church of England really values its theologians, or any number of uncertainties about the future of higher education, there is much to celebrate. And in Dan Hardy I believe we have a worthy role model for an approach to theological education that is deeply pastoral, centred in eucharistic worship, and constantly open to God's surprising revelation through theological exploration.

Dan Hardy quoted from Ephesians as he concluded his address to General Theological Seminary shortly before his death; David Ford used the same verses to close his Blackwell Manifesto. They seem worthy words of inspiration for those of us who seek to love God with all of our minds:

> Now to him who by the power at work within us is able to accomplish abundantly far more than all we can ask or imagine, to him be glory in the church and in Christ Jesus to all generations, for ever and ever, Amen. (Eph 3:20–21)

PART III
The Educational Context

Chapter 8

The Vocation of the Theological Educator: Listening for the Divine Voice

Mark D. Chapman

Divine Book and Divine Society[1]

In a letter to a clergyman, who was evidently deeply troubled by one of his young friends' problems over the question of biblical authority, Henry Liddon, Dr Pusey's biographer and a predecessor of mine as Vice-Principal of Cuddesdon Theological College, offered the following advice:

> We believe in the Bible for a variety of reasons: **partly** external, partly internal. We cannot separate the Bible from the Church which **recognised** and preserved it. The Divine Book and the Divine Society are the two factors of the one Revelation – each checking the other.[2]

Liddon, who went on to become one of the greatest preachers of his age, is here enunciating a principle which the Church in virtually all its historical forms has upheld and continues to uphold: from its very beginnings the Church has endeavoured to maintain a tradition of interpreting Scripture while at the same time subjecting such an interpretative tradition to control by a principle which is itself derived from this Scripture. It seems to me that at its heart the vocation of the theological educator is in part to ensure that those who have a special responsibility to interpret Scripture through preaching and practice are given sufficient critical faculties to question and engage with both the divine book and the divine society: through all the inevitable conflicts, ethical dilemmas and

---

[1]   This chapter develops and builds on the argument first presented in my 'Scripture, Tradition and Criticism: A Brief Proposal for Theological Education' in *Anglican Theological Review* 78:2 (1996), 258–74. I am very grateful to Michael Lakey for making me think again about what I have been doing for the past 23 years. I could have entitled the chapter, 'Why I haven't changed my mind'.

[2]   J.O. Johnston, *Life and Letters of Henry Parry Liddon* (London: Longmans, 1904), 134.

pastoral problems there needs to be a proper set of checks and balances on both the divine society and divine book. Theological education becomes properly theological when both teachers and students are enabled to open themselves and their presuppositions as well as those of their church by subjecting them to the judgement of 'divine voice': indeed, the vocation to serve the Church might be best enabled by criticism and challenge which puts any theologian in an uneasy relationship with those in authority in the divine society. Although a tradition of interpretation is necessary, it can all too easily work to rob the 'Divine Book' of its potency to offer a critique of the 'Divine Society'. Indeed there appears to be an almost constant tendency throughout church history towards ecclesiastical control over scripture. Writing of the Roman Catholic Church, Avery Cardinal Dulles made this clear: 'The ecclesiastical magisterium, making use of Scripture and tradition, is the authoritative judge of the conformity of particular doctrines and practices, including human traditions, with the word of God'.[3] The vocation of the theological educator might perhaps be to question such an understanding of authority: where the divine voice itself is the interpreter the magisterium itself is not immune from criticism. This ambiguity inevitably makes the calling to theological education rather uncomfortable and occasionally disturbing.

This chapter addresses some dangers in some recent understandings of theological education which themselves are based upon a theory of ethical education. These frequently serve to emphasise the practice of living 'correctly' in the Divine Society to such an extent that there is little space left for the openness to the challenge by the 'divine voice'. As I will show when there is frequent talk of living the virtues of the Christian life or developing a Christian 'character' there can at the same time be a corresponding downplaying of the importance of the critical faculties. Correct practice is not necessarily either liberative or creative. It was no doubt in part against the control of scripture by the Church that the Reformers of the sixteenth century erupted, and yet in turn they paved the way for different forms of control which in turn required further critique by the 'Divine Book'. Given this emphasis on repeated ecclesiastical construction and evangelical critique, Church history can be understood (as it was, for instance, by H. Richard Niebuhr) in terms of a repeating cycle of revolutionary change followed by institutionalisation, of critique and construction, where 'the same institutionalism which represents the death of an old movement can be, as history amply illustrates, the pregnant source of a new aggression. It cannot be

---

[3]   Avery Cardinal Dulles, 'Tradition as a Theological Source' in *The Craft of Theology* (Dublin: Gill and Macmillan, 1992), 104.

otherwise with a Church which conserves in some form the kingdom of God'.[4] In this way the institution which develops in response to the critical force of the divine voice heard in Scripture will in turn be subjected to critique by this very principle. Consequently there is a 'genuine back-and-forth communication'[5] between Scripture and Church in the constant attempt to establish an institutional response to the Gospel ever more open to the liberating force of the Gospel itself.

This chapter seeks to emphasise the vital role of theological education in ensuring that a 'back-and-forth communication' between tradition and Scripture remains possible.[6] However, before outlining a proposal for a critical yet constructive model of theological education, in the next section I discuss some recent work on theological education which has stressed the importance of conceiving of the goal of theological education as the cultivation of 'theological wisdom' which is related to the idea of *paideia*[7] or education in the virtues. While agreeing that theological education – and Christian living more generally – is primarily concerned with the assimilation and living out of a particular community's tradition, I will go on to emphasise the importance of ensuring the survival of a critical and even subversive element within this tradition itself which results from the need to listen out for the divine voice in the midst of all the human voices. This should guard against the dangers of mere passive and uncritical acquisition of what might amount to little more than communal prejudice. I will suggest that 'being wise' in the tradition is at once knowing how to criticise that tradition by the cultivation of a critical faculty which in the end subjects all tradition to judgement by the divine voice, that is the Word of God, or more portentously, the judge of all human beings.

---

4   H. Richard Niebuhr, *The Kingdom of God in America* (New York: Harper and Row, 1959), 198.

5   H. Richard Niebuhr, *The Purpose of the Church and its Ministry* (New York: Harper Bros, 1956), 119.

6   See also Leonard Hodgson, *The Bible and the Training of the Clergy* (London: Darton, Longman and Todd, 1963), esp. 89–95.

7   On *Paideia* see the magisterial work by Werner Jaeger, *Paideia: The Ideals of Greek Culture* (Oxford: Blackwell, 1939). For its assimilation into early Christianity see Jaeger, *Early Christianity and Greek Paideia* (London: Oxford University Press, 1961). See also Andrew Louth, *Discerning the Mystery* (Oxford: Clarendon Press, 1983), esp. 77ff.

The Rediscovery of *Paideia*

This section will look briefly at some recent understandings of theological education beginning with the work of Edward Farley (1929–2014),[8] who through a series of writings beginning with *Theologia* dominated the discussion, at least in America. To counter the tendency towards the fragmentation of theology into numerous and only loosely related sub-disciplines, Farley called for the recovery of 'theologia' where all aspects of theological education are unified around a single purpose: theology is thus the mode of 'ecclesial reflection', whose goal focuses on the possibility of ensuring continued ecclesial presence in the world. As such, theology is a vocation rather than simply an academic study. What unifies theological education, in Farley's model, is the 'comprehensive historical phenomenon, ecclesial existence'.[9] Such a vision of theological education as centred on the acquisition of a shared corporate mode of existence is something akin to the Ancient Greek model of *paideia*, that is, education in a continuing tradition borne by society, in this case, the ecclesial society.

The re-invigoration of theological education with the ideals of *paideia* is particularly appropriate in Farley's American context with its traditional sharp division between historical theology and practical theology which, in part, stems from Schleiermacher's justification for theology in the new University of Berlin set out in his classic, *Kurze Darstellung des theologischen Studiums*,[10] which provided the model for much American theological education. According to Schleiermacher, the minister, like the lawyer or the doctor, learns a historical tradition, works out its essence, and then passes this on, using the techniques of practical theology, to the coming generation. The study of theology in the university is thus primarily the acquisition of historical and methodological theory, analogous to the learning of medical or legal theory, for the clerical practitioner,[11] and is justified in terms of the functional requirements of an indispensable activity of the state – the need for the 'cure of souls'. Unlike Farley's *paideia* model, Schleiermacher's is an extreme example of the clericalisation of

---

[8]   Edward Farley, *Theologia. The Fragmentation and Unity of Theological Education* (Philadelphia: Fortress, 1983) and *The Fragility of Knowledge: Theological Education in the Church and the University* (Philadelphia: Fortress, 1988). See also Charles M. Wood, *Vision and Discernment: An Orientation in Theological Study* (Atlanta: Scholars Press, 1985).

[9]   Farley, *Theologia*, 191.

[10]   This was first published in 1811. It was translated by Terence Tice as *Brief Outline on the Study of Theology* (Richmond: John Knox, 1966). See my *Theology and Society in Three Cities: Berlin, Oxford and Chicago, 1800–1914* (Cambridge: James Clarke, 2014), esp. ch. 2.

[11]   See Farley, *Theologia*, ch. 4.

theology whereby a specially trained leadership is equipped with a distinctive professional knowledge to perform a function in the state at large: theology is defined in terms of ministerial practice and thereby becomes a 'technical rationality'. This becomes clearest in Schleiermacher's famous description of the ideal clergyman:

> Imagine the concern for religion and the scientific spirit united, for the sake of theory and practice, in the highest degree and in the most perfect balance, and you have the idea of a 'prince of the church'.[12]

A similar vision of theology very quickly spread to the United States and became the basis of the formal development of theological seminaries of the mid nineteenth-century. It became clear as the century wore on, however, that the natural extension of such a model was to see that the necessary social functions of the minister (the 'cure of souls') was far better performed not by a training in theological theory, but in other disciplines. This model is perhaps best typified by the Chicago model where sociology, and more broadly science, were to become the chief subjects of study in clergy education. As William Rainey Harper, President of the University and an Old Testament scholar, wrote:

> A specific amount of laboratory work in science is in our day as necessary for the prospective theological student as a knowledge of Greek, and if the college does not furnish the student this equipment, the seminary must take the necessary steps to provide it.

Similarly there would be much to gain if the time devoted to the study of the Bible could be devoted instead to English literature. In short, he went on, 'the day has come for a broadening of the word minister, and for the cultivation of specialism in the ministry ... The ministry stands today in this respect where law and medicine stood twenty years ago'. This vision became remarkably influential, especially in the development of practically orientated 'theological clinics', and of the suggestion that seminaries should take account of the situation of learning (their 'context').

The chief problem with such models is that, by defining theology solely in terms of ministerial education, or what David Kelsey calls the 'clerical paradigm',[13]

---

12   Schleiermacher, *Brief Outline*, §9, 21.
13   David H. Kelsey, *To Understand God Truly. What's Theological about a Theological School?* (Louisville: Westminster/John Knox, 1992), 91.

theology ceases to have much purpose in a secular academic university. Still more problematic for such a model, however, is the seeming irrelevance of the ministry itself, at least as defined functionally by Schleiermacher: in much of Europe, at least, the state has usurped much of the social function of ministry. In contrast the model of theological education as the cultivation of the mode of ecclesial existence is quite different from the model of 'professional education', (where a body of theory and method is learnt in order to be put into practice), as well as from those of purely academic education (where the pursuit of scientific research is seen as an end in itself). The primary goal of ministerial education is not a 'technical rationality' which encompasses a number of scientifically based skills, but the acquisition of theological understanding or 'wisdom'. Farley's alternative to Schleiermacher makes no clear-cut distinction between theory and practice. In turn, theology is not defined in terms of the functions of ministry, but instead in terms of the acquisition of wisdom, the 'habitus' of theology.

Thus, against a vision of theology as a body of theory orientated primarily around clergy education, Farley sees it as something which combines theory and practice and which is rooted in the mode of assimilating the historical being of the Church. The unifying feature of theology is thus first and foremost the acquisition of a tradition, an inheritance, a set of rules. This is indeed reminiscent of Augustine (*On Christian Teaching* 2.42), for whom learning and assimilating a communal tradition is an essential human characteristic and is the necessary pre-requisite for any act of communication. Drawing on such a tradition Farley thereby sees historical theology as something which cannot be divorced from practical theology:

> Historical, thus, is theology itself. It may continue to be knowledge, but if it is the wisdom, the understanding, and insightfulness that occur when the human being is shaped in a redemptive way, it occurs in connection with the believer's or Church's responses to things, and as such it has the character of interpretation. ... It is the shift from theology as a cluster of sciences based on a priori authority to theology as historically situated reflection and interpretation.[14]

Paideia in the Church of England

Although this style of theological education as assimilation of 'ecclesial existence' has only recently returned to the centre of the discussion in America, it has shaped Anglican theological education at least since the foundation of the first

---

[14]   Farley, *Fragility of Knowledge*, 128. See also Kelsey, *To Understand God Truly*, 236.

theological colleges in the middle of the last century. Instead of being primarily focused on the education of the clerical practitioner, that is, on the acquisition of historical knowledge coupled with practical skills on the Berlin model, Anglican education has been more vaguely defined in terms of spiritual, pastoral and ministerial 'formation', or the assimilation of an 'ethos', the ownership of a tradition and the development of a pattern of being.[15] Furthermore, it has traditionally been rooted in the praying life of a religious community rather than in the purely intellectual atmosphere of the academic community.

Henry Liddon, Bishop Samuel Wilberforce's choice as first vice-principal of Cuddesdon Theological College (founded in 1854), offers a shining example, this time of the importance of *paideia* in theological education.[16] In a sermon preached at the College Festival in 1868, he remarked:

> A theological college endeavours, so far as human agency can do this, to give the tongue of the learned, the power of spiritual instruction to the future ambassadors of Christ ... It would fain teach them to listen, morning by morning, for the Divine Voice, explaining, deepening, fertilising within them the truth which is thus committed to their guardianship.[17]

Liddon outlines the goal of theological education by drawing from what he calls the 'God-taught wisdom' (*sophia theodidaktos*) tradition of the Greeks. It is this theological wisdom to which everything else is subordinated, and it becomes the goal of theological education: this wisdom is not limited to mere doctrine or knowledge but embraces all aspects of life, thus shaping the very being of the clergyman as he 'lives for God'.[18] Liddon contrasts this form of education with that offered in the secular universities which even in his day, he felt, were already ceasing to 'yield any public homage or honour to the name of our Lord Jesus Christ'.[19] In another sermon preached at the same occasion

---

[15]   See F.W.B. Bullock, *A History of Training for the Ministry of the Church of England, 1800–1874* (London: Home Words, 1955); *A History of Training for the Ministry of the Church of England, 1875–1974* (London: Home Words, 1976); Alan Haig, *The Victorian Clergy* (London: Croom Helm, 1984), 116–176. This emphasis on ethos bears close similarity to the central educational ideal of the Oxford Movement. See Chapman, *Theology and Society*, ch. 3.
[16]   On Liddon's part in the shaping of Cuddesdon, see O. Chadwick, *The Founding of Cuddesdon College* (Oxford: Oxford University Press, 1954).
[17]   Henry Liddon, 'The Work and Prospects of Theological Colleges', in *Clerical Life and Work. A Collection of Sermons* (London: Longmans, second edition, 1895), 49–50.
[18]   Ibid., 62.
[19]   Ibid., 67.

five years later, Liddon further developed his understanding of wisdom as the basis of theological education. The primary task of the theological college, he maintained, was to ensure that theology was undertaken in the context of the Church:

> The absence of [the] fear of the Lord, which is wisdom in the leading Bible sense of the term, is fatal to any living appreciation, if not to any appreciation whatever, of the doctrines of Redemption and Grace ... Dogmatic wisdom has its root and beginning in the culture of those moral and spiritual sensibilities which Scripture calls the 'fear of the Lord'.[20]

According to Liddon, spiritual and theological wisdom required a basis in 'conduct, in life, in conscience' which implied both a 'system' and an 'atmosphere'. It was impossible 'in the case of theology to ignore morals, conduct, life, without the greatest risk'.[21] This required living by a 'rule of love', which would furnish the future clergy with an ideal pattern for living. At the same time, however, 'system' required 'a moral and religious atmosphere'[22] which instilled the sincerest form of friendship rooted in 'consciously common convictions'.[23]

For Liddon, then, education in a theological college was first and foremost the cultivation of a disposition of the heart. This meant that its students were to be 'men who know something of their own hearts ere they preach to others'.[24] It was for this reason that the communal life of system and spirit which was gained through living, praying and eating together became so important in forming the theological disposition.[25] According to Liddon, a theological college was a community entrusted by the Church to develop theological wisdom in those who were to be ordained to preach, to exhort and admonish, and to act in its name. The parallels with the model outlined by Farley are clear: Liddon's idea of a theological college is every bit as far removed from the mere acquisition of pastoral and academic skills, mere 'theory' to be put into practice.

---

[20] Henry Liddon, 'The Moral Groundwork of Clerical Training' in *Clerical Life and Work*, 82–3.

[21] Ibid., 84.

[22] Ibid., 87.

[23] Ibid., 89.

[24] Ibid., 92.

[25] See William Jacob, 'The Development of the "Concept of Residence" in Theological Education in the Church of England' in *Residence – An Education* (London: Advisory Council for the Church's Ministry (ACCM), 1990), 68–91. He develops this in 'An Integrating Theology in Theological Education' in D.W. Hardy and P.H. Sedgwick (eds), *The Weight of Glory* (Edinburgh: T & T Clark, 1991), 185–94.

Liddon's ideals seem to have survived remarkably intact in Anglican theological education despite the many changes of the past century. Indeed, until very recently, most of the changes to the education of the clergy have increased the role of theological colleges, particularly the 1921 requirement that all ordinands should spend a period in residential training. It was only relatively recently that alternative patterns began to develop.[26] Indicative of the persistence of Liddon's ideals, however, is the attention which has recently been paid to the educational procedure for best ensuring that the theological student is able both to learn the tradition but also to make it live. The key-word has been 'integration' where the many aspects of theological education are to be integrated in the light of a coherent vision. This leads to

> an approach to theological education which would hold together in a creative
> relationship the formation of a person's own ministerial formation and character,
> the acquisition of an appropriate and serviceable knowledge of the living
> tradition, and an understanding of the forces operating in contemporary culture
> at the individual and at the social level.[27]

Similarly, in a report of 1987, which had far reaching effects on the academic and personal assessment of students in theological colleges, the approach taken emphasises that 'all parts of the educational programme are to be seen in relation to, or 'relativised' by, the central aim of theological education; and no one part should be seen as the heart of the process'.[28] The central aim was seen as

> to enable the student to grow in those personal qualities by which, with and
> through the corporate ministry of the Church, the creative and redemptive
> activity of God may be proclaimed and realised in the world. One who is to show
> God's activity must know of it, respond to it, participate in it, be animated by
> it in relationships with others and seek to proclaim and realise it in the world.
> This requires that he/she seek to be conformed to the very form of God's being
> for mankind in the world, intellectually, spiritually and practically, and into the
> discipline of thought and life which is implicit in this. He/she must seek to be

---

[26]   The first part-time course was set up by Mervyn Stockwood and John Robinson in Southwark in 1960.

[27]   Peter Baelz, introduction in *An Integrating Theology* (London: ACCM, Occasional Paper No.15), 1983.

[28]   *Education for the Church's Ministry* (London: ACCM, Occasional Paper No.22, London, 1987), §57(1).

incorporated into the truth by growing in wisdom and godliness by the grace which God confers.[29]

Theological education is thus not just about learning the tradition, the story of the creative and redemptive activity of God, but also about engaging with tradition in order to make it live, learning how it is true today, and then making it true today. It is about being formed and conformed to the being of God in the world. 'If we are to be true to a living tradition', wrote Peter Baelz, at the time Chair of the Church of England's ACCM's Committee for Theological Education, 'then we dare not separate so-called spiritual experience from so-called theological knowledge. Neither will live and flourish without the other. Indeed, divorced from each other, both become mockeries of their true selves'. In short, he continued, 'a living tradition, with its roots in the past, is one that sets people free to explore the unrealised potentiality of the future'.[30]

All this goes to show that Anglican theological education is undoubtedly moulded, at least in its ideals, by the model of *paideia*, and resembles something like the union between theoretical and practical implied by its context in the microcosm of ecclesial existence, the theological college itself. Baelz's idea that theology was something to be worn like comfortable clothes and not left hung up unused in a wardrobe, thus describes both the practice and the goal of theological education: theology is a usable wisdom, a *habitus*, which shapes all aspects of life as one is formed into the very image of God by assimilating a mode of 'ecclesial being'.

The Dangers of *Paideia*

Ecclesial being, however, is not without its dangers. The *paideia* model of theological education which centres on the growth of Christian character and the assimilation of divine wisdom can make it difficult to engage critically with the communal structures and language of identity. One might ask whether there is an inherent tendency to stifle the critical faculty of listening out for the divine voice which might challenge those very structures. *Paideia* might even prevent the 'back-and-forth communication' between scripture and tradition outlined in the first section. Is the acquisition of theological wisdom simply the adoption of

---

[29]   *Education for the Church's Ministry*, §45.
[30]   See also introduction by Peter Baelz in *Experience and Authority* (London: ACCM Occasional Paper No.19, London, 1984).

a fixed closed system of ecclesial existence? There is every likelihood that despite the idealistic language of *paideia*, wisdom, and character, theological education is in practice frequently little more than the assimilation of the ideology of an institution dominated by a Church party.[31] Indeed, in its original usage, *paideia* was education for a social form of activity, involving the acquisition of those distinctive virtues which formed the social cement for the city state, the polis, and which served as a basis for its immortality or survival in future generations.[32] As such it appears to have been inherently conservative, lacking any significant critical dimension. Perhaps for similar reasons of social stability (for instance, ecumenical co-existence or Anglican 'comprehensiveness') *paideia* as practised by the Churches is likely to conform the student to a distinctive form of ecclesial being which lacks much of a critical dimension. A Church of England Report on theological education of 1949, for instance, suggested that the 'best theological college is one in which the Chapel, the lecture room and the common room are all working together to make a fellowship of Christian life both natural and supernatural, the power of which shall remain in the memory of the ordinand as a pattern and inspiration for his future work in a congregation'.[33] Without due caution the goal of theological education can become little more than that of instilling the party line of the college into the future clergy: I am very aware that there is a species of 'Cuddesdon man' characterised by a feeling of effortless superiority and who gives thanks daily that he is neither too high nor too low.

In order to avoid this danger of *paideia* becoming little more than a conservative form of indoctrination there seems to be a vital need to ensure that the particularity of the tradition through which one comes to the Gospel, that is a particular mode of ecclesial existence, is not mistaken for the Gospel itself.[34] There must always be room within any ecclesial tradition for the critical encounter to take place, a latent suspicion of all attempts to control the divine voice: that voice, as ultimate judge, thus stands over and against any form of ecclesial existence. Theological integration – *theologia* – must thus be no mere

---

[31]   On the attraction of ideologies, see the classic account by John M. Hull, *What Prevents Christian Adults from Learning?* (London: SCM, 1985), esp. ch. 2.

[32]   See Jaeger, *Paideia*, 379–408.

[33]   *The Purpose and Scope of Clergy Training: An Outline of Current Practice* (London: Central Advisory Council for the Ministry, 1949).

[34]   On this see the programmatic essay by Rowan Williams, 'Does it make sense to speak of pre-Nicene orthodoxy?' in *The Making of Orthodoxy*, ed. Rowan Williams (Cambridge: Cambridge University Press, 1989), 1–23. See, for example, p. 15: 'The convert enters a new world in which, because conflict, constraint and uncertainty remain, learning and exchange must continue, and progress needs to be checked against original inspiration, individually and collectively'.

passive assimilation or conformity to a particular form of ecclesial existence or tradition, but a re-invigoration of that tradition through the often painful business of criticism.[35] This requires an understanding of tradition, not as a closed system or complete 'semantic universe' on George Lindbeck's model of doctrine[36] but one which is constantly subjected to constructive criticism. Consequently, the acquisition of tradition is not a passive assimilation of a language but the active response to a critical encounter with that tradition. This is recognised by Farley himself who sees the clergy's role in this existence as not simply that of passing on the tradition but as a 'situationally oriented dialectic of interpretation', that is, the task of evoking ecclesial presence in the world, which requires a critique of the tradition. In this way a more authentic ecclesial existence will be discerned.[37]

There are obvious parallels here with the celebrated dispute between Gadamer and Habermas.[38] The problem with linguistic or anthropological analogies, which are used extensively by both Gadamer and Lindbeck, is that they seem to lack a criterion to distinguish what Habermas calls 'pseudocommunication' where the inherited tradition itself might be shown to be a distorted form of communication.[39] Linguistic analogies appear to lead inexorably to a 'hypostatisation of the traditional context'.[40] Consequently, the tradition into which we are being assimilated through *paideia* might itself be shown to be an (albeit structured)[41] distortion or pseudocommunication, 'a consciousness forged of compulsion'.[42] In a theory of truth that is wholly 'intra-systematic',[43] however, there can be no room for criticism, no recognition that the system itself is in dialogue with other systems and consequently open to all

---

[35]   See Kelsey, *To Understand God Truly*, ch. 7.

[36]   See Lindbeck's 'cultural-linguistic' model as set out in *The Nature of Doctrine* (Philadelphia: Westminster Press, 1984).

[37]   Farley, *Theologia*, 191.

[38]   The relevant documents are translated in Kurt Mueller-Vollmer (ed.), *The Hermeneutics Reader* (Oxford: Blackwell, 1986), 256–319. For a perceptive analysis, see Werner Jeanrond, *Theological Hermeneutics* (London: Macmillan, 1991), 64–70. Andrew Louth draws out the connection between Gadamer, *Bildung* and *paideia*. See *Discerning the Mystery*, 29–44, esp. 42.

[39]   See Jürgen Habermas, 'On Hermeneutics' Claim to Universality' in *The Hermeneutics Reader*, 294–319, esp. 302. See also Jeanrond, *Theological Hermeneutics*, 67.

[40]   Habermas, 'On Hermeneutics' Claim to Universality', 314.

[41]   See Hans-Georg Gadamer, 'Rhetoric, Hermeneutics and the Critique of Ideology', in *The Hermeneutics Reader*, 274–92, esp. 286.

[42]   Habermas, 'On Hermeneutics' Claim to Universality', 317.

[43]   Lindbeck, *The Nature of Doctrine*, 63–9.

manner of ideological distortion. In such a closed system theological education can only ever be the passive appropriation of the historical structures, symbols and practices of an ecclesial community complete with all manner of ideological distortions, however idolatrous.

Conclusion

To counter this tendency towards absolutising a particular tradition, it might be suggested that the 'system' into which the Christian is socialised through *paideia* is no closed system, but instead is one founded on what Rowan Williams refers to as 'a generative event' which defies 'schematisation into a plan of salvation that can be reduced to a simple and isomorphic moment of self-recognition in reasons to illumination'.[44] It was to counter any 'hypostatisation of the traditional context' that Farley's mode of ecclesial being emphasised a critical dimension which de-absolutises any ecclesiastical-cultural situation in the 'purging and sifting of the mythos', with the proviso that criticism is always 'truth-oriented', that is, undertaken constructively with the goal of moving ever closer to the kingdom of God.[45] The theological educator's task is thus to open up possibilities for the creation of a new situation for faith's dealing with the world, something undertaken in the conscious criticism of all past situations. The Christian 'system' is thus at the same time the constant critique of all systems, including its own ecclesial expressions.

In its emphasis on integration and the living assimilation of a tradition and way of being, the *paideia* model of theological education is attractive, but only when it is no mere indoctrination in the closed semantic system of a Church party. For the Gospel to continue to speak to future generations requires that the 'cultural-linguistic' mode of a particular ecclesial community is itself (in Rowan Williams's phrase) 'open to judgement' and does not instead usurp the role of judge over the scriptural principle, the generative event of the Gospel – the encounter with the life, death and resurrection of Jesus. Although a part of theological education must obviously be concerned with the acquisition and 'ownership' of a cherished tradition, at the same time, if the divine voice is to act as a potent force for the coming generation, it must also seek to awaken the faculty of critical discernment in those who will be authorised to speak and act in the name of the Church, enabling them to hear, preach and proclaim the word

---

[44]   Rowan Williams, 'Pre-Nicene Orthodoxy?', 16.
[45]   See Farley, *Theologia*, esp. 166–7.

of God, even where that word is critical of the ideological distortions introduced by the Church.

Learning the inherited tradition of the community is undoubtedly necessary; it is the vehicle through which the Gospel is mediated and through which an encounter with Christ first becomes possible. But in turn, as the product of human history, any such tradition is bound to be related to what Richard Niebuhr called the 'fragmentary and frail measure of our faith'.[46] It will inevitably be tainted by the destructive tendency towards absolutisation of the fragmentary. Consequently, all historical forms of the Church, all traditions, all symbols and all practices must be subjected to thoroughgoing suspicion, opened up to an encounter with the 'permanently disturbing generative event',[47] if they are to continue to exist as living mediators of the word of God to the coming generation.

This critical task of theological education might usefully be summarised as the practice of ideological literacy, that is, the task of critically dismantling the Church's control over its underlying narrative, thereby allowing the narrative itself to speak afresh to the new generation: the divine society is to be subjected to critique by the divine book as witness to the divine voice. On this model, beyond the preliminary task of understanding the historical particularity, the symbols and practices through which the Gospel is mediated and without which no criticism would ever be possible (that is, the tradition), there are two further aspects which stand together in a dialectical relation and which form the goal of theological education: firstly, there is the need to establish criteria to discern where and when the Gospel is being heard, that is, to open up the possibility for encounter with the central narrative (for Christians a narrative focused primarily on the life, death and resurrection of Christ). Secondly, there is the need to attain a critical faculty to distinguish theology from ideology within the tradition in which the divine word is first mediated. The first aspect calls into question all meaning while opening up new paths of meaning, while the second is a call to judge all those channels through which the tradition is handed on to each generation; this is nothing short of a requirement to challenge and judge the very ecclesial structures which shape Christian identity.

Tradition is thereby perpetuated not by uncritical assimilation, but by critical encounter: what is handed on after such criticism is an attempted refinement of tradition, as the tradition is brought into contact with the divine voice. In this

---

46   H. Richard Niebuhr, *Christ and Culture* (London: Faber and Faber, 1952), 234.

47   Rowan Williams, 'What is Catholic Orthodoxy?', in *Essays Catholic and Radical*, eds Kenneth Leech and Rowan Williams (London: Bowardean, 1983), 19.

way the particular historical tradition which forms the necessary point of departure for the reception of the word of God is radically changed by renewed encounter with the Gospel. In the critical encounter the tradition is transformed as new metaphors and images communicate the 'death and birth of meaning'[48] to the succeeding generation. Far more central to theological education than the acquisition of knowledge, 'theory', or so-called 'practical' skills, is the task of ideological literacy, which means questioning, criticising and suspecting in the light of the highest criterion. Consequently, the primary task of theological education does not involve the acquisition of 'theories' and a 'body of knowledge' which will later be put into practice, but rather it involves the far more painful process of encounter, judgement and conversion. It is by challenging the past and the present that the future is opened up for the divine voice. The most important thing in theological education, then, is the acquisition of the faculty to criticise and to recognise the distortions of the false authorities, 'bastard traditions',[49] under whose malign influence we will constantly fall, and to criticise them in the light of a vision of the truth as free as possible from all authoritarianism and vain conceit.

Though a conclusion to such a task is impossible in that any tradition we hand on to the future generation will itself be permeated by our own perhaps unnoticed prejudice and an often unrecognised ideology, it is still nonetheless the pressing task. Theology is thus focused on critical reflection 'on the ideological distortions of [one's] own group, class, national or cultural consciousness' at the same time as prophetically exposing 'the peril of those who imperil the livelihood, well-being and self-respect of others'. Such criticism becomes constructive, however, 'if it is, and seen to be, from start to finish, self-criticism in the light of the Gospel of Christ crucified and risen'.[50]

What seems lacking in much theological education is a proper critical hermeneutics of suspicion. The vocation of the educator ought to throw into question a cherished past, not out of a relativistic nihilism, but in the light of the life, death and resurrection of Christ where everything will seem suspect: it is this divine voice that provides that 'extralinguistic' ideological critique of all our language, our symbols and our partisan identity. And those with a vocation

---

[48]   Ibid., 19.

[49]   F.J.A. Hort, *The Way, The Truth, The Life: the Hulsean Lectures for 1871* (London: Macmillan, second edition, 1897), 91–2.

[50]   Nicholas Lash, 'Criticism or Construction? The Task of the Theologian', in *Theology on the Way to Emmaus*, (London: SCM, 1986), 3–17. See also Rowan Williams, 'Doctrinal Criticism: Some Questions' in Sarah Coakley and David Pailin (eds), *The Making and Remaking of Christian Doctrine* (Oxford: Clarendon Press, 1993), 247.

to serve the Church as theological educators have a duty to ensure that the Church constantly undergoes what Michael Ramsey called 'an agonizing death to its pride'.[51]

Theological wisdom forces those of us with a vocation to teach to the paradoxical recognition that the greater the degree of wisdom the greater the doubt, the greater the suspicion of our own and every other tradition. Against the natural inclination of all institutions towards self-perpetuation, the tradition of belief which recites and responds to the divine voice is a perpetually self-critical one. Thus although this model of theological education might be hazardous to the health of an institution, it is nevertheless the only possible basis if such an education is to open Christians up to the divine voice in the service of the coming generation. As Richard Niebuhr put it: 'A theory of theological study which does not lead toward new endeavours toward better, more precise and more inclusive understanding of the nature of theological endeavour under the government of God is not a theory of theology but a dogmatic statement backed up by no more than individual authority, that is by no authority at all'.[52] In the same way, *Paideia* without critique usurps this divine reality for the more familiar dwelling-place of the community of faith where one 'learns how to feel, act, and think in conformity with a religious tradition'[53] but forgetting that this community itself is part of the crucifying world. That makes the vocation to theological education critical for the survival of the Church as a witness to the divine voice.

---

[51]   A. Michael Ramsey, *The Gospel and the Catholic Church* (London: Longmans, Green and Co., 1937), 66.

[52]   Niebuhr, *The Purpose of the Church*, 134.

[53]   Lindbeck, *The Nature of Doctrine*, 35.

Chapter 9

The Academic Priest as Teacher and Tutor

Alison Milbank

Wisdom has built her house,
she has hewn her seven pillars.
She has slaughtered her animals, she has mixed her wine,
she has also set her table.
She has sent out her servant-girls, she calls
from the highest places in the town,
'You that are simple, turn in here!'To those without sense she says,
'Come, eat of my bread
and drink of the wine I have mixed. (Prov 9:1–5)

A student arrives for advice on her essay in my normal university office hours. Her hair is shiny and smooth, and her make-up immaculate in a manner unthinkable in my own far-off student days. She has colour-coded notes in an array of formidable files, and her questions for me are well-prepared, and written on her iPad, which she manipulates with easy elegance. Before me is a perfect example of what the philosopher and cultural historian, Charles Taylor, calls the 'buffered self' of the modern era:

> The buffered self is the agent who no longer fears demons, spirits, magic forces. More radically, these no longer impinge; they don't exist for him; whatever threat or other meaning they proffer doesn't 'get to' him. Now the disengaged rational agent carries out an analogous operation on desire.
>
> Of course our desires still impinge, as de facto inclinations. But they are deprived of any higher meaning or aura. They are just de facto solicitations. We ought to be able to stand back from all of them, and determine rationally how we should best dispose them.[1]

---

[1]   Charles Taylor, *A Secular Age* (Cambridge Mass: Harvard University Press, 2007), 135.

In contrast to the pre-modern self who is traversed by forces and is porous to forces and influences, the self of a post-Cartesian separation of mind and body is no longer vulnerable and a part of a cosmic whole. Instead, the self is safe behind its own self-sufficiency and agency: metaphysically buffered just as my student is literally polished and buffered to a high material gloss. Her physical person has become a work-in-progress: almost an external object, which she tends conscientiously.

As in Charles Taylor's description, desires still affect my student. She wants a good degree and job and will work tremendously hard to achieve this aim. Very often, however, this rational aim is all that drives her work. School and a regime of constant examinations have rendered her highly competent but instrumental in her attitude to knowledge. Each essay is planned like a military campaign, and topics chosen for their ease of sources, clarity of method, and likelihood to give a strong mark. When other desires do impinge, however, my student disintegrates. Quite often the breakdown of a relationship will tear the buffered self open, and raw longings rack him or her in front of my eyes. Quite naturally, such love and jealousy and anger dissolve the rational subject, but in the buffered self this loss of poise is wholly negative. Desires are no longer a locus of higher meanings or linked to the sacred. The aura of desire, as Taylor notes, is now regarded as total illusion:

> This agent is in a sense super-buffered. He is not only not 'got at' by demons and spirits; he is also utterly unmoved by the aura of desire. In a mechanistic universe, and in a field of functionally understood passions, there is no more ontological room for such an aura. There is nothing it could correspond to. It is just a disturbing supercharged feeling, which somehow grips us until we can come to our senses, and take on our full, buffered identity.[2]

Passion and emotion have now become secularised but this renders their power all the more unmanageable, and they become a new dark continent for psychoanalytic investigation. Therapy mimics spiritual direction or healing but denies the subject, Taylor argues, the dignity of choice. There is no longer any element of conversion and rejection of evil, just incapacity.[3] The 'talking-cure' may come close to giving the subject some lost dignity but ultimately, its aim is to understand, and in understanding to reduce the force of suffering and psychic conflict: 'On the crucial issue, what we have morally or spiritually to learn from

---

2   Ibid., 136.
3   Ibid., 620.

our suffering [psychoanalysis] is firmly on the therapeutic side: the answer is "nothing".[4]

So what is my role as a priest educator before my buffered student? How can I call her to the feast of wisdom? How can I open in her a desire for God? I teach in a department of theology and religious studies in a secular university and I certainly cannot call her to the altar table. Unlike the lecturers who taught me over 30 years ago, I cannot even appear to teach in clerical dress, or style myself 'reverend' in the faculty list. One wonderful afternoon, a crematorium was running late, so I was deposited by the hearse in surplice and stole in the full gaze of 70 undergraduates waiting for me to lecture on Augustine. Despite the fact that they were about to hear about the autobiography of a bishop, they were as shocked as if I had appeared nude before them, although it may have been the hearse's *memento mori* that offended their assured immortality rather than my voluminous priestly garb. There is in such a context no question of direct evangelism. And yet we live in an intellectual climate in which the days when the great comparative religion scholar, Ninian Smart, could claim to be bracketing his own beliefs, and be talking objectively when he stood to the left of his slide-projector are long gone. The impossibility of separating fact and value is one of the key insights of postmodernism that has been accepted as normative by the academy. We academics make students aware of our pre-suppositions in order that they may be disillusioned out of innocent acceptance of our disinterestedness. And yet, I and my colleagues aim to present ideas and movements with as much faithfulness to the truth as possible.

I cannot here give an account of how to answer coherently all the philosophical problems of post-modernity, but I can share something of my own reflection on how to respond to my buffered student and her needs as a priest and teacher. My first aim for my student is to open his or her desire for wisdom: to offer a vision of the aim of education as knowledge of the true, the good and the beautiful. And already by invoking these transcendentals, I have entered the realm of the religious, since the very acknowledgement of such ideas suggests the existence of a substantive truth to be grasped. To know the Good is to become good, and to desire further participation. In the world of the humanities and social sciences – less so in the pure sciences – 'truth' is now the uncovering of illusion, and the revelation of ideological structures of power. That exercise may have a role in the uncovering of truth, but it is only the beginning, as it was for Socrates, who acted as a gadfly, stinging and testing his students to examine the assumptions they made without examination in their ideas of truth, justice

---

4   Ibid., 621.

and so on. In the Socratic method, this uncovering of illusion is called *elenchus* and is best shown in the early books of Plato's *Republic* in which a sequence of well-born, self-confident Athenian young men are tied up in knots by Socrates as he makes them push their conventional or amoral ideas on the nature of justice to their logical conclusion. The difference between Socrates and contemporary humanities academics is that he acted with a strong apprehension of the Good, whereas nowadays the only good is critical disillusion: a feminist, post-colonial or psychological deconstruction. Socrates instead aimed at an *aporia*: an impasse or dark night of the mind beyond which it cannot think. This then became the basis for rebuilding desire for the Good which would lead to apprehension of the substantial nature of truth.

As a priest I am required to preach the gospel 'in season and out of season' and I think of this as akin to a mode of *elenchus*. This may, indeed, involve reading *A Secular Age* with my students and offering Taylor's account of the changes in the idea of what it is to be human in the last few hundred years. Today students do not encounter different views on reality very often before university, or sometimes at it. We have a somewhat attenuated intellectual culture, a monochrome political landscape, and an increasingly privatised religious conversation. Any of us who work for institutions as well as businesses know how bureaucratic and managerial modes of knowledge and organisation rule our lives, and with them comes a distinct lack of interest in truth. These discourses are interested in method, skills and competence. Church and university are not exempted but, I would argue, are equally affected by these trends, which result from a culture in which moral discourse apart from a playground language of 'fairness' and individual autonomy is noticeably absent. Ironically, my buffered student who seems so unassailable in her self-determination is actually a victim of this bureaucratisation of all aspects of life, as Livio Melina explains:

> When 'reason is silent about values', the individual is left to the emotion of the moment, which he succeeds in surpassing through means of a free self-determination. The 'I' is fragmented into moments and areas of life each quite distinct from the other; it becomes a fragile 'I', easily dominated by different and opposed laws that are imposed on it from time to time by the social organization. The individual is reduced to playing different characters in different scenes with different roles and rules: one sphere is economics, another that of the family, another politics, another concerned with leisure time. The fragmented and

individualistic 'I', unable to become a free subject of action, is the victim desired
by every bureaucratic power.[5]

Without an understanding that there is a truth, moral subjectivism rules and
denies the self that unity and that Good that makes free action possible, and allows
one to channel and direct desires aright.

So my task as teacher and priest in the quest of an opening to the good, the
true and the beautiful is to enable some questioning of assumptions about the
nature of the human person as the fragmented and individualistic 'I'. One might
suggest, for example, as Melina demonstrates, that this sort of subjectivism
denies that there is any truth about a created thing that must be respected,
'so that everything can be manipulated without limits, save those pertaining
to the calculus of one's own advantage'.[6] Such a belief about the world looks
remarkably tawdry in the light of the imminent ecological crisis. The gadfly
method of *elenchus* elicits from the students the implicit values by which they
live and think, subjects these to question, and takes them to their limit. In the
classroom it is a traditional method of teaching, although one that survives more
strongly in the United States, where a liberal sense of the role of education as a
moral endeavour still pertains in universities.

In the tutoring session, this method can also have a role to play as a way of
eliciting a student's true desires. We still in my university call the tutor's role
'pastoral', which suggests a leading and chivvying, as well as a relationship that
is closer and more holistic than that of a mere course advisor. This can make it
hard for a tutor-priest, since it is so like a pastoral visit and yet I cannot pray
with the student or speak using any religious language. One day I had a student
who had done something wrong to some friends about which he felt enormous
and oppressive guilt. The friends concerned had forgiven him but the burden of
shame and guilt remained. How I longed to invite him to an act of sacramental
penance and offer Christ's forgiveness!

What one can do is to direct the tutorial meeting through the classes to be
chosen and the student's intellectual aims so as to enable the student to examine
her own conception of education and what it is for. To understand this task, I
tend to rely on Aristotle's division of the virtues between the intellectual and the
moral. The Catholic artist and critic Eric Gill sums it up succinctly in his essay
'Art and Prudence': 'Doing is an activity directed to an end in view –the end in

---

[5]   Livio Melina, *Sharing in Christ's Virtues: For a Renewal of Moral Theology in Light
of* Veritatis Splendor, trans. William May (Washington DC: Catholic University Press of
America, 2001), 19.

[6]   Ibid., 20.

view being man's good, Heaven. But when a man's deeds are directed not to his own good simply but to the good of a *thing*, then doing becomes *making*. An act that is good, or thought to be good, with regard to oneself is called a *prudent* act. An act that is good, or thought to be good, with regard to a thing to be made is called *art*.[7] When looking at the choice of courses, the student and I are directed towards the good of the thing: the intellectual work; we seek its splendour and apprehension of the good, the true and the beautiful. For Aristotle the height of the intellectual virtues was contemplation, which is a participation in truth itself. This might seem a long way from choosing between modules but having first done some elenchic testing of assumptions, the next step is constructive. In the *Symposium* and the *Thaetetus* Socrates is compared to a midwife as he brings ideas innate in the student to birth. This pedagogic procedure is called *maieusis* in Greek and depends in Plato on the idea of a pre-existent soul, which has forgotten the truths it once knew. The teacher as midwife awakens this memory (*anamnesis*) and helps the student to recognise the truth he knows.

The midwife role is one that has a biblical analogy in St Paul's language of childbirth and labour, as well as in 1 Thessalonians 2:7, where he compares himself either to a midwife or a wet nurse. It is a particularly rich symbol for the woman priest who images Mother Church and Mary as priestly in her giving birth to Christ. (There is a lovely tradition that she confirmed John the Baptist at the Visitation, so acting as bishop as well as priest.[8]) *Anamnesis*, as a mode of memory which renders that which it seeks present is also a term much used in discussion of the action of the Eucharist, being the Greek word used by Christ himself according to 1 Corinthians 11:24–5 and some versions of Luke 22:19: 'do this in remembrance of me'.[9] Similarly, in the *Thaetetus* Socrates struggles to elicit from the eponymous young man busy oiling himself the true nature of knowledge. The kind of *anamnesis* involved in a typical advising session is to talk through work and writing the students have done in the past and to elicit from them what was pleasurable, what is intriguing and what they would like to take further. In this way we begin to uncover what they truly desire to know and what vision of truth they have already experienced. I ask them in what way they feel the different subjects they have studied actually connect, and in this way we begin to orient away from purely instrumental goals and towards a love of knowledge/

---

[7]   Eric Gill, 'Art and Prudence', in *Beauty Looks after Herself*, ed. Catherine Pickstock (Tacoma WA: Angelico Press, 2012), 12.

[8]   Réné Laurentin, citing Jean-Jacques Olier, *Maria, Ecclesia, Sacerdotium* (Paris: Nouvelles Éditions Latines, 1952), 278–82.

[9]   See Gregory Dix, *The Shape of the Liturgy* (London: Dacre Press, 1975 [1945]), 238–47.

wisdom as such. The students begin to realise that they know more than they thought they did, and as I ask them to talk me through the past term's sessions and how each connected to the next, they begin both to understand what they know and to bring new insights to birth. One key task is to help tutees choose a dissertation topic for their third year, and here remembering and connecting is a crucial task if they are to find their own subject and really begin to act and learn independently. What this sort of tutoring aims to do is to unite knowledge and begin to use the intellectual quest as a mode of union in pursuit of a truth that is both glimpsed and yet eludes us. In the letter to the Colossians St Paul writes: 'we ask God that you may receive from him full insight into his will, all wisdom and spiritual understanding' (Col 1:9). The word for 'understanding' is *sunesis*, which means literally the flowing together of two streams. Understanding is therefore a uniting of knowledge and Colossians goes on to show that this is through the illumination of Christ who reconciles all things and all knowledge.

Those of us who have undertaken any kind of independent research know that there is always a personal reason for our choice of subject, although this may not be apparent to anyone else reading the finished work. Learning is always an action of the whole person. Therefore, to return to my Aristotelian division of the good of the person and the good of the work, I cannot neglect the good of the person and his or her 'end', which is, of course, a supernatural one for this Christian application of Aristotle. As Eric Gill puts it, 'Art and Prudence are, as it were, one flesh'.[10] Although my university may be secular and our degrees not given as they are at Cambridge, in the name of the Trinity, Nottingham uses the word '*sapientia*' in its motto, suggesting the foundational role of wisdom for the city: *sapientia urbs conditur*. Hence I can rightly call the students to wisdom as a supernatural value, and one that is ethically inflected as in St Augustine, involving the whole person. Augustine in his book on *The Trinity* (12–14) makes a distinction between what we might now call instrumental knowledge of things, *scientia*, and wisdom, *sapientia*, to which we cleave and by which we are transformed because it is knowledge of the divine (the good, the true and the beautiful etc.).[11] Without some higher view of wisdom we have no way of preventing knowledge being pure instrumental mastery, and thus no longer 'liberal' or free. Liberal education as an idea derives from ancient Greece, when education provided the subjects that would enable a free man to take a full part in civic life in all its aspects, including the religious and philosophical.

---

[10]   Gill, 'Art and Prudence', 16.
[11]   St Augustine, *The Trinity*, trans. Edmund Hill, O. P. (New York: New City Press, 1991), 322–94.

This conception continued and was extended in the medieval and renaissance university in a Christian reordering. The seven subjects of the curriculum, the *quadrium* and *trivium* were the seven pillars of the house of wisdom. The combination of virtue, wisdom and participation as the foundation of the house is shared in all periods. It is still latent in university life and structure today. Once one is a member of a university, one is so for life: an *alumnus* or *alumna*. The word means foster son or pupil but is derived from the verb, *alere*, meaning to nourish. Despite leaving classes and going out into the world, the student is always a foster child, and always nourished by its *alma mater*, or nursing mother.

In this traditional understanding of freedom and liberality, the self is not cast off into autonomous life but is ever more deeply fed by wisdom, as he or she seeks to unite present occupation and challenges with the discipline espoused while a student. Theology as a university discipline is ideal here because it is really a community of disciplines: history, textual exegesis, philosophy, literature, languages, ethics and so on. It thus reaches into work and family in a myriad of ways. Its orientation and unity, however, comes from its rationale (from *ratio*), its seeking to accord knowledge to the Good, the True and the Beautiful. It is always pushing questions as far as they can go metaphysically, while also remaining rooted in the personal and the practical and therefore it is a discipline that impacts upon daily life and the life of work. I have noticed, over the years, that employers quite like students of theology and religious studies: perhaps they feel that they are more ethical and reliable as employees, or have a nuanced understanding of cultural and religious differences? They see that Theology can be practical.

So as tutor, I aim to convey something of this embodiment of the *alma mater*, nourishing and equipping the students, initiating them into the mysteries of a craft in which the whole person is to be called into play. If learning is more than the merely instrumental and is transformative it must change us. So the tutor can quite properly invite the student to reflect on personal questions about what kind of person he or she wishes to become. What kind of learning can help this becoming? What kind of work and experience will develop this self-understanding? On one level I am merely doing the practical task of careers guidance but at a deeper level, my questions are so crafted as to focus upon the development of a lover of wisdom and someone who has already eaten and drunk at wisdom's table.

It is in the university classroom, however, that one has the real work to do. Here, of course, Christian faith is not assumed, and ideas are presented and debated freely. If we believe that Christianity is true, then this should not worry us, and we should just calmly inform our students of our own perspective, so that they may take it into account in judging what we say. My own academic field is that of theology and literature; I am interested in how such texts explore and embody religious ideas not just in their content but in the manner in which they express these ideas. For me stylistics, mode, genre and narrative technique *themselves* do theological work and are modes of argument.

So we look in my classes at different literary genres such as drama or epic to see how each asks different questions, has a particular understanding of what it means to be human, or assumes a different audience. Drama evolves and engages religious ritual, tests limits between humanity and the gods, is transformed by the mimetic nature of Christianity, and so on. The modern novel, in fact, as a form of protestant poetics, tests out the freedom and autonomy of the individual; the ode invokes the absent presence of the divine other. We study Auerbach and the Tel Aviv school's investigation of point of view in the biblical historical books as a device to bring the reader to see the mysterious depths of the human agent, and to mimic a divine judgement. Dante's triple rhyme employed in his *Commedia* is explored as a mode of engagement in ideas about the Trinity. We set up the class room as a playing space and enact bacchic chant; we act out the farcical humour of *The Second Shepherds' Play* to see what a sheep dressed up as a baby has to tell us about typological understandings of Christ. We compare the multiple narrations of *Dracula* to the Bible.

These are just a few examples of the sort of work I do with students, getting them to inhabit the texts we study and to perform them wherever possible. I have never forgotten the time a student dressed up as a pirate to narrate *The Rime of the Ancient Mariner* in a strong west-country accent! Literature makes its effects rhetorically and through the incitement of emotion and passion as well as reason, and so participatory modes of response are appropriate. So students taking my course on religion and fantasy are allowed to write stories, paint pictures and make films to show how the fantastic can engage religious ideas. One student currently has got hold of a door-frame, and is setting it up in different locales to enact the liminal threshold that is so common to much religious fantasy – by George MacDonald or C.S. Lewis, most famously. My aim in allowing creative participation is to help students understand how imagination works, and to understand artistic creation from the inside, as well as to actually embody argument through literary stylistics or musical form for themselves.

In projects like these, we are learning an historical narrative about the division of reason and imagination in the Enlightenment and post-Kantian reduction of religious belief to the secondary level of practical reason. We are studying the deliberate use of imaginative creation by Coleridge and the German Romantics for theological exploration. And later we study fantasy as a mode of apologetics and the rise of the importance of the imagination as a religious mode of truth. Such fantastic tales seek to turn a reader into an initiate: to offer a sense of what it is to experience the divine. These stories offer a world beyond the physical as real, as Lewis does in his solid outskirts of paradise in *The Great Divorce*, or G.K. Chesterton's astonishing *The Man Who Was Thursday*, where the nightmare of nihilism outrageously transforms into a happy ending. So the *subject* the students are studying is one which seeks to make its readers participate in religious experience; and my creative projects mimic that procedure, and thus offer, potentially, a transformative experience.

I spend some of my time teaching more obviously theological material. In our innovative 'Great Religious Texts' first-year seminars, we try to wean students off purely text-book approaches to learning by making them read a whole primary text each week and talk about it in small groups. Such an approach makes them 'live' the text and try to understand its internal logic. This may mean the caste ethics of the *Bhagavad Gita* or the mythic universe of Native Americans. But it also often includes the second theological oration of Gregory Nanzianzus. This makes the claim that a theologian should be pure to apprehend light, to be a particular kind of person. It thus provokes the question of what a student of theology should be like, and how he or she can learn. Gregory was a consummate rhetorician, who sought to persuade and move his readers. So as a teacher I encourage students to analyse how the rhetoric works, while offering a text that seeks to offer an experience of what it is to be caught up in the unspeakable mystery of the divine. Studying theology from the past when it was so much closer to prayer and praise makes the whole exercise much more of a challenge but also much more attractive and moving.

Looking at the way theological texts make their arguments enables us to be aware of their religious value. They can be studied in exactly the same way as a poem. So when I am reading Thomas Aquinas's *Summa Theologiae* with my students, I show them how the form of each individual question, divided into initial statement, objections and 'I answer' sections mimics the shape and drama of Pseudo-Dionysius's negative theology in his *Mystical Theology*. In so doing, I am trying to show that texts are performative: they make things happen. To read a question in the *Summa* is not just an intellectual act but one which is more akin to a wrestling-match or a journey in which our initial certainty is put at risk and the truth hidden from our eyes, so that we may see more clearly. Each question is like Jacob wrestling with the angel, and learning his own name.

The A level syllabus for Philosophy and Ethics often contains a small section on virtue ethics: the moral tradition employed above in relation to the role of the tutor. Believing as I do that our society can only recover some sense of a common good and some moral coherence through a return to virtue, I offer a module to train students in the virtue ethics tradition. We read classical texts by Plato, Aristotle and Aquinas and texts from the modern revival in its non-religious and religious modes, from Sarah Foot to Alasdair MacIntyre and Stanley Hauerwas. Students assess the strengths and weaknesses of this tradition, as well as its instantiation in Homer, Jane Austen and more modern fiction by Iris Murdoch and Graham Greene. They also give presentations on how it might work in different professions, moral questions or communities. One of the great discoveries for me has been their empirical research, in which, for example, one student questioned a range of nurses about the virtues needed to nurse well; another who already assisted in a primary school began to work out how he could live and model the virtues for his pupils; another looked at the ethics of music. They were beginning here truly to become *alumni* and *alumnae*, using their knowledge outside the lecture hall so as to internalise it and make it their own. Virtue ethics depends however, on an understanding of the Good. It involves substantive virtues: justice, temperance, fortitude and prudence/practical wisdom to name the pagan cardinal virtues. How often, however, the students invoked the Christian theological virtues of faith, hope and love. For Aquinas, charity or love is the key virtue by which our ordering through divine love inspires and orders the rest. The students were finding for themselves how central charity/*caritas* is to an ethical life.

Obviously one cannot preach but what I hope students catch is the sheer attractiveness and beauty of such ideas. All I can do is, in the word used by Liugi Giussani, 'propose' the order of charity but by showing it in action in literary texts so that proposing takes on embodied form. Students are forced to use their imagination to enter the experience of a fictional character, and in so doing, to mimic a religious mode of existence. This is foreign not only to atheist students but often to those from a strongly evangelical background, who tend to think only of a Christian 'message' inserted in a text and are uncomfortable in encountering Christianity as a form of life. They scan *Pride and Prejudice* in vain for biblical references and yet are scandalised by the theatrical repentance of Graham Greene's paradoxical sinners. When they do 'get it', however, they can produce some of the most profound and thoughtful responses.

Luigi Giussani, whom I quoted above, is a guide to me as a teacher. He was a Catholic priest and a High School teacher, working like me in a secular institution, though later he also taught at the Catholic University of Milan. He died in 2005. From his books and development of after-school meetings of students there grew a huge lay movement, Communion and Liberation, which is now world-wide. Like me Giussani was a teacher of literature, and used it extensively not so much to convert in any obviously evangelistic way, but so as to show his students reality. Employing music, art and literature, Giussani sought to show that it is only Christ – only the Divine – that speaks to the fullness of what it means to be human. Conversely, reality itself in all its fullness always speaks to us of God.[12] Part of Giussani's technique is to provoke doubt:

> The whole of human religiousness is played out in the recognition that the single, total meaning of life resides in the mystery of God. Therefore, our life's meaning exceeds us and is for us a puzzle: human religiousness is predicated on the fact that our security, our values, and everything 'worthwhile' lie in the mystery.[13]

The gadfly role of the teacher is to provoke this sense of puzzlement: to show that we are more than we appear. It is to lead the student, as Gregory Nanzianzus has his theologian led like Moses into the cloud, but this is not an other-worldly experience but a mystery that appears in the minutiae of our daily lives at every point and in our relationships. It is similarly a reality that can be mediated to us in cultural works of art of all kinds. In showing how they open up to mystery in their fitting themselves to our conception of reality – their *ratio* or proportionality to the Good – I too am mediating the transcendent in *maieusis* and become priestly once again.

In this short chapter, I have tried to lay out my philosophy of teaching and tutoring, as I seek to enable the full human flourishing of my students. It is also predicated at the emancipation of my buffered pupils from their embattled autonomy and subjection to bureaucratic discipline. I want to open them to the idea of mystery, transcendence and virtue, and offer an education of participation, freedom and transformation through the direction of desire. I have made reference to the feast of wisdom in Proverbs 9, which Christians read as a typological anticipation of the Eucharist. Unlike priests in religious institutions, I do not have an ecclesial and Eucharistic role as an academic. I may feed my students, and do my best to offer refreshments and hospitality, and I may feed them with the nourishment of wisdom, but this is worlds away from the Children's Church I run and the sacramental role in the Parish Church Cathedral where I am a priest vicar. All I can do at the university is remember the students silently at the altar, and just occasionally act liturgically at a wedding or funeral for a Christian student. Yet when I 'propose' the thought of a great theologian, or teach a beautiful poem, I do feel as if I am effecting some entrance

---

[12]   Luigi Giussani, *The Religious Sense*, trans. John Zucchi (Montreal: McGill-Queens University Press, 1997), 46–8.

[13]   Luigi Giussani, *The Risk of Education: Discovering our Ultimate Destiny*, trans. Rosanna M. Giammanco Frongia (New York: Crossroad, 1996), 36.

to mystery, if not *the* mysteries; I do feel as if I were offering the world back to God for his transformation. Sometimes I can even feel the class thinking and remembering and something fragile but nascent emerging among the students. If the Eucharist is my source of meaning and hermeneutic, then my sacramental identity and function is not wholly occluded even here. Alice Meynell has a beautiful poem, 'Portugal 1912', which I find helpful:

> And will they cast the altars down,
> Scatter the chalice, crush the bread?
> In field, in village, and in town
> He hides an unregarded head;
>
> Waits in the corn-lands far and near,
> Bright in His sun, dark in His frost,
> Sweet in the vine, ripe in the ear –
> Lonely unconsecrated Host.
>
> In ambush at the merry board
> The Victim lurks unsacrificed;
> The mill conceals the harvest's Lord,
> The wine-press holds the unbidden Christ.[14]

The context is the persecution and proscription of the Church after the Revolution of 1910, when religious practice in Portugal was outlawed in a wave of anticlerical legislation. Yet the unacknowledged presence of Christ in natural and cultural objects – vine and wheat as well as mill and wine-press – is what actually gives meaning to the reality described. Similarly I and my fellow academic priests, unacknowledged as we may be, are there as the priests of an unfulfilled Eucharist. The arms that would bless clamped to our side; our body bent to listen as if in confessional intimacy; the hand pouring tea invoking the flow of baptismal water. And yet our presence as teachers is priestly because it is aimed at formation, and because education as wisdom is food indeed. Christ as illuminator is the mediation of all knowledge, whether people know it or not, just as he shapes our world as Logos. And we are his priests, preaching 'in season and out of season' the good news of salvation, and acting as midwives to bring truth to birth.

---

[14]   Alice Meynell, 'In Portugal 1912', *Oxford Book of Mystical Verse,* ed. D.H.S. Nicholson and A.H. Lee (Oxford: Oxford University Press, 1917), 264.

Chapter 10

Pursuing a Vocation in the Midst of Crisis: Moving from Scarcity to Mission

Daniel Joslyn-Siemiatkoski

Introduction

The state of theological education in the Anglican Communion is at a crossroads. Writing from my perspective within the Episcopal Church, seminaries have been in a state of crisis for much of the past decade. As the number of Episcopalians has declined from a high-water mark of 3.4 million in the mid-1960s to just around 2 million, the enrolment levels at Episcopal seminaries have also declined dramatically. The question then remains, what ought to be the purpose of encouraging a vocation pursued in the context of theological education? Who does theological education serve and how does it advance the mission of the Church?

The American Scene in the Past Decade

The Crisis in the Seminaries

The educational landscape within the Episcopal Church looks different from that in other Anglican contexts, especially when compared with the Church of England. Because of the disestablishment clause of the Constitution of the United States, historically there has never been any state support of seminaries or ministry training programmes. In the absence of such support, many American denominations took it upon themselves to underwrite the foundation and development of theological institutions. Some of these were linked to colleges and universities, such as the Congregationalist roots of Harvard and Yale's divinity schools. Other institutions found their origins in denominational efforts that included direct funding from church coffers, as happened within

Lutheran and Roman Catholic contexts. Alongside financial support, many denominational bodies set standards for instruction and even made efforts to coordinate the work of seminaries that fell under their purview.

The history of the Episcopal Church's seminaries is unique because these institutions have never enjoyed direct financial support.[1] Aside from canons regarding the general outline of areas of competence for those preparing for ordained ministry, the Episcopal Church has not clearly spoken about how theological education ought to relate to the larger life of the Church in a consistent or clear way. The one exception to any sort of focused oversight is the relationship of schools to official bodies of the Church. For example, General Theological Seminary, the oldest of the Episcopal seminaries, was founded by an act of General Convention (the governing body of the Episcopal Church) in 1817. Likewise, some schools such as Church Divinity School of the Pacific and the School of Theology at the University of the South (commonly called Sewanee after its location) are schools that have an official relationship with its province (in this context a geographic grouping of Episcopal dioceses). Although such relationships might create natural sources for students, no commitments of financial support or oversight are directly exercised. In general, most Episcopal seminaries rely on national networks of affiliations, some based on a sense of 'churchmanship' or social and theological commitments. In terms of liturgical sensibility, Nashotah House is known for representing the Catholic wing while Virginia Theological Seminary retains a reputation for maintaining the evangelical wing in the Episcopal Church. Even more pronounced, Episcopal Divinity School is known for attracting students aligned with the liberal wing of the Church while Trinity School for Ministry typically educates students aligned with conservative elements of the Church and even people studying for ordination in break-away Churches such as the Anglican Church of North America, the Anglican Mission in the Americas, and the Reformed Episcopal Church. Most Episcopal seminaries prefer to locate themselves closer to the centre of such continuums. What this means for the vitality of seminaries is that

---

[1]   The ten current Episcopal seminaries in alphabetical order are: Berkeley Divinity School at Yale (New Haven, Connecticut), Bexley Seabury Federation (Bexley, Ohio and Chicago, Illinois), Church Divinity School of the Pacific (Berkeley, California), Episcopal Divinity School (Cambridge, Massachusetts), General Theological Seminary (New York City), Nashotah House (Nashotah, Wisconsin), Seminary of the Southwest (Austin, Texas), School of Theology at the University of the South (Sewanee, Tennessee), Trinity School for Ministry (Ambridge, Pennsylvania), and Virginia Theological Seminary (Alexandria, Virginia). Prior to 2012, Bexley Hall and Seabury Western Theological Seminary were independent entities.

in the absence of a denominational commitment to underwriting and directing theological education in a broad sense, a healthy future for any seminary depends on cultivating as many networks and resources as possible within the Episcopal Church.

Any seminary will reflect in general the health or problems particular to its denomination. Over the past several decades, the Episcopal Church has weathered massive changes and turmoil. While once representing a landed, patrician class, even dubbed 'the Republican Party at prayer', in many sectors the Church now takes a more leftward tilt, with some significant regional exceptions. In the past four decades, the Episcopal Church has lost about a million and a half members. Some of this decline mirrors the general decline of so-called 'mainline' denominations in the United States. Episcopalians can take solace with Lutherans, Methodists, Congregationalists, and Presbyterians who have also seen a decline in their number while evangelical Christianity solidified its place on the national scene. Some of the causes of decline are the result of not replacing prior generations of members. Whether by ineffective catechising or a failure to engage in activities that would bring in new members, attendance could not be maintained. Some of that is the result of members of the Baby Boomer generation (those born between 1946 and 1964) opting out of many forms of organised religion and not rearing their children with strong connections to churches. Alongside these factors, three specific factors also lent themselves to a decline in membership of the Episcopal Church. These were the decision to ordain women to all orders of ministry in 1976, the revision of the *Book of Common Prayer* in 1979, and the rethinking of human sexuality, represented most clearly in the ordination of Gene Robinson as bishop of the Diocese of New Hampshire in 2003. While I am personally supportive of all three of these developments, they led to members and congregations disaffiliating from the Episcopal Church. Many of these went to other bodies, such as the Anglican Church of North America and the Anglican Mission in the Americas, which were established with the cooperation of bishops from other provinces of the Anglican Communion.

The transformations and tensions in the Episcopal Church are reflected in its seminaries. From a purely quantitative perspective, there is a shrinking pool of potential students to enrol in any given seminary's Master of Divinity programme, the traditional degree programme for those pursuing ordination. Between 2006 and 2011, the number of ordinations fell by 26 per cent.[2] In the

---

[2]   *The State of the Clergy 2012: A Report for The Episcopal Church* (Church Pension Group, 2012), 2.

past 60 years the number of ordained priests who had received the MDiv from an Episcopal seminary declined 19 per cent, from 83 per cent in the 1950s to 64 per cent in 2010.[3] The reason for this decline is complex. Surely part of it is that there is a declining number of available full time ministry positions in traditional parish settings (with some local exceptions in parts of the West and South). But alongside this, there have been changing standards for clerical ordination. Currently, diocesan bishops have great latitude in determining what sort of training is necessary for any individual candidate for ordained ministry. In recognition of the wide range of people called to ordained ministry, including people who cannot move large distances to attend seminary or take on the considerable burden of a three year degree programme, many dioceses have chosen to develop local ministry programmes that pool the resources and expertise of local clergy and scholars in order to prepare people for ministry.[4] The twin dynamics of age and cost are considerable.[5] While in the 1950s the average age of a seminarian was 27, by 2010 it was 44. At the same time, those who are aged 35 and under are the most likely to travel any significant distance to attend seminary. Furthermore, in the past decade the average cost of a three year MDiv has risen 16 per cent.[6] The net result is that a large group of potential students has chosen to train locally. Alongside local ministry training programmes, potential students also have the option of enrolling in non-Episcopal seminaries and divinity schools. Some of these schools have begun Anglican study courses to recruit potential students. Between 2001 and 2011, the number of priests graduating from non-Episcopal seminaries increased by 25 per cent.[7]

The net effect of these developments, especially as they have manifested and accelerated since 2000, has had significant consequences for Episcopal seminaries. In 2008 alone, three developments symbolise the changing fortunes of the seminaries. First, Seabury-Western Theological Seminary chose to shut down its Master of Divinity programme because of declining enrolment, choosing instead to focus on its Doctor of Ministry programme. Second, Episcopal

---

[3]   *Whither Thou Goest: Assessing the Current State of Seminaries and Seminarians in the Episcopal Church* (Church Pension Group, 2012), 4.

[4]   Multiple examples of these exist. One of the newest is the Bishop Kemper School for Ministry convened among four dioceses in the American Plains.

[5]   This dynamic is applicable to other Christian bodies in North America and is also mirrored in other places such as Great Britain.

[6]   *Whither Thou Goest*, 6, 15, 32.

[7]   The five non-Episcopal schools with the highest share of Episcopal ordination track students are Candler School of Theology (Emory University), Princeton Theological Seminary, Union Theological Seminary, Duke Divinity School, and Harvard Divinity School. *Whither Thou Goest*, 12–13.

Divinity School sold its campus to Lesley University for $33.5 million. In turn, Lesley leased back some of the buildings on the campus so EDS could continue its programmes. Third, Bexley Hall closed its satellite campus in Rochester, New York consolidating its small campus and faculty in its Columbus, Ohio neighbourhood and deepened its cooperation with the neighbouring Trinity Lutheran Seminary.[8] In 2010, General Theological Seminary announced it was perilously close to exhausting its operating budget. In order to strengthen its financial position, the school chose to sell significant portions of its property to a development agency. Many other schools have seen declines in endowments due to the economic recession that began in 2008. Several schools have seen declines in staffing and teaching faculty. The seminaries were beset by further crises in 2014. At Episcopal Divinity School, the faculty took a vote of no confidence in their dean among debates about the future direction of the school. At General Theological, eight of the eleven faculty went on strike after citing contentious and hostile relations with their dean. In turn the board of trustees declared the faculty had resigned. This led to an outcry, especially among alumni who expressed themselves via social media. Although faculty were restored to their positions, many questions about the relationship between faculty and administration remain unresolved at the time of writing.[9]

The rapidly changing, and at times contentious, landscape for theological education has also emboldened schools to work diligently at ensuring their long-term viability. Virginia Theological Seminary, the School of Theology at the University of the South, and Seminary of the Southwest have all engaged in successful capital campaigns to ensure stronger endowments and greater resources for student scholarships and financial aid. Other schools, such as Church Divinity School of the Pacific, Episcopal Divinity School, Nashotah House, and the Bexley Seabury Federation have responded to the inability of all students to relocate or enrol in a residential Master of Divinity programme by developing online or low residency educational programmes. A number of schools have also chosen to partner with local ministry programmes developed by dioceses either by supplying instructors or agreeing to take students for a final year of residential ministry training. Alongside these strategic and programmatic

8   Elizabeth Redden, 'Seminaries Under Stress', *Insider Higher Ed*, March 11, 2008, accessed 22 October, 2012, http://www.insidehighered.com/news/2008/03/11/episcopal.

9   G. Jeffrey MacDonald, 'Conflict Halts EDS Review', *The Living Church*, June 26, 2014, accessed 13 January 2015, http://www.livingchurch.org/conflicts-halt-eds-review; Sharon Otterman, 'General Theological Seminary Bringing Back Professors It Dismissed', *The New York Times*, November 7, 2014, accessed 13 January 2015, http://nyti.ms/1uIKgTA.

developments, Episcopal seminaries have sought to more clearly articulate the benefits of studying for ministry in the context of a specifically Anglican context.

The Crisis in the Academy

As in the United Kingdom and Europe, higher education in the United States is under enormous stress. Many institutions, especially those that used to receive state support, have found themselves under a burden to establish their relevance. In the area of the sciences, there exists increasing pressure to acquire outside funding, especially from federal government or corporate sources, to support ongoing research. Typically, a percentage of any grant or research funds acquired by any given professor or department will go directly to the operating budget of the institution. This arrangement has led to concern that university and college administrators have begun to look to research itself as a form of income generation. Alongside this concern is the worry that researchers might become beholden to the priorities of those who fund them.

In the shadow of increased funding of the sciences, administrators have turned their eyes to the poorer cousins in humanities departments. Majors and departments have been eliminated in the name of irrelevance or lack of interest. This trend has especially hit hard foreign language, classics and fine arts departments. The unsettling feeling among those in the humanities is that the life of the mind itself is undergoing an increasing commodification. If the work of a particular discipline cannot demonstrate a satisfactory measure of a return upon investment, it faces the budget axe.[10]

A feature of the crisis in the humanities in the United States is the emerging critique of doctoral programmes. Three specific issues are pre-eminent among critics. The first is the charge that doctoral programmes largely exist as self-perpetuating organisms. The administrators and professors within doctoral programmes, it is alleged, largely recruit new students not so much to meet an existing need for an annual stock of newly minted doctoral degree holders in literature, religious studies, or history but to justify the very existence of these programmes. Critics point to the balkanisation of disciplines into smaller and smaller subfields, or at other times the bewildering interdisciplinarity of other fields, as signs that there is not a need for new doctorates every year but instead departments have made deliberate choices to perpetuate the growth of degree

---

[10]   Peter Cohan, 'To Boost Post-College Prospects, Cut Humanities Departments', *Forbes*, 29 May, 2012, accessed 22 October, 2012, http://www.forbes.com/sites/petercohan/2012/05/29/to-boost-post-college-prospects-cut-humanities-departments; Stanley Fish, 'The Crisis of the Humanities Finally Arrives', *New York Times*, 11 October, 2010.

holders for its own sake. The second issue follows closely upon the first. Just as a steady number of freshly minted PhD degree holders come out each year, the past decade has witnessed a decline in the number of tenured positions in the humanities and a steady increase in the number of adjunct teaching positions. Currently, only about one-third of all higher education teaching positions are defined as tenure track. In other words, many qualified applicants for a shrinking pool of permanent positions cannot find steady work in the fields in which they have trained. Third, and again connected with the prior two issues, a growing percentage of new doctoral degree holders find themselves in increasingly untenable financial situations, with some even having to seek government assistance. Here the critique comes full circle. How can doctoral programmes continue to actively recruit new students year in and year out, knowing that there is a good chance a significant portion of its graduates may never secure a full time teaching position or that they might even become financially ruined by the costs of higher education? Ultimately, one arrives at a set of ethical dilemmas that must be addressed if the current educational system is to persist.[11]

Pursuing an Academic Vocation in the Midst of Crisis

When one considers the pursuit of an academic vocation within the context of the current life of the Church, I begin from my American context of the crisis in higher education in general terms and the specific crisis that the seminaries of the Episcopal Church are weathering. These two crises are largely discrete events that emerge from differing factors and thus have different solutions. But each crisis nonetheless has an effect upon those working in theological education in the United States. And the combination of these two crises most acutely influences those that might be considering whether to pursue an academic vocation at all. They are the ones who have to navigate both the complex difficulties of attaining a doctoral degree within the humanities and the uncertainties about its future. And they are the ones who must discern how to employ their learning and skills within a church that is deeply uncertain about how it ought to go about the work of education.

---

[11]   Thomas H. Benton, 'Graduate School in the Humanities: Just Don't Go' *Chronicle of Higher Education*, January 30, 2009, http://chronicle.com/article/Graduate-School-in-the-Huma/44846/; Mary Ann Mason, 'The Future of the Ph.D.', *Chronicle of Higher Education*, May 3, 2012, http://chronicle.com/article/The-Future-of-the-PhD/131749/; Stacey Patton, 'From Graduate School to Welfare', *The Chronicle of Higher Education*, May 6, 2012, http://chronicle.com/article/From-Graduate-School-to/131795/. All last accessed 22 October, 2012.

I also speak to the dilemma of discerning an academic vocation from my perspective as a seminary professor who has trained in a university graduate programme unaffiliated with a ministry training programme. I also speak as one who has helped former students, both lay and ordained, who have chosen to go on for doctoral studies in order to serve the Church through their advanced education. But I also have the perspective of one who has seen colleagues spend years on the job market before finding a job, or colleagues who lost their jobs teaching at seminaries they loved because of fiscal crises, or colleagues who could not find a job teaching but were happy to serve the Church in other capacities that drew upon their skills until those jobs too disappeared for financial reasons. And finally, I write with a particular perspective on the purpose of theological education. I hold that we need both lay and ordained people to pursue an academic vocation within the Church. But in order to serve the wider mission of the Church, educational efforts ought not to stop with the training of those pursuing ordained ministry. Instead, theological education should speak to the widest circles of the Church, lay and ordained alike.

The question that precedes considering how to encourage and prepare people pursuing an academic vocation is how to understand the purpose and role of theological education. This necessarily requires asking how theological education serves a church (and its seminaries) that is in the midst of a crisis. In order to do that, the nature of theological education must be placed within the overarching mission of the Church. If the focus of theological education is not at this time missional it will be unable to adequately serve the Church for which it exists.

From a strategic perspective, the coincidence of an increasing number of qualified people to teach in seminaries with a decline in the stability and viability of seminaries within the Episcopal Church raises the larger question of how the Church as a whole and the seminaries collectively understand the purpose of theological education. Given that the 2012 General Convention of the Episcopal Church featured a renewed commitment to mission and evangelism in the passage of various resolutions and the structure of its triennial budget, I propose that a movement towards understanding theological education as education for mission would help address the crisis featured in this chapter. I do not propose that one abandon a focus on training for ministry as an important aspect of theological education, but suggest that it is not the starting point. Working from this missional foundation for theological education, those discerning an academic vocation would have a clearer sense of how and in what manner they might be able to serve the Church.

A useful point of departure for reflecting on the missional foundations of theological education is to consider the purpose of it. Former Archbishop Rowan Williams has offered this useful definition of a theologically educated person as

> somebody who has acquired the skill of ... reading and interpreting the world in the context and framework of Christian belief and Christian worship ... Theological education is bound ... to be regularly a matter of looking at the pattern of human lives ... And that is why theology is inevitably a component in the business of Christian discernment.[12]

This definition serves as a useful grounding for considering the academic vocation in the context of crisis because it places the task of theological education as primarily providing the training necessary to engage with the world. The competent person trained theologically would be able to engage with the world around her. Locating the theologically educated person as someone fully grounded in the belief and worship of the Church reinforces the purpose of this education as something organic to the very life of the Church. But as an interpreter and reader of the world, the theologically educated person is also trained to be always in a kind of persistently hermeneutical posture. There is a two-fold movement here then. The theologically educated person is able to discern constantly what is holy, true, and good within their own lives and the broader life of the Church. At the same time, they are able to bring these habits of discernment to an engagement with the world beyond the Church.

Anyone pursuing an academic vocation within the life of the Church should be willing to train people in the way Rowan Williams describes: grounded in the deep riches of the Church and postured to engage in the life of the wider world. But this is a difficult prospect given the would-be theological educator's reality poised between the crisis of the Church and the crisis of the humanities. Those discerning an academic vocation likely will receive doctoral training in a university humanities context that focuses on the development of expertise in a particular discipline in such a way that integrating this learning into the wider life of the Church might be difficult. Given this, those training for an academic vocation would need significant vocational counselling and guidance from others in the Church to help them navigate the competing demands on the nurturing of their vocation.

---

[12]   Rowan Williams, 'Theological Education and the Anglican Way', *The ANITEPAM Journal* 55 (2006): 3, 5.

But why does Williams insist on engagement with the world as essential to theological education? Certainly it is possible to educate people who ably serve their communities without an accompanying sense of call to engage the world. This emerges later in this same essay where Williams focuses on obedience. By obedience he has in mind Karl Barth's sense of 'absolute faithful attention to the otherness of what you are dealing with that springs you from the trap of your own preoccupation and preferences'.[13] The primary source of otherness in this sense is God. God, the source of all that is and who is revealed in Scripture and history, constantly encounters the faithful Christian with complete otherness. But, Williams argues, those who attend to the otherness of God are engaged in a form of obedience that compels one to be attentive to the rest of humanity. Through attentiveness to the otherness of both God and other people beyond one's own subjectivity, one is compelled to engage with them as they really are. Out of this obedience and attentiveness is born a mission to proclaim to others the message of God revealed in Scripture and history.

Williams's vision of theological education is inherently a missional vision, the theological educator as witness to God's work and servant to others. The purpose of educating people theologically is so that they can strengthen the Church but also engage the world beyond the Church. But this missional vision does not suggest a blunt approach. It fits with an emerging understanding of mission and theological education in the Anglican Communion that is both traditionally grounded and contextually focused. Recent documents produced by both Theological Education for the Anglican Communion (TEAC), a working group of the Anglican Primates, and the Inter-Anglican Standing Commission on Mission and Evangelism (IASCOME) help us to better situate the future of theological education as primarily a missional endeavour.

The TEAC working group emerged out of a commitment made by the Primates of the Anglican Communion when they met in Brazil in 2003. The Primates affirmed that 'all Anglican Christians should be theologically alert and sensitive to the call of God. We should all be thoughtful and prayerful in reading and hearing the Holy Scriptures, both in the light of the past and with an awareness of present and future needs'.[14] This statement mirrors the definition of theological education provided by Rowan Williams. Again we find a strong sense of education rooted in the Scriptures and traditions of the Church but also necessarily responsive to a wider cultural landscape. In this document

---

[13]   Ibid., 14.

[14]   Theological Education for the Anglican Communion (TEAC), 'Working Briefs and Process of Target Groups', November 2003, accessed October 22, 2012, http://www.anglicancommunion.org/media/109432/briefs080206.pdf.

the Primates underline the importance of both attending to local context in the task of theological education while also emphasising the importance of education as an aspect of expressing communion. As a concrete expression of this reality, the Primates commissioned TEAC to develop common standards for theological education across the Anglican Communion. In the process of defining the constituencies of the Communion who are in need of theological education (from bishops to laity), a key question emerged: 'How can theological education enable the Church to live the relationship between the ministry of the ordained and the ministry of the baptized?'[15] TEAC responds to this question by envisioning ministry in all orders as a holistic enterprise. Working groups have developed grids of educational competency for all the orders of ministry – episcopal, priestly, diaconal, licensed lay ministers, and laity in general. Along with these grids, TEAC proposed specific ways in which people ought to be educated in what they term 'the Anglican Way'. The concern for a firm grounding in Anglicanism especially matters in contexts where Anglicanism is rapidly expanding and where strong networks of educational institutions are less robust, specifically in the so-called Global South.[16]

In constructing these grids covering educational competency and the Anglican Way, TEAC grounds the work of the Church within the realm of mission. The underlying principle is that a primary purpose of theological education is to prepare all people in the Church for mission. The work of mission looks different for a bishop than for a deacon, for a lay catechist or a newly baptised Christian. Nonetheless, part of TEAC's goal is to draw all Anglicans deeper into the life of the Church via education. And at the core of the life of the Church is the mutual work of all the faithful, with the power of the Spirit, to fulfil God's mission in the world. The work of IASCOME further locates theological education as a vital aspect of an Anglican approach to mission. In *Communion in Mission*, the members of IASCOME encourage a focus on mission to attain a more coherent life of the Anglican Communion. Theological education advances the Communion's work because participating in mission is foundational for the task of theology.

> A shared commitment to God's mission is the responsibility of every member
> of the Body of Christ. The implications for theological education and leadership
> development connect discipleship of Christ to the transforming dimensions of

---

15   TEAC, 'Working Briefs'.

16   TEAC, 'Ministry Grids', accessed October 22, 2012, http://www.anglicancommunion. org/mission/theology/educationstudies/ministry-grids.aspx.

> a missional grounding. Discipleship equipping which is isolated from a mission footing is likely to be a deficient discipleship, with loss to the Church.[17]

The clear linking of theological education with mission expressed by both TEAC and IASCOME provides us with a clearer lens for understanding the academic vocation today. And returning to my specific context, it also dovetails with the call for a return to a focus on mission and evangelism expressed at the 2012 General Convention of the Episcopal Church.

Re-imagining the Academic Vocation as a Missional Vocation

The working documents from TEAC and IASCOME mirror a trend in the Anglican Communion to foster networks for ministry. Re-envisioning theological education, and hence the academic vocation, as an expression of the mission of the Church provides a productive answer to the question of how to live out the academic vocation in the midst of crisis. Most people who contemplate the scholarly life in service to the Church, I would hazard a guess, already understand their future role to be, at least in part, in service to the Church. But most of them most likely envision themselves teaching in seminaries or theological colleges or as college chaplains. This might be because of their own presuppositions or because of the advice that they are given. But if we follow trends within the Anglican Communion to conceive of theological education and the mission of the Church in a fundamentally symbiotic relationship, the horizon of what the academic vocation entails must expand.

Expanding the horizons of the academic vocation is not simply a cynical move to justify the existence of seminaries. Rather, it is a way of asking how seminaries and theological colleges can operate as a vital core for the task of theological education. If we turn back to the parameters of ministry competency and Anglican Way grids produced by TEAC, it is absolutely clear that educators holding doctorates in relevant fields are vital for providing the educational foundations that will contribute to the expanding missions and ministry expressed within (and beyond) the Anglican Communion. One obvious place to locate these trained educators is in seminaries and theological colleges. But

---

[17]   IASCOME, *Communion in Mission & Travelling Together in God's Mission*. Report of IASCOME 2001–2005, 2006, §5. Web version, 2010. Accessed 22 October 2012, http://www.anglicancommunion.org/media/108022/IASCOME-Communion-In-Mission-Main-Documents.pdf?tag=IASCOME.

theological educators are also needed to move beyond, or back and forth, from traditional academic venues to different fields.

I especially want to point to the educational needs for two groups: priests and deacons and licensed lay ministers. While it is desirable that all ordained clergy attend seminary, it is possible within the canons of the Episcopal Church for priests and deacons to be trained 'locally' and not enrol in an accredited academic programme. Likewise, other contexts in the Anglican Communion may either have similar canons or operate in areas where there are not optimal education programmes for training. Even for priests and deacons who receive a standard education for ministry, the TEAC grids still reveal the need for continuing education. This continuing education is especially vital in contexts in which it might be necessary to receive training to continue to engage effectively in mission. The need for ongoing education of lay ministers is also evident. For example, TEAC suggests that after three years from licensing, lay ministers have 'some form of theological study' and that they be able to use Scripture in a variety of ministry contexts and display 'understanding of exegetical and hermeneutical principles'. Regarding the category of mission and evangelism, it is recommended that at the point of licensing, lay ministers 'have begun to develop the educational tools to nurture faith in others'.[18] If any province in the Communion is to grow, including in the Episcopal Church, it will be because laity have been empowered to grow in ministry and to participate in the mission of the Church. Yet, it does not seem reasonable to assume that any given parish priest in the congregation of a lay minister can effectively provide all the needed educational resources. Developing educational networks for the education of laity and the continuing educational needs of clergy seems like an ideal trajectory for an academic vocation dedicated to mission.

The academic vocation itself is changing due to technology. The latest move, beyond online courses for degrees, is the development of massive open online courses (MOOCs). Often designed and taught by faculty at prestigious universities, these courses are open to anyone and include thousands of users. The purpose of these courses is not to grant credit but is for as many people as possible to learn. While only now venturing outside the initial fields of the sciences into the humanities, MOOCs have rapidly gained attention (as well as criticism).[19]

---

[18] TEAC, 'Catechists and Lay Ministers Grid', 3, 4.

[19] Jeremy Knox, Sian Bayne, Hamish MacLeod, Jen Ross and Christine Sinclair, 'MOOC pedagogy: the challenges of developing for Coursera', *Association for Learning Technology Online Newsletter*, 8 August 2012, accessed October 22, 2012, http://newsletter. alt.ac.uk/2012/08/mooc-pedagogy-the-challenges-of-developing-for-coursera/. Tamar Lewin, 'Massive Open Online Courses Prove Popular, If Not Lucrative Yet', *New York*

The benefit of launching MOOCs for the purpose of theological education in the Anglican Communion is that it engages people who might not otherwise have access to resources in their own context. It connects those with specific knowledge and skills to those who desire to acquire content and practices. It is also a specific instantiation of the emerging global network into which the Anglican Communion is organically developing. Utilising technology is a solution that can connect educators across the Anglican Communion to students elsewhere. In the Episcopal Church there is an increasing interest in having seminaries embrace online education. Likewise, mobile phone technology is providing important social and economic innovations in developing countries, especially sub-Saharan Africa.[20] In other words, if there is a pool of highly talented but underemployed educators in the Global North, they might be able to live out their academic vocation in part by helping to develop the mission of the Church not only in their immediate context but also globally.

Developing the academic vocation so that its practitioners reach a broader set of people than in the past requires a new institutional attitude as well. First, traditional sites out of which theological educators have emerged need to affirm that this is a desirable goal and that students will be supported in expanding the arena of education. Those already engaged in the vocation need to be willing to shift into new modes of education. The mode and means of education would also have to change to fit new audiences and learning contexts and goals. There would also need to be a willingness on the part of churches to finance such initiatives. Education is expensive. It requires intensive investments that rarely translate into monetary gain. But an investment in education for mission would be a clear expression of the hopes and values of any Church. Moreover, this approach would require more intentionality about who ought to go into academic vocations. This is not a vocation for the life of the mind but for the life of the Church. As such, those who are willing to use their intellectual gifts in service to the Church in as broad a way as possible should be encouraged. Those who are not open to teaching and serving in as wide a range of contexts as is needed should be redirected to other vocational paths.

If the focus of theological education is recognised as a concern of the entire Church, and not solely the preserve of training future priests, the meaning and significance of the academic vocation expands greatly. Theological education

---

Times, 6 January 2013, accessed 31 January 2013, http://www.nytimes.com/2013/01/07/education/massive-open-online-courses-prove-popular-if-not-lucrative-yet.html.

[20]   Monica Mark, 'West Africa's technological revolution driven by mobile phones', *The Guardian*, 24 September 2012, accessed October 22, 2012, http://www.guardian.co.uk/global-development/2012/sep/24/nigeria-mobile-phones-success-technology.

is a concern of the entire Church and for Anglicans a concern for the entire communion. From my perspective within the Episcopal Church, understanding the interconnectedness of theological education within my province with the wider needs of the Communion allows me to perceive better my vocation as fundamentally missional in nature. While the crisis in the seminaries of the Episcopal Church might be a passing issue or presage a fundamental change in the ecclesial landscape, it does not mean that the missional needs for theological education have disappeared or will do so in the future. If the crises of the Anglican Communion in the past decade have shown anything, it is that we are diminished when Anglicans are divided. A renewed focus on the missional nature of theological education may not only revive the academic vocation in various quarters, it might also aid in healing rifts in the Communion itself.

PART IV
Theology and Ministerial Vocation

Chapter 11

The Scholar Bishop: Recovering Episcopal Vows

Stephen Pickard

A Scripture-Formed Episcopate

At the consecration of a bishop, prior to the making of promises, there appears an exhortation (or 'examination'; 'declaration') outlining the responsibilities and challenges relating to the office of bishop.[1] An unmistakable common thread appearing in the many Ordinals of the Anglican Communion concerns the priority of witness to Christ's resurrection and the faithful 'proclamation', 'exposition', 'protection' and 'interpretation' of the Gospel.

Familiarity with the promises made by a bishop at consecration indicates how important the sacred Scriptures are for the office of a bishop. Promises made in relation to the Holy Scriptures are the first promises made by bishops. The Scriptures are the first 'port of call' for a bishop for the very good reason that they 'contain' and 'reveal' everything necessary for eternal salvation through faith in Jesus Christ. Thus in the *Book of Common Prayer* of the Episcopal Church, even prior to the Examination, the Bishop-elect solemnly declares 'the Holy Scriptures of the Old and New Testament to be the Word of God, and to contain all things necessary to salvation' (EC 513). Anglican Ordinals are clear and uncompromising: a bishop's life is marked by the reading, diligent study and teaching of Scripture, and the interpretation of the Gospel. Such engagement is to equip, enlighten, stir up and encourage the people of God. In the process, faith is deepened, and a bishop is made fit 'to bear witness to the truth of the gospel' (CoE 62). A corollary of this calling is the expectation that

---

[1]   For the purposes of this brief chapter I have used three Ordinals: The Episcopal Church, *The Book of Common Prayer* (New York: Seabury Press, 1979), 512–24 (hereafter EC); Church of England, *Common Worship: Ordination Services Study Edition* (London: Church House Publishing, 2007), 54–76 (hereafter CoE); Anglican Church of Australia, *A Prayer Book for Australia* (Alexandria, NSW: Broughton Books, 1995), 799–809 (hereafter APBA).

the bishop will defend and guard the faith; 'refuting error' (CoE 62). The bishop is thus called to 'correct and set aside teaching contrary to the mind of Christ' (AustPB 803). A Scripture-formed episcopal office calls people 'to maturity, to the measure of the full stature of Christ ... ', to 'the truth as it is in Jesus' (Eph 4:13b, 21).

Episcopal vows concerning the study, interpretation and teaching of Holy Scripture may seem simple enough though the fulfilment of the same requires an investment of time, energy and disciplined prayer (as the Ordinals repeatedly make clear). In the busy life of a modern bishop the care of the Church can be so consuming that the study and meditation upon Scripture is short-changed.[2] The Anglican emphasis on Morning and Evening Prayer with the use of the Lectionary is a time-honoured way by which Anglicans might continually 'hear, read, learn, mark and inwardly digest' the Holy Scriptures. This allusion to a well-known prayer used by Anglicans since the Reformation[3] gives credence to the old adage that 'we become what we eat'. A bishop's food for the episcopal pilgrimage is first of all the Scriptures. This also requires familiarity with the rich inheritance of Scripture interpretation as displayed for example in the ecumenical creeds of the early Church, the *Book of Common Prayer* and its various iterations throughout the Communion, and Anglican formularies such as the Articles of Religion, and Catechisms.

It is also the case that a bishop's engagement with Scripture does not occur in a vacuum. To quote an old saying: 'We read the Bible in one hand and the newspaper in the other' (perhaps 'the Bible on an "app" and social media for news', might give this a more contemporary feel). But of course the matter goes deeper than that. Our different cultures and contexts shape the way we hear and interpret the Holy Scriptures and interact with the rich tradition of Scripture commentary. The apostle Paul was forever connecting Scripture with new contexts in his missionary travels, and in this he was simply following in the footsteps of the Jewish Jesus whose teaching, healing, and prophetic ministry was steeped in the Hebrew Scriptures. New situations required new responses and fresh interpretations. A Scripture-formed bishop is a person called to wrestle like Jacob with the Angel (Gen 32:24–31) to discern the truth of God and bear

---

[2]   For a discussion of the tensions between diocesan responsibilities, management mission and the claims of the Episcopal vows see Stephen Pickard, 'The Travail of the Episcopate: Management and the Diocese in an Age of Mission' in *Wonderfully and Confessedly Strange: Australian Essays in Anglican Ecclesiology*, eds B. Kaye, S. Macneil and H. Thomson (Adelaide, ATF Press, 2006), 127–55.

[3]   Originally the Collect for the Second Sunday in Advent (often called Bible Sunday) though it has been shifted in many Anglican Churches a few weeks earlier.

witness to it. Scripture in this sense is more than a 'tool kit' of truth. It is more truly the living voice of God that has to be listened for and prayed with in the company of fellow pilgrims.

Promises to continue to study and deepen faith give gravitas to the teaching office of the episcopate and the bishop's calling as a pastor theologian of the Church. Liturgically this is signified by the giving of a Bible and the wearing of an episcopal ring with stone of amethyst – a symbol of one who seeks wisdom. And such wisdom emerges from within the storms and stresses of ministry at the crossroads of life (Prov 8:1).

If the above reflections on episcopal vows have any weight, then it is clearly the case that a bishop, as far as is possible, according to gifts and capacity, is called upon to exercise a robust and sustained intellectual engagement with the Gospel tradition. In an earlier time, especially in the English tradition, the 'scholar bishop' was not an unfamiliar badge of office. With the rise of Western managerial culture the ancient administrative bishop has been turned into a corporate CEO. This may have a certain inevitability about it, but one thing is sure, the heightened emphasis on organisational management/leadership has impacted on the nature of episcopal life. Look at the diary of any bishop! One consequence of this is that the 'scholar bishop' is now quite clearly an exception to the rule; a luxury which, in the minds of many, the Church can ill afford. The weighting in episcopal appointments in relation to scholarship/managerial leadership in the Church of England might be an interesting if not telling barometer of the decline of the theologian bishop and the ascendancy of the manager bishop.

Of course this belongs to a wider cultural development. Contemporary Western pragmatism and impatience with matters of the intellect has had little enthusiasm for, or apparent need of theologians in the Church. Some kinds of theological activity – overly academic, elitist and irrelevant – might only confirm such prejudice! If theology occupies a somewhat marginal place then perhaps this is as it should be. After all, in a management and market driven world, where resources are scarce and rationalising of structure and work force is uppermost, of what value is theology in the life of the Church? However, the consequences of such a shift in emphasis – not to mention a certain wilful blindness to the imperative of serious theological engagement – are serious indeed for the wellbeing of the Church and its witness. To understand this I turn briefly to consider how John Henry Newman saw the problem.

Repairing the Theological Vocation

In Newman's preface to the re-publication of his famous essays on the *Via Media* of the Anglican Church (1879) – first published as the *Prophetical Office of the Church* in 1837 – Newman identified theology as one of the three fundamental powers of the Church.[4] Theology (Newman's system of philosophy) offered a critical stance in relation to the other two powers, the sacramental and worship tradition (ritual) and ecclesiastical rule (political power). Liturgy and polity required this third power as an essential hermeneutic for the ongoing faithfulness of the Church to the Gospel. Without this third power the Church was easily directed into an unhealthy sacramentalism and/or an unfettered abuse of ecclesiastical power. Church history bore testimony to the conflict that often occurred between these three indispensable elements of the life of the Church. Newman considered that the theological vocation was essential to preserve and foster a critical and reforming spirit. His position had an Anglican feel about it, even though he had long since jumped ship!

But who may presume to pursue such a vocation? In the early twentieth century the reformed theologian Karl Barth remarked that 'every Christian – in however primitive and rudimentary way – can and must be a theologian'.[5] For Barth the theological vocation may well generate scholars but he was equally clear that the theological vocation, so critical to the life and mission of the Church, was the responsibility to some extent of all the baptised.

Rigorous thought bent towards the practice of discipleship in the world was the kind of theology Barth, Dietrich Bonhoeffer and many others pursued, stretching minds and hearts into as yet uncharted regions of God's surprising grace. This dynamic had a long pedigree: it included the apostle Paul exhorting the Christians at Rome to be 'transformed by the renewal of your mind' that they might know what was pleasing to God (Rom 12:3). It had resonances with the Scripture tradition: of the Deuteronomist discerning the providential movement of God's Spirit in the history of Israel; of the Psalmist seeking after wisdom to understand God's ways in the world; of Job and his 'comforters' wrestling with the mystery of evil and the goodness of God; of the parables of Jesus and the life of the new community.

---

[4]   John Henry Newman, *The Via Media of the Anglican Church*, 2 vols, vol. 1, *Lectures on the Prophetical Office of the Church Viewed Relatively to Romanism and Popular Protestantism*, third edition, (London: Basil Montagu Pickering, 1877), 40ff.

[5]   Karl Barth, *Church Dogmatics: The Doctrine of Reconciliation*, vol. 4, part 1, trans. G. Bromley and T.F. Torrance (Edinburgh: T&T Clark, 1956), 765.

Anglicans stand in this long tradition of theology as the active pursuit of wisdom and its radical and transformative impact.[6] It is clearly not an optional extra, nor a luxury the Church can ill afford, nor the preserve of an elite – clergy, seminarians, the experts or 'professionals'. It is a task for the baptised enshrined in their baptismal vows and a corollary of their diverse ministries in the world. This is encapsulated in Cranmer's 1549 'Good Friday Collect':

> Almighty and everlasting God, by whose Spirit the whole body of the Church is
> governed and sanctified; Receive our supplications and prayers, which we offer
> before thee for all estates of men [sic] in thy holy Church, that *every member* of
> the same, in his [sic] *vocation and ministry*, may truly serve thee; through our
> Lord and Saviour Jesus Christ, who liveth and reigneth with thee, and in the unity
> of the same Spirit, ever one God, world without end. Amen.[7]

How, it may be asked, is it ever possible for the people of the Church to fulfil their vocation and ministry unless they are equipped to engage in critical reflection upon their vocations in order that they might more clearly embody faithfulness to Christ in the world? To live a life of faith is to be a pilgrim seeking deeper understanding of the ways of God in the world with the intent to follow such ways after the manner of Jesus Christ. On this account theology has a significant function and therefore it ought to occupy a fairly central place in the life of the Church.

If the Episcopal ministry is a truly representative ministry then minimally a bishop ought, together with the baptised – to the extent that he/she is able – aspire to theological expertise in order to be a good and faithful interpreter of the Gospel. This is not to claim that a bishop has to be the only or the best theologian of the Church. Rather it is to state unequivocally that a bishop is called to fulfil vows in respect of the theological vocation and be accountable to the Church under God for such vows. The theologian bishop is hardly an optional extra but rather ought to be part of the 'standard operating procedure'

---

6   For an important discussion of the ancient tradition of theology as sapiential knowledge see Edward Farley, *Theologia. The Fragmentation and Unity of Theological Education* (Philadelphia: Fortress, 1983).

7   *Book of Common Prayer* (Cambridge: Cambridge University Press, 1662, 2003) my italics. This Collect from the 1549 *Book of Common Prayer* represents Cranmer's re-working of the earlier Roman rite. It presumes that all members of the Church have a vocation and ministry. The reference to 'vocation and ministry' was added in the 1549 Prayer Book and reflects Lutheran influence. This Collect points to a profound mutuality in ministry wherein each ministry bestows life and energy on other ministries.

for the episcopal vocation. To ignore this dimension of a bishop's calling is to abdicate something vital for the wellbeing of the office of a bishop. Within an Anglican episcopal polity this weakens the whole. Recovering the theological vocation for the episcopate is not simply a challenge and responsibility for individual bishops. Certainly it is that, but that is only the tip of the iceberg. A far greater problem has to do with the context in which the episcopal vocation is undertaken and its impact on the capacity of any bishop to be a theologian and scholar for the Church.

Church for the Scholar Bishop?

What happens when the Church does not value the theological and scholarly expertise of a bishop? What happens when the management/therapeutic paradigm so dominates the Church that it influences the selection and appointment of bishops in the Church of God? This is masked somewhat by a heavy mission rhetoric driven by a sense of urgency that the Church of Jesus Christ, in particular in the West, has lost touch and is increasingly irrelevant to society. However, mission talk more often defaults into management. A prevailing culture of anxiety, competition and resource depletion generates new management and rationalising strategies couched in the legitimating language of mission. It would be interesting to survey episcopal appointments over the recent period in the Church of England to see how well the criteria of theological expertise has fared within an anxious Church keen to arrest decline and manage resources more efficiently.

The issue of the bishop as theologian has to be examined within the context of a church impatient for renewal but often lacking the spiritual intelligence and maturity required for the task. Its leadership is often focused on the waves breaking on the sea shore which represent the myriad difficulties regarding personnel, resources and engagement with the world. What is lost sight of or neglected is the direction of the tide. To change the image, what we have at present is an inside/out church; a church which approaches its engagements with the world from the perspective of its inner life and difficulties. This usually generates an attractional model of the Church despite gallant attempts to transcend this. An inside/out church has little energy to attend to the world beyond. And the energy it expends even intellectually is focused on immediate practical questions requiring answers or difficult problems requiring urgent solutions. One consequence is that the Church seeks a leadership focused on managing (or more accurately coping with) transitional times and this skews intellectual engagements. In this context the Church and its councils struggle to discern any real tangible reason for investing in or encouraging a scholarly episcopate to pursue a careful and sustained engagement with Scripture, tradition and the contemporary world. The scholar/teacher bishop will invariably run a distant second to a practically minded, management-savvy, and pastorally credentialed prospective bishop.

Of course the Church of Jesus Christ is a world-wide phenomenon. For their part, Anglicans number over 80 million and can be found in over 160 countries. The regions of significant growth and vitality are to be found in Africa, Latin America and South East Asia. The contexts for episcopal life in such places are very different from what I have described above in the West. Engagements with Islam and other faiths, the reality of persecution, the strong sense of mission and the sheer vitality of Christian life within relatively poorer countries are features of these developing regions of the earth. The needs are great, resources are stretched, and in places such as, for example, Nigeria, the long tradition of the missionary bishop is alive and powerful. In such contexts it is tempting to view the need for a scholarly episcopate as a luxury. Access to books and other literature is often minimal and online *e*-learning is spasmodic. The bishop may hold the scriptures in one hand and the newspaper in the other, but commentaries and other theological resources may be entirely lacking.

However, even a cursory familiarity with the growing edge of the Christian Church – and the Anglican Church in such regions is a good case in point – makes it abundantly clear that one of the greatest and most urgent of needs is good quality theological education for both clergy and laity alike. Who will give a lead in such matters? Given the significance of a bishop in an episcopal polity it is urgent that bishops of the body of Christ provide intellectual as well as pastoral leadership for the Church. This is increasingly recognised by all concerned and raises sharply the issue of resourcing scholarly work in the study of the Scriptures and those disciplines that enable the Church's deeper theological engagement with public life and the mission of the Church. The missional imperative of the Church does not blunt the need for a scholarly episcopate. Rather an informed, intelligent and scholarly engagement with the Christian tradition and the context in which the faith is lived gives vitality and energy to the spread of the Gospel. The challenge felt by those places where the Church is expanding is more often one of lack of resources to fund properly theological education and the work of theology. This in turn highlights the need for increasing collaboration between and among churches across countries and cultures. This would enable resources to be shared more equitably and opportunities created for bishops to be strengthened as pastor-theologians in the Church.

Scholar Bishops for a Church in Transition

It is not enough to seek a scholarly informed episcopate. It is equally important to understand what kind of scholarly work might be required of bishops today. This of course will vary widely depending on local and national context and of course the particular strengths and capabilities of a bishop. However there is an even wider horizon which offers clues about the kind of theological work required of episcopal leadership today. Attention to context is a prerequisite for the renewal of the theological vocation of a bishop. How well does a bishop read the signs of the times? The fact is there are major upheavals in world politics, international developments, conflicts and national realignments, violence and suffering, and movements of people. The immensity of the challenges facing the people of the globe are hard to grasp let alone begin to address. And the Christian Church is part of this wider context. It is inescapable. It can generate a nostalgic longing for an earlier more settled and stable existence (usually an over-idealised earlier state). It can also drive new and innovative engagements with the world and impatience with the past. Bishops as leaders of churches can unthinkingly go with the flow either into the past, burying themselves and their people in the same old ways in a slightly jazzed-up manner, or rush headlong with the next bright idea into yet another ecclesiastical *cul de sac*. The contexts of the modern world vary immensely and the bishop is easy prey to the temptation to embrace relevance for the sake of newness or cling tenaciously to outmoded practices and forms that have long since become obsolete. A bishop needs discernment and wisdom and a collaborative spirit. This means a bishop requires an attentive spirit, and this includes attentiveness to the best scholarship, and to those people and institutions that offer leadership in interpreting the signs of the times and are as abreast as it is possible to be with the explosion of new knowledge that abounds in the world. A bishop needs to do the best she or he can in this regard in order to help the Church of God give careful consideration to questions like: How is the Church of Jesus Christ to grow disciples in the emerging world of the twenty-first century? And how will the Church play its part in fostering a fresh wisdom from on high in a difficult and often disturbed world? We are in transitional times and the Church requires leaders who have thought carefully and intelligently about such matters with the best resources available in order to assist the people of God to live as disciples on the journey.

Critical to this activity is the imagination and capability to draw together traditions of wisdom and knowledge from many fields of inquiry for the purpose of attending to some of the major issues confronting the world – for example, climate change, food, energy and water needs, inequality and poverty, people migration, world religions and peace, violence and corruption. Such concerns are not second-order matters in relation to the study and interpretation of Scripture but are rather bound up with it, a fact clearly evident from even the most cursory familiarity with the content of Holy Scripture. For in this sacred text are uncovered the ways of God with the world where such things abound. Episcopal leadership in theology therefore includes a disciplined imagination and intention to help the people of God reconnect their lives and churches with God's world. This might mean that a bishop could give a lead intellectually in engagement with what have become known as 'wicked problems'. A wicked problem

> is a complex issue that defies complete definition, for which there can be no final solution, since any solution generates further issues, and where solutions are not true or false or good or bad, but the best that can be done at the time. Such problems are not morally wicked, but diabolical in that they resist all the usual attempts to resolve them.[8]

Attending to such problems and challenges requires a transdisciplinary imagination which is not only open to other fields of knowledge and understanding but expects that through interaction fresh wisdom can be found for living together. Can a bishop set an example and give a lead in such intellectual matters that impinge so powerfully on our common life? Is it possible for a bishop today to make a contribution to the public intellectual life of a community and country? Episcopal vows do not close a bishop's intellectual life to the world but rather open up the world through the lens of Scripture and tradition.

Episcopal Leadership and the Logic of the Gospel

'It is of the nature of the Christian faith to generate intellectuals' writes the late Colin Gunton.[9] And the fact is that many of these have been bishops in the long history of the Christian tradition. Gunton's remark draws us into the

---

[8]   Valerie A. Brown, John A. Harris and Jacqueline Y. Russell (eds), *Tackling Wicked Problems Through the Transdisciplinary Imagination* (London and Washington DC: Earthscan, 2010).

[9]   'The Indispensibility of Theological Understanding: Theology in the University' in *Essentials of Christian Community, Essays for Daniel W. Hardy*, eds David F. Ford and Dennis L. Stamps (Edinburgh: T & T Clark, 1996), 277. Gunton is also quick to note that

inner logic of the gospel so well captured in one of the towering minds of the eleventh century, Anselm Archbishop of Canterbury. For Anselm, 'Faith seeking understanding' (following Augustine, the fourth-century bishop of Hippo, North Africa) belonged to the dynamic of Christian believing. The gospel that gave birth to faith, simultaneously gave birth to an ongoing quest to understand the riches of what had been apprehended in faith. This quest in turn expanded and deepened belief. This dynamic could be likened to a spiral of wisdom that was always being stretched further towards the reality of the Divine under the energetic movement of the Spirit. The bishop as teacher of the faith is called to follow the pulse of the Gospel and faithfully follow the logic of the truth of God as far as is possible. Of course this vocation can be refused, denied, avoided, suppressed or undertaken in a half-hearted manner. The 'sin that clings so closely' (Heb 12:1) occurs under myriad guises and there are of course so many claims upon a bishop that it is not surprising that there is often little energy remaining for the work of theological leadership in the Church. Yet this work belongs to the obedience to the gospel and episcopal vows. Certainly the people of God are quite discerning in such matters and can tell when a bishop has stopped reading (and thinking!). Like any other believer, a bishop wrestles with the fundamental temptation of 'distraction' which can be so easily disguised, at least for a time.[10]

Conclusion: Vows for a Teaching/Scholarly/Public Episcopate

I began with the matter of episcopal vows and specifically those vows that require a bishop to be engaged with Scripture and the world in which the gospel is to be lived and witnessed to. It is difficult to keep our promises at the best of times. We are only too well aware of the frailty of human life, the darkness of the human heart and the inevitable 'break at the heart of every promise' that haunts our life, church and society.[11] And episcopal vows are no different in this respect. Often a bishop's study of Scripture and commitment to interpreting the faith in and for the people of God in the world is displaced by other pressing concerns. In our times it is vital that such vows are recovered and the vocation to be a teacher

---

Christianity 'has also its fair share in producing anti-intellectualism, particularly perhaps in England'.

[10]   See the comment by Laurence Freeman OSB in Rowan Williams's *Silence and Honey Cakes: The Wisdom of the Desert* (Oxford: Lion Book, 2003), 12.

[11]   Paul Ricoeur refers to the 'break at the heart of every promise' as a feature of our life as humans in *Oneself as Another*, trans. Kathleen Blamey (Chicago: University of Chicago Press, 1992), 168.

of the faith is embraced. If the conditions are created so that this becomes a real possibility – and this is a question for the whole body of Christ – then the Church of God will be blessed with a more thoughtful, scholarly episcopate which is better able to make a contribution to the public intellectual life of society for the praise of God's holy name.

Chapter 12

Walking with God: Vocational Vignettes from the Gospel of Mark

Martyn Percy

A person set aside for a symbolic, pastoral and priestly role in any community or context is in an increasingly unusual – some would say unique – position today. The work is not paid, at least in the strict sense of remuneration: but there is (usually) a stipend. The role is not 'work', strictly speaking, in the way that the world might understand the concept. There are few proscribed hours, duties and tasks – and yet the role is highly demanding, and at times, intensive. The kind of leadership that one gives in a (largely) voluntary institution is not the same as that given in an organisation with clarity between employers, employees and those whom the organisation serves. Ministry is relatively easy to describe on a day-to-day basis in terms of tasks; and supporting paradigms – rooted in people and practices drawn from the richness of Christian tradition – are numerous. Yet curiously, ministry remains difficult to *define*, and the role increasingly hard to articulate.

What, then is ministry *like*? It is not like teaching, nursing or counselling; nor is it like being a doctor, social worker, solicitor or other profession. It is a role in a community – whether a parish, university, prison or other sector – that is essentially beyond the normal vocabulary for defining work. And what is ministry *about*? It is hard to say. As the poet Stewart Henderson, puts it,

> So, what does a priest do?
> ... visits hospices, administers comfort,
> conducts weddings, christenings -
> not necessarily in that order,
> takes funerals
> consecrates the elderly to the grave
> buries children, and babies,

feels completely helpless beside
the swaying family of a suicide.[1]

It is of course possible for any generation to re-imagine Christian ministry. But before this can be done well, arguably, ministry in the present must first be understood, with some sort of account of that present being rooted in an understanding of the past. Part of the issue before the Church today may lie in the slow and broad expansion of the term 'vocation' that has taken place since the Reformation. Martin Luther broadened the term to include all Christians, however they laboured and worked. John Calvin saw industry and commerce as evidence of God's blessing upon those who gave themselves to the tasks God had assigned them. By the seventeenth century, the English Puritans saw that faithfulness to God could be expressed through fidelity to a job or a trade. So the idea of a vocation changed, in just a few hundred years, from being a special calling to sacred orders or enclosed religious life, to being something that every Christian could practice in their sphere of work. All occupations were now equal callings that came from God – covering anything from the charity sector to teaching (at all levels), and from nursing to humanitarian relief.

This, of course, has meant that the identity of ministry has undergone degrees of specialisation in direct proportion to its marginalisation. This is something that Anthony Russell's work picks up on, suggesting that clergy in the nineteenth and twentieth centuries reinvented themselves as assiduous visitors and preachers, and 'technicians of the sanctuary'.[2] Yet many of the pivotal pastoral functions of the clergy continued to be reassigned to local churches, resulting in a deepening crisis of professional identity. If ministry today is now something 'for the whole people of God', pastoral work something that can be done by locally deployed teams, and many other aspects of ministry carried out by hired-in specialists provided by the diocese, district or region, then the role of the clergyperson shifts, almost imperceptibly from being specialist and essential to being general and managerial.

Professionalisation, in other words, is a double-edged sword for clergy roles and clerical identity. On the one hand it increases the public sense of specialisation – the uniqueness of priest-craft – at a time when the general fabric of civic life is being challenged. On the other hand, its subsequent compression

---

[1]   Stewart Henderson, 'Priestly Duties', in *Limited Edition* (Stratford-upon-Avon, Plover Books, 1997), 18–23.

[2]   Anthony Russell, *The Clerical Profession* (London, SPCK, 1980), 235ff.

lays it open to further marginalisation and rationalisation. In a similar vein, Urban Holmes III comments that

> ... in pursuit of professional status we (clergy) have divested ourselves of a different kind of symbolic role, without ever resolving the question as to what precisely our unique professional competence might be. Every time we think we have come up with an answer, someone has been there before us.[3]

Towler and Coxon also seem to have understood the ambiguity of the role of clergy in the late twentieth century. Their articulation of a crisis of identity and function is worth reflecting upon:

> the clergyman, more than anyone else on the contemporary scene, is a jack of all trades. He occupies a unique position, but the uniqueness of his position has nothing to do with unique skills, or even with unique competence. There is nothing which he does that could not be done equally well by a lawyer or bricklayer in the congregation whom the bishop had ordained to the Auxiliary Pastoral Ministry. He does not have a job at all in any sense which is readily understandable ... and today, more than ever before, a person must have a job in order to fit into society. The clergyman, however, is in a position which is marginal to society and at the same time highly visible. He is a public person who, alone in our society, wears a distinctive uniform at all times. When he discards the uniform, as many clergymen do today, he evades the problem posed by his marginality, but he does not solve it ... [4]

So, before ministry and vocations can be sketched, one has to acknowledge and understand some of the cultural forces and shifting tectonic plates of social change that have shaped ministerial identity in the past, and do so now in the present. This is important, because sometimes our attempts to reimagine the Church are misconceived. The French Dominican theologian, Yves Congar, was deeply troubled that the Church's ongoing tension with the secular world was leading it 'to adopt very much the same attitudes as temporal power, to conceive of itself as a society (or organisation), as a power, when in reality it was a communion of ministers and servants.'[5]

---

3   Urban Holmes, *The Future Shape of Ministry* (New York, Seabury, 1977), 245.
4   R. Towler and A. Coxon, *The Fate of the Anglican Clergy: A Sociological Study* (London: Macmillan, 1979), 54–5.
5   Yves Congar, *True and False Reform in the Church*, (Paris: Editions du Cerf, 1950), 11.

At present, and in our attempts to organise the Church and manage its diversity, we are often guilty of trying to 'give unto thy servants that peace which the world cannot give' to ourselves. But it is a gift of the Spirit, grafted through conversation, conflict and slow consensus that gradually build us into communion. The genius of Christianity lies in its contestability. If diversity could have been managed, the Apostles and Early Church Fathers would probably have led the way, and the New Testament could perhaps have been clearer on issues that can be almost stubbornly divisive in ecclesial life (gender, sexuality, polity, governance, and so on).

And yet women and men still continue to be 'called' into what we term 'ministry'. And we still speak, quite properly, of vocations. In what follows, therefore, I want to offer three sketches rooted in the *Gospel of Mark* that might provide some clues as to what a vocation for 'academic ministry' might be about. In offering these three sketches, I have deliberately focused on the 'past-present-future' aspect of calling, and the 'interior, surface-exterior' dimensions of a vocation. In other words, how they begin inside a person (often by the calling from far beyond), and how they then take to the flesh, before finally becoming public and therefore socially embodied. When we speak, therefore, of 'public ministry', we speak of a process of gestation that first of all began with a seed planted deep inside the soul of the self. Unsurprisingly, perhaps, this chapter makes use of poetry. To modify a Swedish proverb, 'good theology is not science-minus, but poetry-plus'. And poetry, sometimes, is the best sense we can make of how God calls us and shapes us.

Offering Up Ourselves: Mark 1:16–20

A vocation is not a career, but a life surrendered to God. Every Christian has a vocation. But just as every life is unique, so is every calling. No two are identical, and while you can often discern clear patterns and several similarities, in the end it comes down to each individual, their relationship with God, and then to the wider Church and world. Wisdom, the mystics tell us, is knowing your place before God. And a vocation is about finding that place, and then knowing what to do next. An academic calling is a vocation to inhabit wisdom – to grow in truth through searching, re-searching, teaching and being taught. It is a dynamic rooted in humility and truth.

But it is never clear cut. As Woody Allen once quipped, if you want to make God laugh, just tell him about your future plans. Vocations can be quirky, unsettling and uncertain. For most people it's not a question of hearing a clear voice from heaven, but rather piecing together shards of evidence: insights, affirmations and nudges from all over. It can take years to discern.

And callings aren't always instantly recognisable. It is pretty typical of God, if you think about it. He comes to us in unexpected ways: a child in a manger; a still small voice; a thick silence; a bush alight. Not all signs are easy to read. And this is perhaps what Isaiah is wrestling with when he sees his vision of God (Isa 6:8). It ends with the oft repeated rhetorical question: 'whom shall I send; who will go for us? Here am I. Send me'.

'Send me'? Surely God is kidding. There must be better qualified, nicer folk that God could choose, reasons Isaiah? But the invitation is clear. It resonates with some words Jesus will utter to his disciples hundreds of years later: You did not choose me; I chose you. Which is why a vocation is not like a career. It is simply a life surrendered to God.

Like Isaiah, we often cannot fathom God's wisdom, or his reasoning. But vocations often start in marginal places and with ephemeral events. God, the seemingly capricious conductor, seems to orchestrate vocations in unusual ways. As one poet, Emily Dickinson, puts it, truth is often a superb surprise – because 'the truth must dazzle gradually, or every man be blind'.[6] Vocations often sneak up on us. Others see them in us before we do. Few are granted the blinding light. A vocation is simply what happens when we stop running, and surrender ourselves to God.

One of the really arresting things about Mark's gospel is that you never get time to settle. You don't have the luxury of the well-drawn and skilfully crafted stories of Matthew and Luke, or the long conversations and dialogues that John gives us. With Mark, you are straight into the action; and then onto the next scene, and then the next. It is breathless. The disciples are called in chapter 1 verse 16 – and it is pretty well straight down to business.

This is because good news is here, now (Mk 1:14–15). And it requires your immediate attention, and a response. Here, now. So the tone of abruptness in the message of Mark is also his theme. There is no time to cogitate and deliberate. Choose Jesus. Drop everything you are doing, right now, and follow him. Come.

Yet what is so intriguing about Jesus is the range of people he chose to share in this work. It included women and men – and not all of great repute – along with fishermen, tax-collectors and others. The ensemble was hardly the cutting edge of leadership and eloquence. Yet in choosing widely, we gain a foretaste of

---

6   Emily Dickinson, 'Truth', in *The Single Hound* (1914), reprint (New York: Dodo Press, 2008).

what the kingdom will be like, and the Church might become: a place both of diversity and unity; a true home for all.

And this is why vocations are so diverse. God does not call any one 'type'. God calls all types. Some are gifted in particular ways; others bring different talents to the table. But as our reading from Ephesians suggests, the gifts are not competitive, but rather complementary. The gifts are bestowed from grace, so all may be benefit. The unity of the Church flows from diversity, not uniformity. So from the very beginning of the gospels, the story about vocations is a testimony to the extraordinary range of people that God uses to share in the work of the kingdom.

Vocations often come gradually – emerging from the dawns and dusks of our experiences. It was a gradual illumination that eventually made some sense to me. I had no thoughts of ministry or priesthood until I was in my mid-teens. I first twigged that I might be called to ministry when I was sixteen – a rebellious, recalcitrant and slightly reckless youth. Perhaps not quite the teenager from hell; but definitely one that knew how to put his parents through some purgatory. Despairing of their eldest son, my parents made me sit a two-day multiple choice career test to help determine my future. The theory was that if I had a goal in life, I might actually take aim at something. And what did the random-tick-this-box-careers-test conclude might lie ahead? First, consider a career in teaching. (This pleased me – a chance to get my own back on the system.) And the second option was to consider becoming a clergyman. This idea horrified me, truly. But I could not shake it off. Try as I might to leave it, it would not leave me.

It was to be another 10 years before I was ordained. And that time and space was important. Vocations are rarely sudden, complete epiphanies. It takes time to come to a mind; for the heart to be still; and for the soul to be attuned. But as far as God is concerned with vocations, you can run all you like, but you can't hide. Vocations can be like the proverbial *Hound of Heaven* from Francis Thompson's wonderful poem (written in 1893):

> I fled Him, down the nights and down the days;
> I fled Him, down the arches of the years;
> I fled Him, down the labyrinthine ways ...
> From those strong Feet that followed, followed after ... [7]

But if it is true that every Christian has a vocation, what are the next steps? How would you know you were called? How could you be sure? You can't, of course, but there are a few simple things to bear in mind.

---

[7]   Francis Thompson, *The Hound of Heaven* (New York, Morehouse Books, 1981).

First, have courage. Many vocations never take root because of fear. Fear of failure, or of perhaps just of getting it wrong – suppose someone rumbles that I am just ordinary? Suppose I really make a mess of it? But mistakes happen, and I think the best thing we can try to do is learn from these things. Failure is not the worst thing; letting it defeat you is. It takes a special kind of wisdom and courage to face failure and defeat, and to then try and move on from this.

Second, have patience. The Christian life is a marathon, not a sprint. And vocations are weighed and measured over the entire course of a life, not just a few moments of success or glory. It takes a long time to appreciate just how much God has called us too. It takes daily devotion to see that our calling is not about affirmation or success, but rather faithfulness. We are not primarily called to win things – even for God; but simply to *walk* with Christ.

Third, have humility. A vocation is not about the trappings of power and privilege in ministry. The gospel is always about eternal rewards, not the temporal baubles of the Church. The call is that we have our eyes fixed on Jesus, who is, by the way, coming back to do an audit. We do not, therefore, need our focus to be on a career path. Ultimately, a true vocation is something of a release – not something that is to be grasped.

These cardinal virtues play out in academic life too. As we noted earlier, rooted in humility and truth, the pursuit of wisdom is something that requires searching and re-searching, teaching and teach-ability. The call to academic ministry recognises that just as no-one is ever fully converted (a Christian is always in a perpetual state of conversion – so never completely finished), so no one person can ever fully arrive at truth on their own. We need the counsel of others in order to begin to apprehend and comprehend the height, breadth and depths of God's being and love. No one mind can attain the fullness of this. All we have are glimpses.

This is why the Apostle Paul's well-known phrase is so vital to remember: 'his power is made perfect in our weakness' (2 Cor 12:9). We do not belong to a faith where power finds expression in perfectionism. Or where our vocations – whatever they may be – raise us up several feet beyond contradiction. Rather, we look for the God who is incarnate; who comes to the world, and is found in human form. God *uses* our weaknesses – the foolish and base things of the world – to bring about change. Which is why he says to each and every one of us today, as he did to the fisherman at the beginning of Mark's gospel: come, follow me.

Walking with God: Mark 9:30–37

Committing ourselves to a new future in which there are risks and uncertainties is something few of us relish. Yet it is a daily reality for us all. It is often necessary to make a distinction between real and illusory religion. It is tempting at such times to cling to comforting certainties and false hopes. Yet we know that deep down, the future is open, and that sating the craving for certainty is no substitute for faith. The philosopher John Macmurray tells us that the maxim of illusory religion runs like this: 'Fear not; trust in God and he will see that none of these things you fear will happen to you'.[8] But that of real religion is quite contrary: 'Fear not; the things you are afraid of are quite likely to happen to you – but they are nothing to be afraid of'.

Perhaps our best-known psalm, Psalm 23, captures the essence of our assurance. God will be with us – in whatever shadows or valleys we walk through. But we are never offered a detour. There is no way around the difficulties we face in life. Rather, Christian faith offers a way through these things. So as we face the challenges and opportunities of new starts, we step out in trust and in hope. We don't know what our future looks like. But we don't need to, either. As one poet, Minnie Louise Haskins put it, many years ago ('God Knows' – more usually known as 'The Gate of the Year', 1908):

> I said to the man
> who stood at the gate of the year,
> 'Give me a light that I may tread safely
> into the unknown'.
> And he replied,
> 'Go out into the darkness
> and put your hand into the hand of God.
> That shall be to you
> better than light
> and safer than a known way'.
> So I went forth
> and finding the hand of God,
> trod gladly into the night.[9]

---

8   John Macmurray, *Persons in Relation* (London, Faber & Faber, 1961), 171.
9   Minnie L. Haskins, M., 'God Knows' in *The Desert* (London: Hodder, 1908).

One of the great conundrums that faces all those who find themselves caught up in or called into ecclesial life is how to resolve questions of authority and power. And the great temptation – always, I think – is to try and resolve the miscibility of ecclesial life with a clarity that ends up oppressing more that it frees; of bondage more than liberty. This is why meeting, dialogue, conversation and debate are essential components in the formation of wisdom – not just for theology (and discipleship), but in fact any sphere of study. True authority welcomes critical deliberation – not merely receiving faith passively. Theology, when constructive, can be forged in the crucible of conflictual conversation.

I think that the disciples arguing on the road to Capernaum are, by the way, well-motivated. They are doubtless looking at the motley crew that Jesus has assembled, and quickly concluded that what is needed is structure, leadership, clear lines of authority and appropriate concentrations of power in persons and offices. And as they are the first to have this epiphany, they naturally nominate themselves. It does not seem to be such a bad idea. It is tempting too, just to look around you for a moment here. You can understand why God called you – and my, hasn't he equipped you well? But as for one or two of my neighbours, well, I am sure God can see the potential. But I can't quite...

Moreover, such 'problems' in ecclesial life have continued to germinate well beyond the New Testament. Christians agree about what the Bible says; but not what it means. And the resolution to this dilemma, at least apparently for some, is to have leaders who can proscribe the meaning. After all, why settle for confusion when you can apparently have clarity? Yet Jesus' response to this is to refuse and rebuke the choice between clarity and confusion. Instead, he draws us quite properly to complexity.

Which is why Jesus deals with the argument the disciples are having in two complementary ways. Firstly, by pointing out that the leader will suffer and die. And second, by picking up a child, and setting the infant in the midst of the group, and reminding everyone that the leader will be the one whose attention is fixed upon the most innocent and vulnerable in our society, and not on those who merely aspire to high office. So, by drawing their and our attention to the topsy-turvy world of the Church, Jesus changes the way we look at each other, and at God. Leaders must be servants. Teachers must be learners. Rulers must be slaves. It is complex; and not as simple as it seems.

In other words, Jesus will not adopt the hierarchy 'of the gentiles'. The kingdom he preaches and practises will be riddled with teasing contradictions, and knotty dilemmas. It will be the proverbial Gordian knot; but not one that you can cut through.

I often admire the patience and composure of church leaders, who when pressed to be assertive and directive on delicate or controversial matters, find the grace and strength to hold back. Some call this weakness, dithering or foolishness. But it seldom is. For such leaders, in practising hesitancy (or willed spiritual patience), allow the necessary space to develop which permits discussion and deliberation – even if it might call into question their own power, authority and leadership.

So, secure in what they are called to, they do not need to 'lord it over' anyone; nor do they need to assert their primacy. They let the space become. And the Church then breathes, even as it finds its voice – and might begin to argue. But this is, of course, not a bad thing. Christians, like all human beings, disagree. That is in the nature of collective and social gatherings. The moral question for Christians is not 'why do we not agree?' (it is inevitable we sometimes won't), but, rather, *how* do we disagree? How do we conduct ourselves? With assertive power and oppressive authority? Or with dignity, patience and humility?

Jesus, and graciously to the disciples, does not chide them for their ambition. Nor, I suspect for their nascent vocation. But rather, he gently reframes it. The kingdom of God will be led by acts of service, humility and the practice of virtues. Jesus says that the leadership he is looking for will often *not* be clear, directive, structured and concrete. We simply won't be able to get the kind of clarity that the disciples suppose is needed.

Rather, the life of the kingdom and the Church is bound to be one of messy contingency; a miscible muddle in which things will get done by love, service, grace and gentleness. Sometimes there will be decisions, and leaps forward; and leaders may take us there. But most of the Church is about love and service; the practice of virtues and the raising up of exemplary lives of holiness, charity, hope, faith and deep spiritual joy. This is what James has to say in our epistle: 'this wisdom from above is pure, then peaceable, gentle, willing to yield, full of mercy and good fruits, without a trace of partiality or hypocrisy'.

And when you perceive this, you won't want a place on the left or the right of Jesus, staring down at your adoring flock of submissive and compliant devotees. You'll want to be on your knees, towel in hand, with a bowl of water at your side. The academic calling is, ultimately a vocation of service, not of mastery. The truth sets us free; it does not enslave us. The handmaids of truth – deacons of the academy, as it were – serve by teaching and illuminating. The call to be a teacher and academic is rooted not in domination of the other, but in service to the world.

Ministry to the Margins: Mark 7:25–30

If I had to be reincarnated as an animal, I would come back as a St. Bernard dog. I have my reasons. First, I'd like to be a saint, and this is as about close as I'll get. Second, I believe in searching for the lost. Third, everyone loves a good dog, so there is a chance of being both liked *and* gainfully employed, and you can rarely do *both* of these in the Church – trust me on this. And finally, a rescue mission that involves a hip flask full of malt whisky can't be all *that* bad. Indeed, find or lose your victim, it still ends with a well-deserved drink.

One of the more famous quotes from another saint of the same era as Bernard is from Benedict: 'Before all things and above all things, care must be taken of the sick; so that the brethren shall minister to them as they would to Christ himself; for he said: 'I was sick and ye visited me'. (*Rule of St. Benedict*). Benedict had read his gospel: 'Jesus went forth and saw a great multitude and was moved with compassion towards them, and he healed their sick' (Matt 14:14). The *Rule of St. Benedict* is, of course, the oldest constitution in history by which groups still live. Its opening words invite us to listen and be attentive to the needs of others. The invitation to become fully human – never mind any vocation – begins here.

So we neglect our neighbours at our peril. Listening and paying attention to the margins of humanity is crucial. In 1996 I published an article on the healing miracles of Jesus which pressed the question, not about whether or not these miracles ever happened, but what they meant to their audiences either as events, or as written narratives. It caused a bit of a storm – at least for theology. Friends, and one or two critics, accused me of drafting the gospel according to New Labour. One or two felt it might be the gospel according to Old Labour, but just with a bit of spin – but I'll leave that for you to decide on whether this is Blue Labour or Red Tory today.

The paper effectively argued that the healing miracles of Jesus were not in themselves particularly important, either as historical events or as narratives. What was more significant about the miracles were the political implications that flowed from them. I drew attention to the fact that in the forty or so healing miracles recorded we hardly ever learn the name of the person who is healed. This seemed to me to be in itself quite significant, pointing to the insignificance of the subject. What was arguably more revealing about the nature of the miracles was the gospel writers' willingness to tease the reader by naming the category of affliction: leprosy, mental illness, single mothers with dead children, orphans, people of other faiths, the elderly, the handicapped.

I could go on. Jesus hardly ever heals his friends, and rarely ever heals anybody with any significant social or moral political status. In nearly every case, the healings of Jesus are directed towards those who are self-evidently on the margins of society, or who have been excluded in one way or another from the centre of social, political, moral or religious life. Not only that, the friendships that Jesus made also suggest that he was more than willing to share his time and abundance with this same group of people.

This observation is not particularly interesting in itself, but it does start to raise a question about what the healing miracles were for, if they are in effect 'wasted' on groups of people who appear to be unable to make a significant response. Yet when one turns to the sorts of encounters that Jesus has with religious and political authorities, particularly when they are accusing other people of betrayal, (a woman caught in adultery springs to mind; equally, the prostitute who anoints the feet of Jesus in the middle of a dinner, recorded in Lk 7), we begin to see that Jesus' healing activity was, for the authorities, a dangerous, even subversive activity. Jesus consorts with the *wrong* sorts of people in the eyes of the righteous; he's not in church, but down the pub. Moreover, Jesus gets no return for his investment in 'the lost' or 'the unclean'; he wilfully loves the loveless, and seeks out those who everyone else has given up on. In all of these healing encounters, the remarkable thing about Jesus' ministry is that it discriminates – *for* the unknown, the lost, the marginalised and the victimised. And almost nobody else.

For example, the syro-phoenician woman is one of several people that Jesus heals who do not belong to a Jewish faith community. She is distraught. There is no price for her miracle: she does not have to come to church now. Nor does she have to become a Jew. No. She simply receives the compassion of God poured out in Jesus Christ. She's not defiled in Jesus' eyes at all. Which explains why the stories are linked together. After Jesus' careful lecture on purity, the disciples still want to send this woman away – she's not one of their kind. But she persists.

This is only a brief summary of the article, but it concluded by offering some reflection on the then state of the National Health Service, which at the time was being re-shaped by a Conservative government. There was a general attack on the rhetoric of praising and blaming patients for 'their' illnesses, which ranged from exploring the appropriateness of criticising obese people for eating the wrong foods, to young, single teenage mothers in certain kinds of housing, and social welfare benefit. All very ugly and irksome.

In my conclusion, I simply said that this kind of approach to healing and health care had no place in a modern society, and little place in the gospels, since the healings of Jesus, although miraculous, nearly always interrogated the *social* causes of dis-ease. That is to say, Jesus was interested not just in healing, but how people had been classed as 'ill' in the first place, and what or who kept them there. He was, I suppose, in modern idiom, tough on illness, and tough on the causes of illness.

We need to remember that when Jesus heals the leper, he makes himself unclean by touching a source of impurity. The radical demand of Jesus is that the Church is required to assume the pain and impurity of the excluded, the demonised and the (allegedly) impure. That's why there are prison chaplains; that's why the Church works *for* and *with* asylum seekers; that's why the Church questions common sense, social control and prevailing political powers. It is just carrying on the job of Jesus, namely looking for the lost, rejected, marginalised and fallen, and trying to, with the love of God, bring them back into the fold of society and the arms of God. Moreover, the Church always asks: 'how did you get here? Who excluded you?' Or, what kind of society is it that *rejects* people – for being too ill or infirm, or the wrong kind of people. Jesus, the friend of tax-collectors, prostitutes and other undesirables – but it's not how we like to think of Christ, is it?

In some respects, this does allow us to reflect on the kinds of discourse that are sometimes excluded from the academy. It is easy, sometimes, to use categories such as 'literature' to demarcate between 'classical' and 'popular'; or 'orientalism' to place 'otherness' at a distance from what is deemed to be the 'default-normative'. Here, feminist insights (including in the theology) and those rooted in sexuality, politics or ethnicity (such as liberation and black theology) can act as powerful and necessary correctives to the conscious and unconscious domination and hegemony of established power interests. Sometimes, this just requires clergy and academics to notice the small things. In other words, to pay a fuller attention to the everyday, and notice the details of human existence. I like Hilary Greenwood's poem, 'Knotty Nineties', and the vocational invitation it issues:

> What I like about being a priest
> is nothing to do with the cultic beast
> or having a message to write on the leaves
> or offering charms to the heart that grieves
> or counting the sheep in a pitch-pine fold
> or wearing a shirt of cloth-of-gold,
> no, none of these – but marrying
> the glory to the little thing:
> to eavesdrop on a monologue
> delivered to a woolly dog;
> to hear the tones of righteous rage

excite the prophet of schoolboy age;
to sit down in a bus behind
four lots of fingers intertwined;
to see the boy's face in the man's
blush when he comes to put up the banns:
to watch rheumatic ladies pat
a blessing on the pampered cat –
what I like about being a priest
is turning everything to the east.[10]

This noticing of the other – and sometimes the seemingly ordinary – requires, in terms of discipleship, a far fuller Christian consciousness. Noticing and paying attention is a vocation that academics and clergy share. But to practice this well, a vocation has to start from a place of humility and human solidarity. The trouble with Christians, arguably, is that we only regard ourselves as honorary sinners, and the Church as a haven for the saved and secure. The rest of the world is therefore 'other'. But the Church, like the Kingdom of God, is for everyone – and especially the lost and the loveless. And the way Jesus *sees* the world is a way that invites all those called to a vocation – of inhabiting and practising wisdom – to take a second look, and *see and perceive* more deeply.

In view of this, there are three lessons to learn about Jesus and his healing of the syro-phoenician woman, and countless others like her. First, each of the healings seems to indict witnesses, crowds and others who appear to have colluded with the categories of sin and sickness which have demonised individuals and groups. Jesus' healing ministry is decisive in that it questions these categories ('Who told you this person is unclean?'; 'He who is without sin may cast the first stone'). Jesus appears here to be a barrier breaker, eschewing the normal categories that dumped people in 'sin bins', or constructions of reality where they are deemed to be less than whole or suitable. In effect, he turns the tables on his audience on almost every occasion, and asks in whose interests is this person being categorised as ill or evil? This is why he's crucified in the end; Jesus breaks down the barriers between clean and unclean; he re-orders society; the old rules no longer work.

Secondly, and correspondingly, Jesus often insists that a person returns to the centre of the community from where they were originally excluded. One of the best examples of this is the mentally ill man who has been chained up in a graveyard, and who nobody visits, recorded in Luke's gospel. Jesus' healing of

---

[10]   Hilary Greenwood, SSM, 'Knotty Nineties' (unpublished poem, 1969).

the person is extraordinary, precisely because he insists on returning this person to the community that expelled him from their midst in the first place. Even in today's gospel, Jesus sends the healed leper back to the people who would have cast him out of the community for his leprosy and uncleanness – and soon everyone knows that the leper is back.

Thirdly, touching is also an extraordinary feature of Jesus' healing ministry insofar as he seems willing and able to take on the associated stain, stigmas and taboos of his society by getting his own body and soul 'dirty'. Social anthropologists like Mary Douglas[11] have had much to say about this and point out, quite rightly, that categories such as 'pollution' and 'cleanliness' surface particularly in relation to our bodies, which she identifies, of course, as a matter of politics. Correspondingly, what flows into and out of bodies, or what is deemed to be 'unclean' and tainting of individuals or communities (such as leprosy), assumes a special character in nearly all societies, from the most primitive to the most sophisticated. Jesus seems to have no fear of touching and healing a woman who is haemorrhaging, of touching lepers, and of embracing people whose bodies are leaking sin and pollution, for which they are excluded from mainstream society. He inculcates their stain, stigma and suffering, rendering them whole by embracing their exclusion.

Today, we often forget that visions and missions in virtually every religious tradition in the world are not constructed by disciples or religious groups. They are in fact given – in effect, revelations. These revelations do not offer *choice*, but rather *obedience* in the context of a proper *vocation*. And perhaps our only way forward is to underline the imperative of vocations as an essential fundament in the proper ordering of a humane society. So our task – in our mission – is to look out for today's lepers. To look out for the excluded; the 'impure'; the demonised. This is where Jesus will be, always before us. And as the gospel says – he reached out, and he touched. Or perhaps like our St. Bernard dog – he searches for lost causes. And he comes with warmth and a drink.

Conclusion

The application of these sketches to the academic vocation is, I hope, at least inferred, if not perhaps obvious. The vocation to ministry is, *per se*, also an invitation to develop an academic mind. At best, it can be about embarking upon some potentially thrilling intellectual adventures. But more often than not, the

---

[11]   Mary Douglas, *Purity and Danger* (London: Routledge, 1966).

new thoughts and ideas that emerge in training, formation and development challenge (and may destroy) existing paradigms, including ones that are cherished. So the academic vocation – integral to any spiritual one – is, in other words, an invitation into risk-taking. Vocations do not leave us unchanged, unchallenged or un-journeyed. So our minds will be expanded by the walk with God; and old ideas expended.

We also discover, in the process of walking with the Lord of the Journey, that (to coin a phrase from J.B. Philips), our God is too small. Vocations enlarge our vision of God; they deepen our wisdom. So the imperative in a vocation is to let go and trust; not to try and cling to the familiar and (hitherto) true – because God will show us more. This is not to abandon orthodoxy for the uncharted and choppy waters of liberalism. It is, rather, to affirm and acknowledge that no Christian possesses all the truth. Rather, the truth possesses us. Therefore, we are to walk humbly with God, knowing that the God who reveals himself in the things we find comforting and affirming also comes to us in the dis-comforting and disturbing – something the Apostles Peter and Paul knew all about in their visions and revelations. God will not be bound by our constructions of orthodoxy. He will reveal himself both in and beyond our frames of reference. As Simone Weil famously remarked:

> For it seemed to me certain, and I still think so ... that one can never wrestle enough with God if one does so out of pure regard for the truth. Christ likes us to prefer truth to him because, before being Christ, he is truth. If one turns aside from him to go toward the truth, one will not go far before falling into his arms.[12]

All vocations need wisdom. And what better way to resource wisdom than through learning? Wisdom is not just know-how; it is an inward journey that raises our self-awareness and consciousness. It deepens our sense of what we do not know; it prompts humility, grace and truth. It prevents pride. To think you know one religion back-to-front and inside-out is really to know none at all. Wisdom teaches us that our knowledge is partial, and only starts to become more complete when we open up to others, and to God. But wisdom is a journey, not a destination. The more we learn, the better we wrestle. And the better we wrestle, the more humble we become before the face of God, who alone is the source of true wisdom.

And of course the deeper purpose of these three sketches – rooted in the Gospel of Mark and in poetry – has been to help us see something of the inward to

---

[12]   Simone Weil, *Waiting for God* (New York: Harper, 1973), 69.

outwards journey that each vocation takes. The inner sense of calling crystallises into personal embodiment, before finally becoming public and performative. Yet despite this movement, hesitancy and fear remain. This is no bad thing, I suspect. For just as Mark's gospel began abruptly, so it ends in the same way. He ends his narrative with these words – *ephobounto gar* in Greek – 'for they were afraid' (16:8). What kind of conclusion is that to the greatest calling of all – to begin to preach, proclaim and personify the resurrection of Jesus? The salvation of the world set in motion – but 'they were afraid' does not inspire confidence. Yet as Eugene Peterson points out, this word *gar* is transitional; no Greek writer would end a sentence with *gar*.[13] It is a word that gets you ready for the next part of the sentence – except there isn't one. So Mark 16:8 is an end; but not a very good one, which is why other later revisions of the text soon began to supply their own, including the disciples running off into the sunset, happily believing and rejoicing.

But I much prefer the original director's cut. Mark finishes mid-sentence, I think, deliberately. *Gar* leaves us off-balance, mid-stride; where will the next step be? This is artful reticence; a conclusion is withheld from the disciples and the reader. It is up to you to say what happens next. In other words, the Christian faith cannot be wrapped up as a finished product. The frame is open; the picture not completed. As Peterson says: 'write a resurrection conclusion with your own life'. Quite so. That is the invitation Mark poses to us for each and every one of us in our own vocations. What will your next step be?

---

[13] Eugene Peterson, *Under the Unpredictable Plant* (Grand Rapids: Eerdmans, 1994), 195–6.

Chapter 13

Called to Account: Signposts from the Letter to the Hebrews

Joy Tetley

'*In the name of our Lord we bid you remember the greatness of the trust that is now to be committed to your charge ...* ' So says the Bishop to Church of England ordinands shortly before they are to be ordained priest.[1] Being an ordained minister in the Church of God, whatever the ecclesial context, carries a responsibility of no mean dimensions. The spiritual authority conveyed by ordination is accompanied by a far-reaching accountability which has its essential locus in no less than the person of God. Answering to human hierarchies is one thing. Rendering an account before the judgement seat of God is of quite another order. By very definition, nothing could be more searching. Yet this is what the ordained commit themselves to, both publicly and before God, and it ever holds true, whatever the setting and character of their ministry. The academic context is no exception. In ordination, the whole of life is offered into the being and service of God and that most certainly includes the activity and explorations of the intellect. Should this dedication make any difference, then, to the way academic life is approached and exercised? What might God require of the academic ordained? In what does their 'accountability' consist?

In the Ordination service quoted, the Bishop continues thus: 'Remember always with thanksgiving that the treasure now to be entrusted to you is Christ's own flock, bought by the shedding of his blood on the cross. It is to him that you will render account for your stewardship of his people'.[2] In whatever way these words are to be precisely interpreted, their substantial import is clear. Ordained priesthood is directly connected with the sacrificial love of Christ and the deepest well-being of those for whom Christ died. Though this is to be embraced with thanksgiving – for responding to the call of God always draws

---

[1]   From the Declarations in Church of England, 'The Ordination of Priests', in *Common Worship: Ordination Services* (London: Church House Publishing, 2007).

[2]   Ibid.

the respondent into God's essential joy – it is nonetheless and quite evidently a serious business. Like marriage, it is not to be entered into 'unadvisedly, lightly, or wantonly'.[3] Like marriage also, the commitment applies at all times and in all places, for better, for worse. It has major implications, wherever the minister is located, for the way life is lived. At their ordination, priests declare that, 'by the help of God', they will fashion their own lives and that of their households according to the way of Christ, that they may be a pattern and example to Christ's people. That is, indeed, a tall order. But it is not the only promise made. There is also a firm commitment to 'be diligent in prayer, in reading Holy Scripture, and in all studies that will deepen [their] faith and fit [them] to bear witness to the truth of the Gospel'. Further, the ordained undertake to 'faithfully minister the doctrine and sacraments of Christ ... so that the people committed to [their] charge may be defended against error and flourish in the faith'.[4]

In the summary of the seventeenth-century poet-priest, George Herbert, ordained priesthood carries both 'dignity' and 'duty': 'The Dignity, in that a Priest may do that which Christ did, and by his auctority, and as his Viceregent. The Duty, in that a Priest is to do that which Christ did, and after his manner, both for Doctrine and Life'.[5]

For those whose priestly vocation incorporates an academic emphasis, this must be a subject for no little pondering. Where, fundamentally, are one's priorities? How are the solemn commitments entered into at ordination to be defined and delivered in any given situation, not least in 'secular' employment contexts where the overt mixing of faith and work is regarded as, at best, inappropriate? There is also the question of *how* intellectual endeavour is to be pursued. For the ordained academic theologian, for example, should 'detached study' be in any sense qualified by ministerial commitment? In a radical search for 'truth', what might it mean (if anything) to 'defend against error' and, more positively, to foster a 'flourishing of faith' in those with whom one has to do? In the interests of integrity, and even more importantly, in the interests of accountability to God for a trust bestowed, these questions matter.

What shall we say, then? If the ordained are given over, body, mind and spirit, to God and God's service, then what this God might be like is of crucial significance. Indeed, we may say that it makes all the difference in the world. Questions such as those raised above are most fruitfully looked at in the light

---

   3   From the Introduction to the Marriage service in the Church of England, *The Book of Common Prayer* (Cambridge: Cambridge University Press, 1662, 2003).

   4   Ibid., 38.

   5   George Herbert, *A Priest to the Temple* (Norwich: Canterbury Press, 2003), Chapter 1, 'Of a Pastor'.

of who it is who has claimed the ordained for that expression of ministry. The character of 'the Calling One' (1 Thess 5:24) is a theological issue of far more than 'academic' interest.

In Christian conviction, the character of God is none other than the person of Jesus (see Heb 1:3). It is in looking to Jesus that we see most clearly into the being and 'behaviour' of God. Such, certainly, is the vision which has captivated the anonymous author of the Epistle to the Hebrews. In this intriguing figure, we find a telling paradigm of the integration of intellectual and ministerial calling. It is a paradigm which, like the written communication to which it has given expression, is both heartily encouraging and profoundly challenging.

The Author of Hebrews as Exemplar

One commentator has described Hebrews as emerging from 'the passionate conviction and brilliant imagination of a single mind', going on to suggest 'that in the first decades of the Christian movement, another remarkable mind and heart besides Paul's was at work in interpreting the significance of the crucified and raised Messiah Jesus for the understanding of Scripture, of the world and of human existence'.[6] As we ponder on this author[7] and (in all probability) 'his' work, we may perhaps discern some key indicators which are not without relevance for those who come after. In the author of Hebrews, we encounter someone who, when all is said and acknowledged about particular contextual influences, does his own thing. As we shall see, his is an original mind, working creatively on traditional material. The driving force behind his 'lively oracles', however, is not the urge to establish his academic credentials and certainly not the desire to make a name for himself. He works under the overwhelming and primary impetus of covenant relationship with the living God, the God who has 'in these last days' spoken definitively in Jesus (Heb 1:1–3). In close partnership with that reality is the motivation of his urgent pastoral concern for a community which, in faith terms, seems to be seriously losing its way. Here is the interweaving, the dynamic interaction of contemplative, vital spirituality with intellect, passion, poetry and pastoral urgency. It issues in a compelling and radical theology which is yet the source of profound encouragement for all who will engage with it.

---

6   L.T. Johnson, *Hebrews, A Commentary* (London: Westminster John Knox Press, 2006), 30.

7   See further J. Tetley, *Encounter with God in Hebrews* (London: Scripture Union, 1995), 14–22.

Though the identity of this author has been (and still is) the source of much speculation and critical detective work, the most reliable conclusion remains that of Origen back in the third century: 'Who wrote the Epistle to the Hebrews, God alone knows' (Eusebius, *Hist. Eccl.*, 6.25.11–14). Whoever did produce it, however, was clearly known also to the original recipients. He (the masculine form of the participle in 11:32 tells strongly against female authorship, despite Harnack's otherwise attractive suggestion of Priscilla[8]) felt no need of identifying himself to them, nor did he feel it necessary to adopt the not uncommon practice of cloaking himself in apostolic pseudonymity. Indeed, his failure to do either was a major cause of Hebrews' difficulty in finding a place in the canon, especially in the West. For writings to be judged 'canonical', it was important that they had sound apostolic connections. This church leader, however, was evidently not looking towards posterity or the establishing of a 'legacy'. What mattered to him was that he had an urgent message to get across to a particular community in crisis and he had no doubt of his authority to do so. He expected to gain a hearing. His 'word of exhortation' (13:22) – much more of a sermon than a letter – is inherently authoritative. He does not need to remind this community (as Paul so often has to do in his letters) of his right to address them. That is taken as read.

This is a preacher on fire with God and with pastoral zeal. Yet his passion is expressed through a work that is carefully structured and carefully argued. At no point does he lose control of his text. Both mind and heart are very much engaged but in effective harmony with one another. The cerebral and the affective, rigorous thought and experiential faith, have, so to speak, met and kissed each other. They belong together and they bear fruit – fruit that has 'lasted' for many generations. The author of Hebrews was clearly well educated, both in terms of matters Jewish and of Greek rhetoric. He knew how to put an argument together and express it effectively – witness, for example, his use of alliteration and metaphor, his capacity to communicate heights and depths, encouragement and fear, to touch the feelings as well as search the mind. He is, *at the same time*, contemplative pray-er, spiritual visionary, theological poet, committed pastor, acute thinker, attractive writer, powerful preacher and, above all, devoted lover of the God of Jesus Christ. It is all of these qualities which, together, make him the first-rate theologian that he is. His work cannot easily be divided into discrete categories. It has to be taken as a whole, received as a complex, multi-faceted unity. Theology emerges from the entirety of his being

---

[8]   See P. Ellingworth, *The Epistle to the Hebrews*, New International Greek Commentary (Grand Rapids: Eerdmans, 1993), 19f.

and experience, provoked into articulation by looking to Jesus and seeing the dire situation of his community in that light.

Theological Exploration in Hebrews

The author of Hebrews has a passion for his subject, and that subject is Jesus, perceived as the very self-expression of God. It is the contemplation of Jesus which leads Hebrews into the bold and creative theology which we encounter in his 'word of exhortation'. There are assuredly many secondary factors but this is the essence of the matter. Nor is his contemplative activity defined by detached reflection. Rather, it is characterised by a committed engagement with his subject – an engagement which involves investing not less than everything in relationship with the living God, now self-revealed 'once for all' in Jesus. This is the heart-to-heart New Covenant relationship which the author expounds so powerfully and at length in the course of his communication (see especially chapters 8–10). The whole tenor of his work suggests that this is an author given to practising what he preaches. The name of Jesus features prominently in his writing, often with no further qualification and invariably in an emphatic position in the Greek sentence. In particular, the recipients are urged to see Jesus (2:9), to pay careful attention to Jesus (3:1), to look to Jesus (12:2) and to consider Jesus (12:3). These exhortations come, tellingly, towards the beginning and towards the end of the sermon. They constitute the crucial task urged upon the community.

The preacher speaks from the heart as well as the head. The overwhelming impression is that in speaking of Jesus he speaks of someone he knows, and knows intimately; someone in and through whom, he is convinced, we can meet directly with the living God, no holds barred and all barriers gone. Furthermore, the Jesus who can be approached in this way is one who is utterly acquainted with human weakness and suffering, something the beleaguered and struggling Hebrews community needed, urgently, to discover afresh. That conviction and insight is why the author begins his sermon with a resounding (and daring) affirmation of faith in the *divine* character of the Son of God. It becomes obvious as the sermon progresses (4:24, 8:1) that *Jesus* is the Son of God in the way spoken of in the opening section (1:1–14). When we look to Jesus, we see someone bearing all the characteristics set out in 1:1–14. Indeed, we see God. That is critically important to remember when contemplating the suffering and humiliation of Jesus. His experience of rejection, pain and death is also, according to Hebrews, showing us something vital about the character of God. Divine majesty and heavenly exaltation have to be re-envisaged in the light of the mission and ministry of Jesus the Son of God. 'Glory and honour', it seems, are to be directly related to a willingness to go through appalling suffering and shame on behalf of all others (2:9, 12:2). This is divine grace indeed, the radiance of God's glory and the ultimate expression of divine priesthood.

It is also bold and adventurous theology. Focused attention on a direct relationship with God through Jesus, issues, it seems, in ground-breaking insight and courageous communication. Looking to Jesus has led to clear-sightedness and vitality of thought. Where it has not led is into 'safe' territory. Instead, the direction is 'outside the camp' (13:10–16) – outside secure limits, outside the boundaries of the traditionally holy and on to risky, not to say dangerous ground. Jesus the 'Pioneer' (2:10, 12:2), as Hebrews perceives him, works out God's salvation by negotiating the most challenging of terrain – and it is not his intention that he should occupy it alone. Those in committed relationship with Jesus are called to be faith (and faithful) explorers not dug in behind defensive walls. Indeed, as Jesus is the 'fleshing out' of *God's* pioneering character, it has ever been the case that the divine call is to seek to know God and therefore ever to be on a spiritual pilgrimage, a searching enterprise which may at times be distinctly uncomfortable (see the catalogue of faith pilgrims in Chapter 11). For the author of Hebrews, like Anselm of Canterbury amongst many others after him, the process of 'theology' is none other than 'faith seeking understanding'. It is a quest to be undertaken in honest conversation with the One in whom all 'understanding' has its source (see also, for example, Ps 119). In the language of Hebrews, that means constantly drawing near to the throne of grace, where all is laid bare – and on both sides (4:12–16). Just as we are radically exposed before God, so, in Jesus, is God radically exposed before us. Who knows what may come of that encounter? Whatever, we can be sure that it will issue in mercy and grace. And fresh visions of the living God.

The kind of understanding vouchsafed through this knowing relationship, however, may prove difficult to swallow. Such was the case, it seems, with the Hebrews community. Their concerned leader castigates them for not growing up in the faith (5:11–6:3). For whatever reason, they have become 'dull of hearing'. They can't take the teaching they are being offered and they are not prepared to persevere in chewing on it. All they want is milk, a diet which, at their stage of Christian life, is hardly going to give them sufficient nourishment, especially when they are facing many and great dangers. By now, their leader tells them, they should themselves be teachers and, therefore, faith explorers. Yet they want to stay as babes-in-arms rather than walking on their own two feet.

The author of Hebrews in no way wants to infantilise his ailing and failing community. He believes they are capable of spiritual adventure, even in the midst of their fear and doubt. Indeed, leaving their false security and going with Jesus the Pioneer is in truth that which will bring them through to the joy that is set before them. So he makes no concessions to their reluctance. Precisely because he cares passionately about them and their circumstances, he exhorts them to follow through on the implications of looking to Jesus. In human terms this is, to be sure, a risky enterprise. It could take them anywhere and, in all likelihood, ask them to let go of old and familiar certainties. But always it will catch them up into the life of God, the God who, whatever is asked of them, will never fail them or forsake them.

Whoever produced Hebrews most certainly wanted to guard the community against 'error'. He clearly takes his 'ministerial' responsibilities very seriously and is utterly committed to doing all he can to keep these wavering, fearful folk on the way of Christ. He knows that, like the leaders he refers to in 13:17, he, too, must render an account of his ministry to the living God. But his understanding of 'error' is not so much a matter of embracing false doctrine as of 'wandering away' from faith and thus betraying the most important relationship there could ever be. It is breach of covenant faith. It is abandoning God. To 'err' in such a way is the most serious of sins.

Such a stance, when brought into conjunction with the condition of the recipients, helps us to understand the 'severe passages' in Hebrews – notably 2:1–3, 6:4–8, 10:26–31, 12:25–29. They are the warnings of one keeping spiritual watch (13:17), one who feels keenly his responsibility for the 'soul health' of his community. For him, apostasy is the great potential disaster, not adventurous theology. As he sees it, the kind of apostasy he fears is nothing less than the callous betrayal of God, the God who has not only spoken but gone through extreme suffering in Jesus, in order that all might truly 'know' God from the inside and enjoy the transforming benefits of the new covenant. It should perhaps be remembered in this context that a horrifying act of treachery by one of Christ's chosen disciples had deepened the darkness of Christ's passion. The 'Judas factor', so near the centre of the gospel story, must have made apostasy seem especially abhorrent to the early Christian communities. Certainly, the language used of apostates by Hebrews is decidedly personal, not to say emotive, and has its focus on the crucified Lord. They crucify the Son of God afresh, and hold him up to open shame (6:6). They trample on the Son of God, treat the blood of the covenant (the blood of Jesus) as something profane, and outrage the Spirit of grace (10:29). They have deliberately chosen to become enemies of God (10:26, 27). They will have their reward (10:27, 30–31).

Such fierce and heartfelt warnings are also part of a pastoral strategy, designed to keep a faltering community on course. That involves showing graphically how much can be lost, thereby further highlighting the inestimable blessings to be enjoyed at God's hands. It is only a fearful thing to fall into those hands (10:31) if you have treated what they offer with utter and savage contempt (10:29). As Hebrews puts it immediately after one of his diatribes, 'Even though we speak in this way, beloved, we are confident of better things in your case ... ' (6:9). Here is a preacher making telling use of what we might call the 'worst-case scenario' – not to create an effect but because he cares passionately about their spiritual welfare and knows all too well his own responsibility in this regard. He cannot wash his hands of it. What he says and where he leads, matters.

It is with this understanding that Hebrews pursues his theological quest. Indeed, the primacy, in his eyes, of an intimate and searching relationship with the living God through Jesus, propels him further in his exploration. Healthy relationships are ever in a state of development. And to stay healthy they need to stay faithful. They need to persevere through thick and thin. So, *par excellence*, in relation to God. The end of theological endeavour, therefore, is to see God more clearly and to follow wherever that might lead. God is the subject rather than the object of study. What is more, the process is mutual. In examining God we are also examined by God. The questions flow in both directions. The dialogue, even when strained or fiery, is one of commitment rather than detachment.

Theological Exploration in Hebrews – A Focal Example

It is from this matrix that the radical theology of Hebrews is born. We may illustrate this by looking at one of the author's most striking theological insights, that of Jesus as great High Priest. It is a distinctive vision and one which, treated so explicitly and at such great length, is found nowhere else in the New Testament. It is also decidedly bold, not least in relation to that godly tradition which, in all probability, would have been the living, Jewish heritage of both the author and his community. He knows that those he addresses are going to find this exceedingly difficult (5:11) but he is also convinced that if their eyes can be opened to it, they will not only be able to endure their situation but, even in the midst of it, enter into the joy of God. So, skilled preacher that he is, he prepares the way carefully, unfolding his vision in stages throughout the sermon and saving its *most* disturbing dimensions until his word of exhortation is well underway.

It is first signalled in his astounding opening sentence (1:1–4) – a sentence packed full of theological significance and challenge, containing material sufficient for a lifetime's contemplation. In the midst of it comes the phrase, 'when he had made purification of sins'. This is not a throwaway remark. Already it is opening up questions and making bold claims. Such cleansing of sin was priestly business. Here, the one doing the cleansing is none other than God's Son and God's defining and definitive self-expression. The implication is clear. We have a priestly God – a God who not only brings forth creation but who yearns and acts to bring all created life into communion with the divine life. This preacher has no hesitation, right from the outset and knowing full well the dispirited condition of the community, in pushing at the boundaries of their understanding. He is determined to make them *think* in order that they may *feel* the salvation of God more deeply.

His next reference to the priesthood of Jesus comes at the end of what we know as chapter 2. What is contained in these first two chapters constitutes, in effect, an overture to the sermon, rehearsing themes which the preacher will develop over the course of his communication. At the overture's climax, he makes explicit what he has alluded to in his opening sentence, adding in the process a further challenging dimension. Jesus, 'made like his brothers and sisters in every respect', is to be seen as 'a merciful and faithful high priest', making expiation for the sins of the people (2:17–8). The contextual reference here, as the community would be well aware, was to the annual ritual of the Day of Atonement, when the high priest, after stringent rites of purification and carrying sacrificial animal blood, would enter the Holy of holies, representing the people of God and seeking to make atonement for their sins. In Hebrews' view, this ritual was God-given and served an important human need but it was only a shadow of what it could be and had now been rendered obsolete by its fulfilment in Jesus. Jesus is the perfect self-expression of God (1:1–14) and Jesus is the perfect expression of humanity as God intended it to be (2:6–10). Jesus, therefore, and he alone, can perfectly realise the essential priestly vocation of bringing together for good a holy God and a sinful people. He does not do this with ritual caution but with wholehearted involvement, and at the cost of his life. Even more awesome, when we look at Jesus we see right into the character of God. It is no less than the holy God who, shockingly, enters the realm of the unholy and makes full and decisive atonement for the sins of the people.

That is underlined by the description of Jesus the high priest as 'merciful and faithful'. Although there is one highly interesting reference to God's raising up of a 'faithful priest' (1 Sam 2:35), those adjectives are not used in the Old Testament in relation to the high priest. They *are* used frequently of God. God's mercy and faithfulness are inherent in the priesthood *God* expresses in Jesus. This is priestly ministry of the highest possible order. Yet, as Julian of Norwich might put it,[9] it reaches down to the lowest point of our need. That is emphatically underlined when Hebrews begins explicitly to develop his priesthood theme at the end of chapter four (what precedes it is a further preparing of the ground). At this stage, the author graphically presents his community with the truth that Jesus, the great High Priest and Son of God, can identify with them completely, even in their weakness, a faith reality which should encourage them to approach God directly, with confident boldness, so opening themselves to the mercy and grace they so badly need. (4:14–5:10). It is at the end of this section that the next significant feature of the author's vision is revealed: Jesus is 'a high priest after the order of Melchizedek'. As he immediately makes clear (5:11) he knows that this is going to be even more difficult to take in, given the community's unreceptive condition. It will go against what is deeply ingrained within them. He does not pursue it, therefore, until he has attempted to open their eyes with a hortatory passage which pulls no punches (he could certainly fulfil the requirement of the Ordinal that ministers should 'admonish' as well as teach!) By the end of chapter 6, he, at least, is ready to move on.

Where he goes to is, most certainly, pioneering territory. The author of Hebrews is making a revolutionary claim. God has done a new thing, and in the process has, as it were, broken divinely established rules. In a nutshell, the priesthood of Jesus is irregular. As Hebrews underlines in chapter 7, Jesus is not from the right tribe to be a priest. He does not fit the sacred regulations. The author puts it starkly in 7:14: '*For it is evident that our Lord was descended from Judah and in connection with that tribe Moses said nothing about priests*'. Here is tradition being reinterpreted within scripture. On the face of it, this constitutes radical discontinuity with what has been required by God. More profoundly, however, it shows the sovereignty and consistency (if also the unpredictability) of the covenant God.

God, it seems, is showing that love, forgiveness and truth are of the essence. The covenant God who longs for all to know him is willing to go to any lengths to get that message through, to get to the heart of things, even if that means breaking through traditional barriers to expose the full truth. Jesus, our great High Priest and Son of God has 'once for all ... put away sin by the sacrifice of himself' (9:26). Jesus is both priest and victim. His life, 'without blemish' (9:14) but certainly not without struggle, constituted the perfect offering: life

---

9   Julian of Norwich, *Revelations of Divine Love*, trans. Elizabeth Spearing (London: Penguin Classics, 1998), Longer Text, chapter 6.

given over totally to God, life poured out on behalf of all others, the ultimate expression of vicarious repentance and pure love (10:5–10).

Jesus did what no one else could do, in order that everyone might know forgiveness and enjoy life with God, the very blessings of the new covenant. Through the tearing apart of the 'curtain' of his flesh (10:20), the way is opened for *all* to enter the Holy of holies. Jesus does not get in the way. Jesus is the way – a 'new and living way' (10:20). This high priest in no sense reserves the most sacred space for himself. All are welcome in God's nearest presence. From God's perspective, that is the point of it all.

Jesus does not qualify to be a high priest in the traditional sense. Rather he is, in the perception of Hebrews, a high priest 'after the order of Melchizedek'. What might this mean? In using Melchizedek, Hebrews is exploring part of the tradition already there but somewhat obscure, hidden, not (apparently) of mainstream significance – a by-way, we might say. Melchizedek was a mysterious priest, greatly honoured by God, but not a member of the tribe of Levi nor even of the chosen race. He was an outsider who played an extremely marginal part in the history of the people of God (mentioned only in Gen 14 and Ps 110:4). Yet, as Hebrews sees it, Melchizedek resembles the priestly Son of God (7:3). It is this figure from the edges of tradition who, for Hebrews, provides the paradigm for God's decisive intervention in Jesus. Jesus is, of course, far greater than Melchizedek, but it is this strange king's sort of priesthood that Jesus expresses to perfection – and for ever.

Melchizedek contributes dimensions that the mainstream Aaronic priests could not. His priesthood, Hebrews argues, might be tangential in terms of sacred tradition, but it was of a different and superior order, rendering him greater than Abraham, the founding patriarch of God's people. Not only did his name and title express the messianic qualities of righteousness and peace, but also, Hebrews asserts, using a common form of argument from silence, he is without father or mother or genealogy. In terms of the Levitical tradition, based firmly and without exception on genealogical credentials, Melchizedek is a 'non-starter'. In terms of the character of the eternal, ungenerated God, he is a perfect typological fit.

Jesus did not come from the right tribe to be a priest and Jesus died in disgrace '*outside* the camp' (13:13). Yet in a far deeper sense, the 'genealogy' of Jesus is impeccable. He is, after all, the Son of God, and is so after the manner of what is asserted in Hebrews' opening chapter, where, as Richard Bauckham underlines, the Son is presented as sharing the identity of God.[10] When bringing the blessings of salvation, God does, indeed, do a new thing. Such a 'change in the law' (as Hebrews puts it at 7:12) is not always easy to come to terms with. Nor is the God who will not be bound even by holy rules – or by anything else, except steadfast love (6:13–20). It is this covenant love which is God's ultimate and unchanging priority and the motivating heart of God's life and mission. It is the source and fulfilment of the priestly imperative to enable unhindered communion. Anything which gets in the way of that must be broken through, though it be hallowed and in place for centuries. Tradition is not God.[11]

Ongoing Implications

This is truly radical theology addressed to a community in a dire and vulnerable spiritual condition. Their fragile state has not caused this undoubtedly highly able and learned leader to 'cease from exploration', nor to refrain from encouraging his addressees along the same path. Indeed, he is firmly convinced that this is their route to salvation. But only if they look to Jesus and stay in faithful relationship with the God he reveals. Even if they do not know precisely where they are going (11:8) their direction should be clear. Whatever their outward circumstances, they are travelling with God and to God. They are not engaged on an aimless pilgrimage. Nor are they being exhorted merely to play with interesting ideas. The author of Hebrews is in no doubt that their souls' health depends on their risking everything by committing to Jesus in new covenant relationship. That will stretch them on every level, not least that of the mind, but it will also bring joy in the depths of earthly life, not to mention eternal security. It is this relationship which is primary and which leads to everything else. All else is to be seen in its light.

For the author of Hebrews, the discipline of 'theology' is the ongoing exploration of a fundamental relationship. Because that relationship has God as partner, it is fully comprehensive in scope and reach. Not only does it involve the emotions, it also engages and searches the mind, challenges the will and stirs the spirit – all of these dimensions, whether consciously recognised or not, being in

---

[10]   Richard Bauckham, 'The Divinity of Jesus Christ in the Epistle to the Hebrews', in *The Epistle to the Hebrews and Christian Theology*, eds R. Bauckham, D.R. Driver, T.A. Hart, N. MacDonald (Grand Rapids: Eerdmans, 2009), 15–36.

[11]   For a discussion of how this perspective in Hebrews might relate to the ordination of women as priests and bishops, see J. Tetley, 'For God's Sake', in *Apostolic Women, Apostolic Authority*, eds M. Percy and C. Rees (Norwich: Canterbury Press, 2010), 114–23.

constant interplay. And, just as it embraces the whole of being, so it also turns its attention to the whole of life – to 'everything under the sun' and beyond (see Heb 1–2). There is nothing outside its purview. It is thus immensely exciting and at the same time profoundly fearful, bringing together as it does, the intimate and the cosmic. Such relationship expresses the essence of the Gospel. Essentially contemplative, it is therefore characterised, in one way or another, by creative activity. 'Seeing Jesus' is no static phenomenon. It provokes as well as stills – a reality echoed much later in the words of a well-loved yet acutely challenging hymn of Charles Wesley:

> Jesus, confirm my heart's desire
> To work and speak and think for thee;
> Still let me guard the heavenly fire,
> And still stir up thy gift in me.[12]

Thus understood, theology is quite an enterprise – risky and adventurous, yet (paradoxically) anchored (Heb 6:19) in a personal God who is both utterly dependable *and* ever on the move. If also undertaken within the commitment of ordained ministry, it carries a yet more daunting responsibility. A searching relationship with the living God through Jesus has to be both modelled and fostered among those with whom the minister has to do. How precisely that responsibility is to be incarnated will depend on particular circumstances. Always it will involve regular excursions to the throne of grace, frequent personal conversations with the living God in and about the business of work, constant 'looking to Jesus' as both pioneer and companion on the journey and the cultivating of a healthy awareness of the 'here we have no abiding city' (Heb 13:14). Always, too, it is to be exercised within the fundamental reality of solemn promises made, promises which carry with them the inescapable requirement to render an account to the Lord of all.

It is as well that the Bishop reminds ordinands at the time of their ordination: 'You cannot bear the weight of this calling in your own strength, but only by the grace and power of God ... Pray earnestly for the gift of the Holy Spirit.'[13]

The ministerial leader who produced Hebrews (though he would not have been happy with the title of 'priest'!) would surely have said a wholehearted 'Amen' to that.

---

[12] Verse from Charles Wesley, *O Thou Who Camest From Above* (see English Hymnal, no.343).

[13] *Common Worship: Ordination Services*, 39.

PART V
Concluding Reflections

Chapter 14

Places of Encounter:
Hanging Out Where God Shows Up

Samuel Wells

A couple of months after I began work at Duke as Dean of the Chapel in 2005, I made my most important purchase. It was the chair I would for the next seven years keep in the far corner of my office. That's the chair towards which I would direct all who came for counsel, direction, supervision, study, or conversation. Of course this was America, and no one was obliged to sit there. Some would take the more spacious sofa or one of the other chairs in the room. But that chair became the focus of my pastoral efforts at Duke, and is the symbol of what I want to describe in this chapter. What I want to do is to envisage a whole institution, in this case Duke, occupying that chair in the corner of my office.

My father was a pastor. Where I had a chair, he had a sofa. In England, the pastor's office is invariably in the pastor's house; this means the members of the pastor's family inevitably become part of the pastor's ministry, for good and ill. From an early age I used to overhear conversations taking place in my father's study – and when I was feeling curious I would bring in a cup of tea. That's how I knew the significance of his sofa. One thing my sister and I loved to do when we were growing up was to dress up. One of my earliest memories is of when I was six years old. I can work out the date because it was during the war between India and Pakistan that led to the formation of an independent Bangladesh out of what had previously been East Pakistan. My sister and I dressed up as Bangladeshi refugees. With a great number of blankets and some headgear recycled from the previous year's nativity play, we assembled ourselves outside the front door and timidly rang the doorbell. When my father answered, we muttered, dolefully, 'Our husbands are in Dhaka' – referring to the capital of Bangladesh.

At that point we realised we had no plans for what to do next. Nevertheless my father played his, completely unanticipated and unrehearsed, part in the drama. He had compassion on us, showed us gently into his study, sat us down on the well-worn sofa, and sat opposite us in a chair, asking us helpful questions, like whether we were cold, or frightened, and how long we expected the war to go on, and would we like to stay with him and his family for a few days. In short, he took us a little more seriously and a little more playfully than we took ourselves. And that, I have come to discover, is one of the secrets of ministry. I had that childhood memory in my thoughts when I made my most important purchase on coming to Duke.

I'm now going to describe my years at Duke through the sequence of events made up by a conventional pastoral conversation. All kinds of people would make appointments to see me. They were in despair about their health, in confusion about their marriage or children or parents, in bewilderment about their present or future employment, ambivalent about their sexuality, in grief about a lost loved one, in pain about a troubling incident or pattern of events from the near or distant past, at their wits' end about their boss or their neighbours, in a crisis of decision about an abortion or the care of an aging relative, or in the wilderness of lost faith or lost love. In almost every case they were looking not just for practical support and counsel, but for a sense of where God was in their story, and where their story was in God. It's that combination, of heart-searching and faith-searching, that I'm calling a conventional pastoral conversation.

Let's begin with the visitor's hand on my office door, about to knock, and my backside on my desk chair, awaiting their arrival. The reason therapists are expected to receive therapy themselves is that the pastoral relationship must be characterised by a great deal of self-awareness. That means perhaps the majority of the work the pastor does in a pastoral encounter is done before the chair in the corner of the room is occupied – indeed, before the visitor enters the room or the appointment is even made. I understand four elements of this self-awareness as it applied to my post at Duke.

Let's start with my desk chair. My desk chair represented the convictions I brought to the encounter and to the whole philosophy of ministry. I am someone who has been deeply formed by growing up in the Church of England. Worship, especially a rhythm of daily prayer and a weekly corporate Eucharist, is the principal way I know who I am. Those people who gather for corporate worship on a Sunday don't do so for themselves alone; they represent the whole population of the neighbourhood in which the church building sits. Just as a spire points an entire building to heaven, so a gathered congregation directs the hearts of all the residents of the neighbourhood to God. That congregation worships on behalf of everyone in the neighbourhood – Christian, other faith, or no explicit faith. The role of the pastor is to blend the diverse energies and idiosyncrasies and commitments and charisms of the gathered community and to make something beautiful out of them – to make the congregation more than the sum of its parts. Meanwhile the pastor also walks the permeable boundary between the gathered community and the wider neighbourhood, and speaks a language that can help each understand, be challenged, and be enriched by the other. The pastor is there for the whole neighbourhood – not just those who identify with the Christian faith. It is these convictions that lead to the gathered community being called a church and the wider neighbourhood being called a parish. And so when I sit down with a visitor in my office or in their living room or wherever it may be, I am assuming in every dialogue – whether the conversation be serious or apparently trivial – that my role is to help the person discern their role in that interaction between neighbourhood and community, that chemistry between Holy Spirit and human heart, that dynamism between divinity made humanity in Christ and humanity not yet made divinity on the last day, that moment of poise and place of encounter called the kingdom of God. And as Dean of the Chapel, I was there for the whole university, not just those who looked to the Chapel as a focus of faith, not just for the students and faculty, but for the office staff and housekeepers. I couldn't know everyone – but I could try to ensure that everyone knew me.

Now let's move to my listening chair – the chair near to the chair in the corner. This second element of self-awareness refers to what I have learned about myself through my own times of discernment, through my own journeys through the interactions in which I try to guide others. Of those discoveries, two seem pertinent to mention here. One is that I spent my childhood and adolescence with a mother who was very sick and who eventually died when I was 18. Terminal illness became my default mode of experiencing reality, and death was my every second thought. I never expected that anything would last forever. I assumed all relationships, institutions, friendships, passions, convictions would in due course pass. In fact I felt most at home with those whose existences were the most fragile – with those who were most obviously aware that their lives, or marriages, or careers, or livelihoods were not likely to be around for long. These are the poor. And thus the second discovery was that I assumed the gospel was about these poor. Jesus seemed to spend most of his time in the gospels talking about them. There were those who had poverty thrust upon them – through exploitation, oppression, cruelty or bad luck. These needed redemption. And there were those who had become poor largely at their own hand – through recklessness or foolishness or hastiness or poor judgment. These needed forgiveness. Jesus obviously knew the difference between the two, but he surrounded himself with both. And he still does. I spent 10 years living and working in socially disadvantaged neighbourhoods in England, and what I learned was that poverty isn't fundamentally about money. It's about not having any relationships, resources, or realities you can trust. I articulated a motto – 'If it can't be happy, make it beautiful'. I assume in every pastoral encounter, that is what I am helping a person see their way to doing.

Next let's consider the air in my office which both I and my visitor breathe. This third element of self-awareness refers to the cultural web of projections that cluster around the pastor and lead the first-time visitor to exclaim, 'I never expected you, or your office, or your sense of humour, or your perspective on alcohol [or whatever it may be] to be anything like this!' Particularly after coming from England to Duke, I had to learn that my demeanour leads many people to assume that I am effortlessly intelligent, unconsciously patronising, irredeemably stuffy, relentlessly censorious, and unswervingly solemn, as well as addicted to damp weather, royalty and afternoon tea. There's no point in fighting such projections. All I can do is try to play with them, incorporate them into self-deprecating humour, and stay around long enough for people to see past them. In every pastoral encounter I try to remind myself that I am doubtless bringing an equally absurd and generalised assortment of projections to bear on my perception of my visitor, and so to refrain from hasty judgment as much as possible.

And let's complete this introductory tour round my office by considering the small table separating my chair from my visitor's chair in the corner. This fourth element of self-awareness refers to the dynamics of power and status and expectation that are going on when my role and story come into interaction with my visitor's needs and energies. Again, these dynamics can't and perhaps shouldn't be dismantled, so I have to find ways to make them useful to a greater purpose. Most people who come to my office have, just a few seconds earlier, experienced a frisson at entering the spectacular architectural structure and revered ecclesial space that is Duke Chapel. Most people know I'm a dean and a professor, and so assume I'm busy, and always thinking beyond them to my next appointment or lecture or sermon. They've usually tried out their concerns with someone else, perhaps many people, before they come to me. I find their anticipation, or nervousness, or projection is usually hugely helpful. It means we don't spend a lot of time with introductory details, and when I ask them to tell me the whole story, they generally do, succinctly and without long digressions. And when I ask them to tell me the story again, this time just including the parts they really want to talk about today, we can go straight to the point pretty quickly. And when I ask them what's the worst thing that can happen, they usually know; and when I ask them what's the best thing that can happen, already, within a half-hour sometimes, they're beginning to talk their way toward their own way forward. Unlike a lot of pastors, who try to reduce the distance between them and their people, by dressing down and having a friendly ambience in their office, I present myself formally and keep my office looking as tidy as I can, because I want all my unspoken messages of dress and posture and setting to say, 'I'm going to bring all my experience and understanding and prayerful attention to this encounter, and if you tell me the truth, and open your life to the Holy Spirit, then something exciting and wonderful really could happen here'.

So what did it mean for a whole institution, in my case Duke University, to be sitting in that chair in the corner of my office? Well, let me take you once again more briefly through the four levels of awareness I described in relation to myself and look at what Duke was 'bringing into the room' in this encounter, and how as a pastor I responded to such things.

The first one, you'll remember, is what Duke thinks it is. Fifty years ago Duke was a provincial university. During my first couple of years I talked with as many people as I could about how in the subsequent 30 years Duke was transformed from a provincial college into a truly national university. The answers came down to two. One the one hand the civil rights movement made the South a less foreign place to the rest of the country. It was not just that African Americans could enrich the institution with their wisdom, talent and grace. It was that a university like Duke ceased to be a place where privileged elites sought to maintain their stranglehold on power, prestige and routes to political influence, but instead became a theatre where a whole new society could be imagined, a laboratory where previously unthought ideas could be tested, a crucible where diverse people, faiths, convictions and identities could be forged into exciting new configurations. On the other hand there was the most important invention in the history of the American South: air conditioning. I love hot weather, but there are one or two days each year in July or August where I wonder if I'm about to burst. Civil rights made it possible for the rest of America to *identify* with a place like Duke. Air conditioning made it possible for the rest of America actually to *live* there. The combination of the two helped to make Duke a truly national university. And right now Duke is at the beginning of a similar transformation. Duke is a truly national university that's beginning to be transformed into a truly global university.

The first thing I did when I became Dean of Duke Chapel was to ask, 'What is this university for?' In other words, how does Duke avoid becoming a sprawling organisation whose primary orientation is to harness resources and produce goods and services that are highly valued, thus increasing its corporate prestige, but meanwhile gradually losing the quality of its mission in the quantity of its operations? A gentler way of asking the question is to say, 'Where is the heart of this university?' There were many candidates to be the answer to that question, because Duke is famous for many things. But I quickly settled on one answer above all others: the undergraduate classroom. Take any other feature of Duke away – its hospital, its athletic teams, its research programme, its architecture, even its chapel – and you still have a lot of operating parts; but take away the undergraduates, whose raison d'être is most succinctly expressed in the professor–student relationship in the classroom, and you've removed the keystone in the Gothic arch.

From this insight I derived a number of conclusions that guided my ministry at Duke. One was that Duke Chapel should not think of itself as the heart of the university. Others could call us that, if they chose, but it should never describe itself in such terms. To do so would suggest it was pining for or even seeking to restore a lost era when Protestant faith went hand in hand with social, economic, political, and cultural dominance, an era when Christian faith became dragooned into and entangled within a social vision that included some and excluded others. That's not what a university should be for, and that's not what the Church is for. There is a place for Christianity on a campus like Duke, but not if it assumes it is the normal, unquestioned, civil religion everyone should subscribe to. So I coined the mission statement, 'Keeping the heart of the university listening to the heart of God'. This started with a note of continuity ('Keeping') that honoured many decades of ministry at the Chapel. It spoke of the 'heart of the university' but left open the question of where that heart lay. It used the term 'listening', to ensure a break from an era when Christianity was about anything but listening, but also to honour the great musical and preaching traditions of the Chapel as ways in which divine wisdom has long been shared and experienced. And it addressed in a non-sectarian way the person of God. In a subtle way this was designed to reiterate Augustine's point in chapter 19 of the *City of God* that without right worship there can be no true justice. That's to say, as a Christian, I believe unless we are listening to God there can be no flourishing of any life or institution. There is an important statement in the use of the term 'listening' that stresses God as the true agent in all our life's endeavours, and ourselves as simply small characters in a narrative whose protagonist has been fully disclosed in Jesus. But the phrase 'listening to the heart' also, in a more popular way, spoke of a co-curricular role for the Chapel in addressing the heart of an institution that could otherwise tend to get a little too focused on its mind.

Another conclusion that arose from identifying the centrality of the undergraduate classroom was the role of student ministry. The Sunday morning worship service at Duke Chapel had a very large congregation. Around 600 attend each Sunday during the breaks, rising to 900 or 1,000 on semester Sundays, with perhaps 1,200 on major Sundays, and maybe 4,000 at Christmas and Easter. And yet on regular semester Sundays there were seldom more than 50 or 100 undergraduates present. One could rejoice in the nearly 20 Christian campus ministries and simply assume students would find their way to something that suits them. But with the rapidly changing and diversifying demographic of students at Duke, that approach would doom the Chapel to becoming in the medium-to-long-term a liturgical museum. I came to realise that the Chapel had to offer a vibrant student ministry of its own – one that made lively connections between faith, intellect, and worship.

And linked to this, I concluded that if the heart of the university lay in the undergraduate classroom, that's where I needed to be. For my last four years I taught a course in the Public Policy school called 'Ethics in an Unjust World', which looked at three models of social engagement. I called the course 'Everything I was cross about when I was 19'. Christianity played a significant but not dominant part in the course. At a university where the Religion department doesn't approve of confessional teaching and the Divinity School is not routinely at liberty to teach undergraduates, this is one of the few chances an undergraduate gets to think seriously about engaging with poverty and addressing major social questions in ways that can challenge and stimulate their faith. I also hired colleagues who were qualified and able to teach undergraduates in similar areas such as religion and politics and interfaith partnerships.

Duke is in a unique geographical and cultural position because it's on the longitude of the Ivy League and on the latitude of the Bible Belt. What that means is that it is an elite research university but that it's in a place where religion is almost always a legitimate part of the conversation. Duke's motto is the Latin phrase *Eruditio et Religio*. It comes from a line of a hymn written by the great eighteenth-century Methodist Charles Wesley, which goes, 'Unite the two so long disjoin'd, Knowledge and vital piety'. What Wesley is talking about is the combination of faith and works, wisdom and service, knowing and doing. My role was to ensure that the Duke motto wasn't harking back to an outmoded notion of a Christian college – it was a perennial and ever-new appeal to faculty, staff and students to make sure what they thought was never just words and ideas, but became actions and relationships, and meanwhile what they did was never just activity, but was always material for reflection and analysis and better living. One way in which I sought to do this was to inaugurate a series known as the Dean's Dialogues, where two or three times a semester I interviewed a leading campus figure, usually the dean of a professional school, and quizzed them about what they were seeking to achieve, what challenges they were facing in their discipline, and how they saw the future of university and society. Another way was to preach sermons each Opening Sunday considering one aspect of the university's life such as medicine or athletics or research or science, and each Founders' Sunday considering the role of faith and intellect and the new shibboleth, service.

When I became Dean of Duke Chapel I was aware of two kinds of expectations. One was that I would be fervently trying to drag Duke back to an earlier era of Protestant cultural dominance. Another was that I would become a self-styled champion of minority causes, much as many chaplains were during the heyday of the sixties. What instead I tried to do was to help Duke become a model of what America in general and its universities in particular might seek to become. That is, a place where it was assumed that everyone needed faith to live each day and what was interesting about meeting a person different in some respect from oneself was not getting cross about what they didn't believe, but becoming intrigued and fascinated by what they did. A place where it was clear how respectfully and generously faith enriched and broadened and deepened the life of the intellect, and where it was equally obvious how the life of the intellect challenged, refined and in the end strengthened faith. The most visible token of this philosophy was to establish a Faith Council, made up of at least one representative of each of the major global faiths, and the appointment of a Muslim (as well a Buddhist and a Hindu) chaplain. There was an unspoken assumption inside and outside the Church that mainline Protestantism was doomed and the job of someone in a role like mine was to hang on to as much as I could for as long as I could. By saying I wanted Duke to be as well known for its interfaith interaction as for its Christian ministry, and that what's interesting and fruitful about the faiths isn't what they have in common but where they differ, I tried to suggest that the tasks and opportunities of the future might be different but just as rewarding as those of the past.

Going back to the chair in the corner of my office, beyond what my visitor is aware of about themselves, the other three kinds of self-awareness refer to more subtle dimensions of consciousness – what they are learning about themselves, what others project onto them, and what dynamics tend to take place when they interact with others – what I earlier called my chair, the air in the office, and the small table. Duke faculty members live with the knowledge that, for all their remarkable research, outstanding teaching, and noted publications, their institution is primarily known locally as a hospital and nationally as a basketball team. The fact that the American healthcare system is riddled with anomalies, injustices, and compromises, and that NCAA sporting culture is swathed in suspicion, hypocrisy and multiple standards, is known to all involved, insider and outsider alike, and frequently pointed out by academics such as the faculty at Duke. But both are the best systems the nation's best efforts have arrived at to supply the need for healthcare and sporting aspiration. And thus they both provide fitting metaphors for the wellbeing of almost every visitor to the chair in my study, every one of whom is, like you and me, a mass of noble ideals, faltering endeavours, half-formed convictions, somewhat-articulated needs, divergent feelings, confused desires, and boundless capacity for self-deception.

So far we've only explored four dimensions of the pastoral encounter – the knock on the door, my chair, the air in the room, and the small table between me and my visitor. I want now to resume my pastoral encounter with Duke University, as this grand institution takes its seat in the chair in the corner of my office, and I sit close by, my chair carefully angled to allow for trust and intimacy without becoming confrontational. I want to take you through the stages of our conversation and illustrate how I went about my work once I had taken stock of what both I and my visitor were bringing into the room and how that room affected the conversation.

For all that I've said about the advantages of formality, most conversations begin with small-talk. I therefore need to be able to put people at their ease. Pastors invariably make people feel guilty, and judged, and foolish; thus everything I say in the first few moments of a pastoral encounter is designed to alleviate these anxieties, each of which seems in the North Carolina imagination to be exacerbated manifold by the presence of an educated Englishman. And so I'm looking to offer a simple compliment, to avoid passing an unsolicited negative opinion on anything, even the weather, and gently to divert attention from similarities or difference in status to the precious gift of this time now together. And that's exactly what I tried to do when I first took up my post. I won't deny that I easily tired of jokes about the UNC and Duke basketball rivalry, or a thousand other staples of daily conversation, but the point is to build the relationship and earn trust and the only way to do that is to communicate the words, 'I care about what you care about', as subtly and swiftly as possible. Needless to say, my visitor may be much better served by some more specialised help than I can give, and if that's the case it usually becomes obvious in these first few general remarks.

But when they're done, I want to go straight to the moment of truth. And I tend to be very direct. I'll say, 'So, tell me all', or maybe, 'When does the story begin?' or, if I'm less sure why the person has come, something like, 'How would you like to use the time?' Almost always the visitor will hesitate, and say, 'Oh, I don't know about *all*', or some such step backwards. But then, as gently as I can, I try to reassure them that 'all' is fine, which is really a way of encouraging them to make the most of this opportunity to put into words their deepest anxieties and fears and hurts and regrets. And that's exactly what I tried to do when I went to Duke. Every time I've moved to a new post there's always been a crisis or event very early in my ministry that's made me wish I'd been there longer so that I'd know what to do or say. In each case, the relationships formed have been more important than what I did or said. Sure enough, at Duke in August 2005, three weeks after I first sat down in my office chair, it was Hurricane Katrina. Preaching about the event on Opening Sunday I challenged the congregation to identify what this crisis had told them about nature, about America, about God, and about themselves. It was a bit like saying, 'Tell me all'. A few weeks later in my installation sermon I had a chance to reiterate the invitation, asking the congregation to locate their story in the story of Duke, the story of the south, the story of the American university and the story of God.

Once the visitor has begun to articulate their story, their feelings, and their gropings toward perception and insight, my pastoral role is then to be with them as they find words and weave together silences. They need to know that they're not alone, that the painful things they say make me wince, that the terrible things they've done sadden but don't shock me, that the awful things they've suffered grieve me, and that the unresolved situation they're in doesn't make me rush in with a solution to fix it or a rapid remedy to settle it or a joke or a story to distract from or belittle it.

I noted earlier that my own biography is not one of greatness building upon dizzying greatness. My personal story is one of terminal illness. It's one of death, and fragility, and doubting all relationships and institutions. And I don't think it's betraying too many confidences to let you know that a very great number of those who've sat in the chair in the corner of my office tell me that their story isn't the Duke story of greatness building upon dizzying greatness. Everyone is obsessed with GPAs, or tenure, or whatever the symbol of success might be, but, inside, this person in the chair knows failure, and has profound fears, and wonders if they can keep up the pretence and play the public game anymore. And yet more than a little bit of this person craves and yearns for this culture of competition and striving and envy and accumulating they've known all their life, otherwise they wouldn't be here; because these are the energies that make the university swing. And that is my role at the university: to reflect back its glories and its absurdities, gently to bring its self-importance face to face with its private doubts and complex despairs, and generally to eye with scepticism its efforts to make itself immortal, while offering compassion on the occasions when it confronts its own mortality.

In the pastoral encounter the shortage of time is a blessing because it focuses the mind. I say 'Tell me all', but we both know we only have time for the highlights. And the blessing of this is that it reduces the impulse to crowd in more and more detail. The metaphor of resumé-building dominates so much of university existence. I once read 37 pages into a faculty applicant's CV, and, after the endless publications, and embedded amid a list of distinguished presentations given, I saw the words, 'Does anyone read this far?' At the start of my first undergraduate class of the semester I would ask the students, who had ever been on a mission trip or similar extended service opportunity. Every hand would go up, and venues from Ulan Bator to Tierra del Fuego would be mentioned. It turned out the students' lives had been end-to-end service trips, and every one of their high schools was nationally famous for them. Then I would ask, 'And how many of you have written a 12- or 20-page paper reflecting on the experience?' No hands. We anxiously accumulate more and more experience, but are slower to take time to turn this experience into wisdom. That's the time I seek to give my office visitor. That's part of my role: to seek to inject that time into the life of the university – the time for letting experience percolate into wisdom.

When my visitor reached the end of their story, I would try to demonstrate and check that I'd heard and understood by inviting my visitor to explore further and explain more fully. Like an osteopath or a chiropractor passing a gentle hand over a patient's back, I'd be stroking in one place and pushing in another, trying to find the tender area and see which movements made it worse and better. I would say, 'I wonder which was your lowest moment in this whole saga', or, 'I wonder what it's like to realise you don't come from a happy family', or, 'Do you still dream about what happened?' What I'd be trying to do was to give permission to say the scariest, most embarrassing, shameful, or bitterly painful thing and then show that it's possible to live beyond it, outside it, around it, and then begin to face it down together and make a story that was not poisoned or dominated by it. I was still relatively new to the campus when the lacrosse crisis[1] arose in March 2006, but this was the role I thought it best to adopt. I shelved my prepared sermon and addressed a particularly large congregation without a script from the chancel steps, seeking to set a tone of vulnerability and shared ambiguity. I tried my best to articulate why this crisis was so troubling and how it could be a way of putting us in touch with the deepest values of the university. But what I was really trying to do was to dwell in the tender areas until the fear was faced. That's one of the most important roles I had at the university: to be a person who was not afraid to name what was really going on, and yet was able to do so without bitterness or rancour. Perhaps the most visible times this role was called upon was at moments of personal grief, such as the death and funeral of a student, or of public pain, such as the Virginia Tech shootings. These were

---

[1]   See http://today.duke.edu/showcase/lacrosseincident/ (accessed 19 August 2015).

extraordinary opportunities to dwell in places of heightened sensitivity and awareness, and model every element in the process I am describing.

Then comes the crucial moment in the pastoral conversation with my visitor. I say 'Is that the whole story?' Of course it never is. I stay silent for a while, to indicate it's ok to say more. That silence is the crucial moment in the whole conversation. It's a moment of hovering, a stretching out of the hands and dwelling over the sensitive place – a moment that reminds me of the way, during a Eucharist, pastors hold out their arms over the bread and wine when asking the Holy Spirit to infuse these earthly elements with heavenly grace. It's an invitation to my visitor to go deeper, to go way down to the bottom of the pond if that's where the mystery lies and the pain resides. It's a promise that I'll be here as they go way down there. That's the gift every pastor needs more than almost anything else. That's what their people will remember – not the fine sermon or the marvellous fundraising programme, but whether they were willing and able to stare down to the bottom of that pond. And how can one demonstrate that on a campus? Only by being present in the unfashionable places at the unrewarded events and being willing to name and ask the uncomfortable things in ways that seek not exposure and humiliation but learning and understanding. Only by avoiding superficiality and false bonhomie and at every opportunity, allowing others to say it's awful if it really is. You can't do this overnight. But when it's something people deeply want and have maybe never had before, they'll tell you.

And this is the point, the point where my visitor has named the elusive, incorrigible thing, where I take a risk. I listen to my gut, and I say what comes. All the time I'm gauging permission from my visitor and only saying what I sense they may be ready to hear. I'm usually doing one of two things (which I outline at length in my book *Improvisation: The Drama of Christian Ethics* (Grand Rapids: Brazos 2004)). One is to try to tell the person's story back to them in a way that highlights the way these negative moments and incidents may resurface in their present or future in a form that might be somehow redemptive, or at least might not be wholly worthless and lost. That's what I call reincorporation: when previously discarded elements reappear later in a story in ways that enable the story to continue. The other thing I'm usually doing is called overaccepting. That means placing the person's own story within a much larger story, in relation to which the events of their story take on significantly different proportions and resonances. Rather than trying to suppress the sadness and disappointment, or simply resigning themselves to it, overaccepting encourages my visitor to see their portrait on a much larger canvas in which it can have much richer poignancy. The story may still be sad and painful, but reincorporation addresses the fear that all might be lost, while overaccepting addresses the additional fear that none of it really mattered. These were the signal tasks I would take on when I preached sermons on major university occasions like Baccalaureate or led prayers on days like Convocation or MLK. I was trying to re-present the university and the society's past, including its less savoury flavours, and render it not a burden or a lie but a blessing and a gift. These were occasions when I had an opportunity to preach the gospel, even if it sometimes seemed inappropriate to use the word 'Jesus'. And this is how I understand salvation: Jesus takes our past, gives it back to us as a gift, and fits our tawdry story into his wondrous glory. Reincorporation and overaccepting – or, if you prefer, forgiveness and eternal life. That's the gospel.

The next moment in the pastoral visitation is to seek to ensure the conversation ends on an empowering note, by inviting the visitor to craft some kind of plan of action based around this new insight that has emerged through the dialogue. This isn't primarily to suggest there's a simple step to make anything better. It's more about as a pastor ensuring the initiative lies with the visitor, and they depart full of insight or resolve of their own, rather than dependent on whatever contribution I have made. On a campus level I sought to play this role by sitting on and chairing various university committees, where the wellbeing of the university in its various dimensions could be discussed, representations made, recommendations offered, and policy ideas implemented. I was glad not to have an executive role in the running of the university as a whole: this would have made the rest of my work much more difficult.

The penultimate activity in the visit might be the one most associated with the role of pastor. I usually end a conversation with a person who has shown at least some inclination toward the Christian faith by offering to say a prayer. It may sound surprising, but I was slow to realise that modelling how to pray and relate to God by the way I led public prayers was one of the most important things I had the opportunity to do. In the prayer I was seeking to reiterate the key elements of our conversation – the naming of the tender areas, the uttering of the unspeakable words, the hints of reincorporation and the possibility of overaccepting. I've left this point till the very end – but a chaplain without the witness of a lively and faithful Chapel, let alone a host of energetic and engaging campus ministries, is like a pastoral visit without a prayer. Christianity is fundamentally not an idea, nor an ethic: it's more than anything a way of life made possible by the forgiveness and eternal life established by Jesus and shared by the Holy Spirit. I don't know how I could have done my job without constantly being able to point to a congregation and a body of students and colleagues whose lives showed what God could do. By inviting either an individual, or the whole gathered university community, to pray, I was ushering them into the company of worship, the angels and saints around the throne of grace, the constant enjoyment and glorifying of God, and encouraging them to dwell, bask, and remain there. The gospel is toothless if there is no one you can point to who is living it.

And finally, every pastor knows the 'door-handle moment'. I've learned not to put too much furniture near the door to my office, because a great many people will say the most important thing of all just as they are about to run away from the consequences of having said it, and others will only discover why they came in the process of finding words to say thank you and goodbye. And so I need to be prepared to stand by the door for long enough to establish whether this parting shot is truly a part of the conversation or not. And what that meant for my ministry to the campus was to try to appear to be someone who was not in a hurry, who was not looking beyond each person I talked to for the more influential or attractive person behind them, who was able to enjoy the present tense and not see it as a trial run or a stepping stone or a resumé enhancement for what the future might hold.

And so this, in summary, is how I saw my ministry at Duke. It was to dwell in places of encounter. It was to know myself and my people well enough that I had a reasonable understanding of the dynamic between us. It was to show people that I cared about what they cared about. It was to hover over the place of fear and tenderness long enough to know that pain and anxiety would not have the last word. It was to be comfortable with silence, and to listen to people's stories not just once, but a second time, when they'd identified the parts that really mattered. It was to sit with them as they stared all the way to the bottom of the pond, tender and mysterious as the sight might be. It was to speak a word of truth, perhaps a word of hope, that reconfigured what had seemed to be unalterable givens, such that they may become gifts. It was to tell a larger story in which all our stories find their true context. It was to empower, and encourage, and watch people find their own futures. It's to pray, and open out a world of worship and glory to each person I met. And it was not to rush, but to be still present even if the truth only emerged after the conversation was supposed to be over. Most of all, it was to do all of these to a whole community, a whole neighbourhood, on high days and ordinary days, in sunshine, cloud, and rain. That's ministry. That's who I am and what I do.

Bibliography

Except where otherwise stated, all quotations from biblical sources are taken from: *The New Revised Standard Version*. Oxford: Oxford University Press, 1989.

An Integrating Theology. London: ACCM, Occasional Paper No.15, 1983.

Anglican Church of Australia. *A Prayer Book for Australia*. Alexandria, NSW: Broughton Books, 1995.

Aquinas, Thomas. *Summa Theologica*, 3 vols. London: Burns & Oates, 1947.

Archbishops' Council Working Party. *The Hind Report*. London: Church House Publishing, 2003.

Aristotle. *Nicomachean Ethics*. Translated by H. Rackham. Vol. 19 of *Aristotle*, eds T.E. Page, E. Capps, W.H.D. Rouse, L.A. Post and E.H. Warmington. 23 vols. Loeb Classical Library. London: Heinemann, 1926–1970, 1982.

———. 'On the Soul'. In *On the Soul. Parva Naturalia. On Breath*. Translated by W.S. Hett. Vol 8 of *Aristotle*, eds T.E. Page, E. Capps, W.H.D. Rouse, L.A. Post and E.H. Warmington. 23 vols. Loeb Classical Library. London: Heinemann, 1926–1970, 1957.

———. *Politics*. Translated by H. Rackham. Vol. 21 of *Aristotle*, eds T.E. Page, E. Capps, W.H.D. Rouse, L.A. Post and E.H. Warmington. 23 vols. Loeb Classical Library. London: Heinemann, 1926–1970, 1967.

Assmann, J. *Kultur und Gedächtnis*. Frankfurt / Main: Suhrkamp, 1988.

———. 'Collective Memory and Cultural Identity'. *New German Critique*, No. 65. Spring-Summer (1995): 125–133.

Augustine. *St. Augustin's City of God and Christian Doctrine*. Vol. 2 of *The Nicene And Post-Nicene Fathers, First Series*, eds Philip Schaff and Henry Wace. 14 vols. Edinburgh: T&T Clark, 1886–1890, 1887.

———. *The Trinity*. Translated by Edmund Hill, O.P. New York: New City Press, 1991.

———. *The City of God against the Pagans*, ed. R.W. Dyson. New York: Cambridge University Press, 1998.

Austen, Jane. *Emma*, ed. Ronald Blythe. London: Penguin, 1966.

———. *Mansfield Park*, ed. Tony Tanner. London: Penguin, 1966.

————. *Pride and Prejudice*, ed. Vivien Jones. London: Penguin, 1969.

————. *Sense and Sensibility*, ed. Tony Tanner. London: Penguin, 1969.

Barth, Karl. *Church Dogmatics: The Doctrine of Reconciliation*, Vol. 4, part 1. Translated by G. Bromley and T.F. Torrance. Edinburgh: T&T Clark, 1956.

Barton, Stephen C. 'New Testament Interpretation as Performance'. *Scottish Journal of Theology*, 52/2 (1999): 179–208.

Bauckham, Richard. 'The Divinity of Jesus Christ in the Epistle to the Hebrews'. In *The Epistle to the Hebrews and Christian Theology*, eds R. Bauckham, D.R. Driver, T.A. Hart and N. MacDonald. Grand Rapids: Eerdmans, 2009.

Behm, Johannes. '*dianoia*'. In *The Theological Dictionary of the New Testament*, ed. Gerhard Kittel. 10 vols. Grand Rapids: Eerdmans, 1964, Vol. 2, 963–7.

Bennett, Zoë, and Christopher Rowland. 'Contextual and Advocacy Readings of the Bible', in *The Bible in Pastoral Practice*, eds Paul Ballard and Stephen R. Holmes. Grand Rapids: Eerdmans, 2005, 174–90.

Bloch, M. *The Historian's Craft*. Manchester: Manchester University Press, 1992.

Brown, Raymond E., S.S. *The Birth of the Messiah*. London: Geoffrey Chapman, 1977.

Brown, V.A., J.A. Harris and J.Y. Russell (eds). *Tackling Wicked Problems Through the Transdisciplinary Imagination*. London and Washington DC: Earthscan, 2010.

Brueggemann, W. *Theology of the Old Testament: Testimony, Dispute, Advocacy*. Minneapolis: Augsburg Fortress, 1997.

Bullock, F.W.B. *A History of Training for the Ministry of the Church of England, 1800–1874*. London: Home Words, 1955.

————. *A History of Training for the Ministry of the Church of England, 1875–1974*. London: Home Words, 1976.

Burkert, Walter. *Homo Necans: The Anthropology of Ancient Greek Sacrificial Ritual and Myth*. Berkeley: University of California Press, 1983, 119.

Catchpole, David. *Resurrection People*. London: Darton, Longman and Todd, 2000.

Chadwick, O. *The Founding of Cuddesdon College*. Oxford: Oxford University Press, 1954.

Chapman, Mark D. *Theology and Society in Three Cities: Berlin, Oxford and Chicago, 1800–1914*. Cambridge: James Clarke, 2014.

Charry, Ellen T. *By the Renewing of Your Minds. The Pastoral Function of Christian Doctrine*. New York: Oxford University Press, 1997.

Church of England. *The Book of Common Prayer*. Cambridge: Cambridge University Press, 1662, 2003.

———. *Common Worship: Ordination Services*. London: Church House Publishing, 2007.

Cicero, Marcus Tullius. *On Duties*. Translated by Walter Miller. Vol. 21 of *Cicero*, eds T.E. Page, E. Capps and W.H.D. Rouse. 30 vols. Loeb Classical Library. London: Heinemann, 1913–2002, 1913.

Congar, Yves. *True and False Reform in the Church*. Paris: Editions du Cerf, 1950.

Conti, Charles. *Metaphysical Personalism: an Analysis of Austin Farrer's Metaphysics of Theism*. Oxford: Clarendon Press, 1995.

Curtis, Philip. *A Hawk Among Sparrows: A Biography of Austin Farrer*. London: SPCK, 1985.

Danker, F.W. *A Greek-English Lexicon of the New Testament and other Early Christian Literature*. Chicago: Chicago University Press, 2000.

Davies, Philip. *Whose Bible is it Anyway?* 2nd edition. London: T&T Clark, 2004.

Davis, Ellen F. *Wondrous Depths. Preaching the Old Testament*. Westminster: John Knox Press, 2005.

Dickinson, Emily. 'Truth'. In *The Single Hound*. 1914, reprint. New York: Dodo Press, 2008.

Dix, Gregory. *The Shape of the Liturgy*. London: Dacre Press, 1945, 1975.

Dougherty, Carol, and Leslie Kurke (eds). *The Cultures within Ancient Greek Culture*. Cambridge: Cambridge University Press, 2003, 80–81.

Douglas, Mary. *Purity and Danger*. London: Routledge, 1966.

Dulles, Avery Cardinal. 'Tradition as a Theological Source', in *The Craft of Theology*. Dublin: Gill and Macmillan, 1992, 87–104.

Dunbabin, Jean. 'Careers and Vocations', in *The History of the University of Oxford*, vol. 1, *The Early Oxford Schools*, ed. J.I. Catto. Oxford: Oxford University Press, 1984, 565–605.

Dunn, J.D.G. 'Criteria for a Wise Reading of a Biblical Text', in *Reading Texts, Seeking Wisdom*, eds David F. Ford and Graham N. Stanton. London: SCM, 2003, 38–52.

Eaton, Jeffrey, and Ann Loades. 'Austin Marsden Farrer', in *For God and Clarity: New Essays in Honour of Austin Farrer*, eds Jeffrey Eaton and Ann Loades. Allison Park, PA: Pickwick, 1983, xi-xiii.

Education for the Church's Ministry. London: ACCM, Occasional Paper No.22, London, 1987.

Ellingworth, P. *The Epistle to the Hebrews*, New International Greek Testament Commentary. Grand Rapids: Eerdmans, 1993.

Epictetus. *Discourses*. Translated by W.A. Oldfather. Vol. 1 of *Epictetus*, ed. G.P. Goold. 2 vols. Loeb Classical Library. London: Heinemann, 1925–1928, 1925.

Episcopal Church, The. *The Book of Common Prayer*. New York: Seabury Press, 1979.

Eusebius. *Eusebius: Church History, Life of Constantine the Great, and Oration in Praise of Constantine*. Vol. 1 of *The Nicene and Post-Nicene Fathers, 2nd Series*, eds Philip Schaff and Henry Wace. 14 vols. Edinburgh: T.&T. Clark, 1890–1900, 1890.

Experience and Authority. London: ACCM Occasional Paper No.19, London, 1984.

Farley, Edward. *Theologia. The Fragmentation and Unity of Theological Education*. Philadelphia: Fortress, 1983.

———. *The Fragility of Knowledge: Theological Education in the Church and the University*. Philadelphia: Fortress, 1988.

Farrer, Austin. *Finite and Infinite: A Philosophical Essay*. Westminster: Dacre Press, 1943.

———. *The Glass of Vision. The Bampton Lectures for 1948*. Glasgow, the University Press, 1948.

———. *Faith and Speculation: an Essay in Philosophical Theology*. London: Adam & Charles Black, 1964.

Feiling, Keith. 'Transformation of England, 1066–1154', in *A History of England: From the Coming of the English to 1918*. London: MacMillan & Co., Ltd, 1950, 107.

Fitzgerald, Allan, and John C. Cavadini. *Augustine through the Ages: An Encyclopedia*. Grand Rapids: Eerdmans, 1999.

Ford, David F. *Christian Wisdom. Desiring God and Learning in Love*. Cambridge: Cambridge University Press, 2007.

———. *The Future of Christian Theology*. Oxford: Wiley-Blackwell, 2011.

Fowl, Stephen E. *Engaging Scripture*. Oxford: Blackwell, 1998.

Gadamer, Hans-Georg. 'Rhetoric, Hermeneutics and the Critique of Ideology', in *The Hermeneutics Reader*, ed. Kurt Mueller-Vollmer. Oxford: Blackwell, 1986, 274–92.

Gerhardsson, Birger. *Memory and Manuscript*. Lund: C.W.K. Gleerup, 1961.

Gill, Eric. 'Art and Prudence', in *Beauty Looks after Herself*, ed. Catherine Pickstock. Tacoma WA: Angelico Press, 2012, 11–29.

Gittoes, J. *Anamnesis and the Eucharist*. Aldershot: Ashgate, 2008.

Giussani, Luigi. *The Risk of Education: Discovering our Ultimate Destiny*. Translated by Rosanna M. Giammanco Frongia. New York: Crossroad, 1996.

———. *The Religious Sense*. Translated by John Zucchi. Montreal: McGill-Queens University Press, 1997.

Greenwood, Hilary, SSM. 'Knotty Nineties'. Unpublished poem, 1969.

Gunton, Colin. 'The Indispensibility of Theological Understanding: Theology in the University', in *Essentials of Christian Community, Essays for Daniel W. Hardy*, eds David F. Ford and Dennis L. Stamps. Edinburgh: T & T Clark, 1996, 266–77.

Habermas, Jürgen. 'On Hermeneutics' Claim to Universality', in *The Hermeneutics Reader*, ed. Kurt Mueller-Vollmer. Oxford: Blackwell, 1986, 294–319.

Hackett, M.B. 'The University as a Corporate Body', in *The History of the University of Oxford*, Vol. 1, *The Early Oxford Schools*, ed. J.I. Catto. Oxford: Oxford University Press, 1984, 37–95.

Haig, Alan. *The Victorian Clergy*. London: Croom Helm, 1984.

Halbwachs, Maurice. *On Collective Memory*. Chicago: University of Chicago Press, 1992.

Hardy, Daniel W., and David Ford. *Jubilate: Theology in Praise*. London: Darton, Longman and Todd, 1984.

Hardy, Daniel W., with Deborah Hardy Ford, Peter Ochs and David F. Ford. *Wording a Radiance: Parting Conversations on God and the Church*. London: SCM Press, 2010.

Harries, Richard (ed.). *The One Genius: Readings Through the Year with Austin Farrer*. London: SPCK, 1987.

———. 'We Know on our Knees … ': Intellectual, imaginative and spiritual unity in the theology of Austin Farrer', in *Divine Action: Studies Inspired by the Philosophical Theology of Austin Farrer*, eds Brian Hebblethwaite and Edward Henderson. Edinburgh: T & T Clark, 1990, 21–33.

Harrison, Carol. *Augustine: Christian Truth and Fractured Humanity*. Oxford: Oxford University Press, 2000.

———. *The Art of Listening in the Early Church*. Oxford: Oxford University Press, 2013, 147.

Haskins, Minnie L. 'God Knows', in *The Desert*. London: Hodder, 1908.

Hauerwas, Stanley. *Unleashing Scripture. Freeing the Bible from Captivity to America*. Nashville: Abingdon, 1993.

———. 'Remembering as a Moral Task', in *The Hauerwas Reader*. Durham: Duke University Press, 2003.

Hein, David, and Edward Hugh Henderson (eds). *Captured by the Crucified: The Practical Theology of Austin Farrer*. London: T&T Clark, 2004.

Henderson, Stewart. 'Priestly Duties', in *Limited Edition*. Stratford-upon-Avon, Plover Books, 1997.

Herbert, George. *A Priest to the Temple*. Norwich: Canterbury Press, 2003.

Hodgson, Leonard. *The Bible and the Training of the Clergy*. London: Darton, Longman and Todd, 1963.

Holmes, Urban. *The Future Shape of Ministry*. New York, Seabury, 1977.

Hooker, Richard. *The Works of Richard Hooker*, Vol. 2. Oxford: OUP, 1841.

Hope, David. 'Prayer and the Scriptures', in *Bishops on the Bible*, eds John V. Taylor et al., London: Triangle/SPCK, 1993, 75–6.

Hort, F.J.A. *The Way, The Truth, The Life: the Hulsean Lectures for 1871*. 2nd edition. London: Macmillan, 1897.

Houlden, Leslie. 'Editor's Preface', in *Austin Farrer, A Celebration of Faith*, ed. Leslie Houlden. London: Hodder and Stoughton, 1970, 9.

Hull, John M. *What Prevents Christian Adults from Learning?* London: SCM, 1985.

Inter-Anglican Standing Commission on Mission and Evangelism. *Communion in Mission & Travelling Together in God's Mission*. Report of IASCOME 2001–2005, 2006. Web version, 2010. Accessed 22 October, 2012. http://www.anglicancommunion.org/media/108022/IASCOME-Communion-In-Mission-Main-Documents.pdf?tag=IASCOME

Jacob, William. 'The Development of the "Concept of Residence" in Theological Education in the Church of England', in *Residence – An Education*. London: Advisory Council for the Church's Ministry. ACCM, 1990, 68–91.

———. 'An Integrating Theology in Theological Education', in *The Weight of Glory*, eds D.W. Hardy and P.H. Sedgwick. Edinburgh: T & T Clark, 1991, 185–94.

Jaeger, Werner. *Paideia: The Ideals of Greek Culture*. Oxford: Blackwell, 1939.

———. *Early Christianity and Greek Paideia*. London: Oxford University Press, 1961.

Jeanrond, Werner. *Theological Hermeneutics*. London: Macmillan, 1991.

Johnson, L.T. *Hebrews, A Commentary*. London: Westminster John Knox Press, 2006.

Johnston, J.O. *Life and Letters of Henry Parry Liddon*. London: Longmans, 1904.

Joslyn-Siemiatkoski, D. *Christian Memories of the Maccabean Martyrs*. New York: Palgrave Macmillan, 2009.

Julian of Norwich. *Revelations of Divine Love*. Translated by Elizabeth Spearing. London: Penguin Classics, 1998.

Kelsey, David H. *To Understand God Truly. What's Theological about a Theological School?* Louisville: Westminster/John Knox, 1992.

Ker, Ian. *John Henry Newman: A Biography*. Oxford: Oxford University Press, 1988, 2009.

Kirk, Alan, and Tom Thatcher. 'Jesus Tradition as Social Memory', in *Memory, Text and Tradition: Uses of the Past in Early Christianity*. Leiden: Brill, 2005, 25–42.

———— (eds). *Memory, Tradition and Text: Uses of the Past in Early Christianity*. Leiden: Brill, 2005.

Lakey, Michael J. *Image and Glory of God*. Library of New Testament studies. London: T & T Clark, 2010.

————. 'Body', in *Dictionary of the Bible and Western Culture*, eds Mary Ann Beavis and Michael J. Gilmour. Sheffield: Sheffield Phoenix Press, 2012, 64–65.

Lash, Nicholas. 'Criticism or Construction? The Task of the Theologian', in *Theology on the Way to Emmaus*. London: SCM, 1986, 3–17.

————. 'Performing the Scriptures', in *Theology on the Way to Emmaus*. SCM: London, 1986, 37–46.

Lathrop, Gordon W. *Holy Things. A Liturgical Theology*. Minneapolis: Augsburg Fortress, 1993, 43–53.

Laurentin, Réné. *Maria, Ecclesia, Sacerdotium*. Paris: Nouvelles Éditions Latines, 1952.

Liddon, Henry. 'The Moral Groundwork of Clerical Training', in *Clerical Life and Work. A Collection of Sermons*. 2nd edition. London: Longmans, 1895, 73–92.

————. 'The Work and Prospects of Theological Colleges', in *Clerical Life and Work. A Collection of Sermons*. 2nd edition. London: Longmans, 1895, 46–72.

Lincoln, Andrew T. *Born of a Virgin?* London: SPCK, 2013.

Lindbeck, George. *The Nature of Doctrine: Religion and Theology in a Postliberal Age*. Philadelphia: Westminster Press, 1984.

Livy. *History of Rome*. Translated by B.O. Foster. Vol. 1 of *Livy*, eds T.E. Page, E. Capps and W.H.D. Rouse. 14 vols. Loeb Classical Library. London: Heinemann, 1919–1959, 1919.

Louth, Andrew. *Discerning the Mystery*. Oxford: Clarendon Press, 1983.

Lyons, Nan, and Ivan Lyons. *Someone is Killing the Great Chefs of Europe*. London: Jonathan Cape, 1976.

————. *Someone is Killing the Great Chefs of America*. New York: Random House, 1995.

McCabe, Herbert. *The New Creation*. London: Contiuum, 2010.

McConville, G., and J.G. Millar. *Time and Place in Deuteronomy*. Sheffield: Sheffield Academic Press, 1994.

MacCulloch, Diarmaid. *A History of Christianity*. London: Allen Lane, 2009.

MacIntyre, Alasdair. *After Virtue*, 2nd edition. London: Gerald Duckworth & Co., 1985.

MacMurray, John. *Persons in Relation*. London, Faber & Faber, 1961.

Malherbe, Abraham J. *Paul and the Popular Philosophers*. Minneapolis: Fortress Press, 1989.

Melina, Livio. *Sharing in Christ's Virtues: For a Renewal of Moral Theology in Light of Veritatis Splendor*. Translated by William May. Washington DC: Catholic University Press of America, 2001.

Merton, Thomas. *Bread in the Wilderness*. London: Burns & Oates, 1976.

Meynell, Alice. 'In Portugal 1912', in *Oxford Book of Mystical Verse*, eds D.H.S. Nicholson and A.H. Lee. Oxford: Oxford University Press, 1917.

Migliore, Daniel. *Faith Seeking Understanding*. Grand Rapids: Eerdmans, 1991.

Misztal, Barbara. *Theories of Social Remembering*. Maidenhead: Open University Press, 2003.

Mitchell, Basil. 'Austin Marsden Farrer', in *Austin Farrer, A Celebration of Faith*, ed. Leslie Houlden. London: Hodder and Stoughton, 1970, 13–16.

Mitchell, Margaret. *Paul and the Rhetoric of Reconciliation*. Louisville: Westminster John Knox Press, 1991.

Molesworth, Mike, Elizabeth Nixon, and Richard Scullion (eds). *The Marketisation of Higher Education and the Student as Consumer*. London: Routledge, 2011.

Morrill, B. *Anamnesis as Dangerous Memory: Political and Liturgical Theology in Dialogue*. Congeville: Liturgical Press, 2000.

Mueller-Vollmer, Kurt (ed.). *The Hermeneutics Reader*. Oxford: Blackwell, 1986.

Newman, John Henry. *The Via Media of the Anglican Church*, 2 vols. Vol. 1, *Lectures on the Prophetical Office of the Church Viewed Relatively to Romanism and Popular Protestantism*. 3rd edition. London: Basil Montagu Pickering, 1877.

———. *The Idea of a University*. London: Longmans, Green & Co., 1907.

———. *The Arians of the Fourth Century* with an introduction and notes by Rowan Williams. Gracewing, 2001.

Niebuhr, H. Richard. *Christ and Culture*. London: Faber and Faber, 1952.

———. *The Purpose of the Church and its Ministry*. New York: Harper Bros, 1956.

———. *The Kingdom of God in America*. New York: Harper and Row, 1959.

O'Donovan, Oliver. *The Problem of Self-Love in St. Augustine*. New Haven: Yale University Press, 1980.

'Of Polycarp', in *Acts of the Christian Martyrs*, Vol. 2, ed. H. Musurillo. Oxford: Clarendon Press, 1972, 2–21.

Paddison, Angus. *Scripture: A Very Theological Proposal*. London: T&T Clark International, 2009.

Peterson, Eugene. *Under the Unpredictable Plant*. Grand Rapids: Eerdmans, 1994.

Pickard, Stephen. 'The Travail of the Episcopate: Management and the Diocese in an Age of Mission', in *Wonderfully and Confessedly Strange: Australian Essays in Anglican Ecclesiology*, eds B. Kaye, S. Macneil and H. Thomson. Adelaide, ATF Press, 2006, 127–55.

———. *Seeking the Church*. London: SCM, 2012, 183–4.

Pieper, Josef. *Leisure, the basis of culture*. Translated by Alexander Dru. New York: Pantheon Books, 1952.

Ramsey, A. Michael. *The Gospel and the Catholic Church*. London: Longmans, Green and Co., 1937.

Reagan, Charles E., and David Stewart (eds). *The Philosophy of Paul Ricoeur*. Boston: Beacon Press, 1978.

Ricoeur, Paul. *Oneself as Another*. Translated by Kathleen Blamey. Chicago: University of Chicago Press, 1992.

Rodriguez, R. *Structuring Early Christian Memory: Jesus in Tradition, Performance and Text*. London: T & T Clark, 2010.

Rogerson, John. 'The Gift and Challenges of Historical and Literary Criticism', in *The Bible in Pastoral Practice*, eds Paul Ballard and Stephen R. Holmes. Grand Rapids: Eerdmans, 2005, 121–34.

Russell, Anthony. *The Clerical Profession*. London, SPCK, 1980.

Sanders, E.P. 'Paul Between Judaism and Hellenism', in *St. Paul Among the Philosophers*, eds John D. Caputo and Linda Alcoff. Bloomington, Ind.: Indiana University Press, 2009, 74–90.

Sayles, G.O. 'Religious and Intellectual Revival', in *The Medieval Foundations of England*. London: Methuen & Co, Ltd., 377.

Schleiermacher, Friedrich. *Brief Outline on the Study of Theology*. Translated by Terence Tice. Richmond: John Knox, 1966.

Schwartz, B. *Abraham Lincoln and the Forge of National Memory*. Chicago: University of Chicago Press, 2000.

Seneca. *Epistles*. Translated by Richard M. Gummere. Vol. 4 of Seneca, eds T.E. Page, E. Capps and W.H.D. Rouse. 10 vols. Loeb Classical Library. London: Heinemann, 1917–2004, 1917.

Southern, R.W. 'From Schools to University', in *The History of the University of Oxford*, Vol. 1, *The Early Oxford Schools*, ed. J.I. Catto. Oxford: Oxford University Press, 1984, 1–36.

Stuckenbruck, L., S. Barton and B. Wold (eds). *Memory in the Bible and Antiquity*. Tübingen: Mohr Siebeck, 2007.

Tate, W. Randolph. *Biblical Interpretation. An Integrated Approach*. Peabody: Hendrickson, 1991.

Taylor, Charles. *A Secular Age*. Cambridge Mass: Harvard University Press, 2007.

Taylor, John V. 'Divine Revelation through Human Experience', in *Bishops on the Bible*, eds John V. Taylor et al. London: Triangle/SPCK, 1993, 2–3.

Terdiman, Richard. 'Memory in Freud', in *Memory: Histories, Theories, Debates*, eds Susannah Radstone and Bill Schwarz. New York: Fordham University Press, 2010, 93–108.

Tetley, J. *Encounter with God in Hebrews*. London: Scripture Union, 1995.

———. 'For God's Sake', in *Apostolic Women, Apostolic Authority*, eds M. Percy and C. Rees. Norwich: Canterbury Press, 2010, 114–23.

The Purpose and Scope of Clergy Training: An Outline of Current Practice. London: Central Advisory Council for the Ministry, 1949.

'The Shorter Westminster Catechism', in *The Confession Of Faith: Together With The Larger Catechism And The Shorter Catechism*. Atlanta: Presbyterian Church in America, 1990.

The State of the Clergy 2012: A Report for The Episcopal Church. Church Pension Group, 2012.

Theological Education for the Anglican Communion (TEAC). 'Ministry Grids'. Accessed 22 October, 2012. http://www.anglicancommunion.org/ministry/theological/teac/grids/index.cfm.

———. 'Working Briefs and Process of Target Groups'. November 2003. Accessed 22 October, 2012. http://www.anglicancommunion.org/media/109432/briefs080206.pdf.

Thiselton, Anthony C. *New Horizons in Hermeneutics*. London: HarperCollins, 1992.

Thompson, Francis. *The Hound of Heaven*. New York, Morehouse Books, 1981.

Towler, R., and A. Coxon. *The Fate of the Anglican Clergy: A Sociological Study*. London: Macmillan, 1979.

Turner, F.M. 'Religion', in *The History of the University of Oxford*, Vol. 8, *The Twentieth Century*, ed. Brian Harrison. Oxford: Oxford University Press, 1994, 293–316.

Weil, Simone. *Waiting for God*. New York: Harper, 1973.

Wells, Samuel. 'How Common Worship Forms Local Character'. *Studies in Christian Ethics* 15 (2002): 166–74.

Wesley, Charles. 'Hymn 461, For Children', in *The Works of John Wesley*, Vol. 7, *A Collection of Hymns for the Use of the People Called Methodists*, eds Franz Hiderbrandt and Oliver A. Beckerlegge. New York: Oxford University Press, 1983; reprint Nashville: Abingdon Press, 7: 643–44.

Whither Thou Goest: Assessing the Current State of Seminaries and Seminarians in the Episcopal Church. Church Pension Group, 2012.

Williams, Rowan. 'What is Catholic Orthodoxy?' in *Essays Catholic and Radical*, eds Kenneth Leech and Rowan Williams. London: Bowardean, 1983.

———. 'Does it make sense to speak of pre-Nicene orthodoxy?' in *The Making of Orthodoxy*, ed. Rowan Williams. Cambridge: Cambridge University Press, 1989, 1–23.

———. 'Newman's Arians and the Question of Method in Doctrinal History', in *Newman after a Hundred Years*, eds Ian Ker and Alan G. Hill. Oxford: Clarendon Press 1990, 263–86.

———. 'Doctrinal Criticism: Some Questions', in *The Making and Remaking of Christian Doctrine*, eds Sarah Coakley and David Pailin. Oxford: Clarendon Press, 1993, 239–64.

———. *A Ray of Darkness*. Cambridge, Mass.: Cowley Publications, 1995, 152.

———. 'The Judgement of the World', in *On Christian Theology*. Oxford: Blackwell, 2000, 29–43.

———. 'The Sermon', in *Living the Eucharist*, ed. Stephen Conway. London: Darton, Longman and Todd, 2001, 44–55.

———. *Silence and Honey Cakes: The Wisdom of the Desert*. Oxford: Lion Book, 2003.

———. 'Theological Education and the Anglican Way'. *The ANITEPAM Journal* 55 (2006): 3–16.

———. 'Maurice Wiles and Doctrinal Criticism', in *Wrestling with Angels*, ed. Mike Higton. London: SCM Press 2007, 275–99.

Wittgenstein, Ludwig. *Philosophical Investigations*. Translated by Elizabeth Anscombe, Peter Hacker and Joachim Schulte. 4th edition. Oxford: Wiley-Blackwell, 2009.

Wood, Charles M. *Vision and Discernment: An Orientation in Theological Study*. Atlanta: Scholars Press, 1985.

Wright, Stephen I. 'Preaching, Use of the Bible in', in *Dictionary for Theological Interpretation of the Bible*, eds Kevin J. Vanhoozer et al. Grand Rapids: Baker Academic, 2005, 617–21.

Zerubavel, E. *Time Maps: Collective Memory and the Social Shape of the Past*. Chicago: University of Chicago Press, 2003.

Index

Printed in Great Britain
by Amazon